Sunset
How to Grow
Fruits, Nuts
& Berries

By the Editors of Sunset Books and Sunset Magazine

Lane Publishing Co. • Menlo Park, California

Research & Text:
Bob Thompson

Coordinating Editor:
Linda J. Selden

Design:
Roger Flanagan

Illustrations:
Ginny Mickelson

Photo Stylist:
JoAnn Masaoka

Photographers

California Tree Fruit Agreement: 54 bottom, 69. **Derek Fell:** 8 bottom left, 22, 23, 30 top, 34, 42, 52, 54 top right, 62, 74. **Michael Landis:** 20, 30 bottom. **Jack McDowell:** 1, 2, 3, 6, 10, 16, 18, 43, 46, 75. **Muriel Orans and Arthur Norman Orans:** 7, 8 bottom right, 54 top left, 64. **Norman A. Plate:** 66, 68, 73. **Bill Ross:** 8 top. **Teri Sandison:** 4, 26. **Michael Thompson:** 24, 50, 60, 78. **Darrow M. Watt:** 36. **Tom Wyatt:** 38 top and bottom, 45.

Climate Maps: Rik Olson

Cover: Photograph by Tom Wyatt. Photo styling by JoAnn Masaoka. Design by Naganuma Design & Direction.

Editor, Sunset Books: David E. Clark
First printing October 1984

How to Grow Fruits, Nuts & Berries has been designed for home gardeners in every part of this enormously complex continent. It gives ranging advice not only for those looking for a new plant but also those looking for better results from one already in the ground. In every case the emphasis is on growing food more than becoming an expert in botany.

Sometimes the advice is in the form of the right question to ask a local expert, sometimes in the form of specific answers. In both instances, the editors are deeply indebted to the following sources of information:

Agricultural Experiment Stations of Kansas State University, University of California, University of Georgia, University of Massachusetts, University of Missouri, Virginia Polytechnic Institute, Virginia State University, and Washington State University; Agricultural Extension Services of Cornell University and New York State University;

Wilbur Bluhm, Professor Emeritus, Oregon State University; John Bracken, Dallas, Texas; California Almond Growers Exchange, Sacramento, California; California Avocado Commission, Irvine, California; California Kiwi Fruit Commission, Sacramento, California; California Tree Fruit Agreement, Sacramento, California; Alan D. Cook, Senior Horticulturist of Dawes Arboretum, Newark, Ohio; Andrea du Plessis; Philip Edinger; Filoli Gardens;

Fred Galle, Retired Director of Callaway Gardens, Hamilton, Georgia; Dr. Richard A. Jaynes, Botanist, Hamden, Connecticut; Gene Joyner, Urban Horticulturist, West Palm Beach, Florida; J. Van Cleve Lott; Michael MacCaskey; John McCarthy, McCarthy Tree Specialties, Redwood City, California; Pacific Kitchens, Seattle, Washington; Roger's Gardens; Robert H. Savage, Horticulturist, New Windsor, New York; Spencer Shropshire; Dorothy Woodruff.

Contents

INTRODUCTION

Apples, chestnuts, blueberries, almonds, cherries, apricots, raspberries, grapes — these are just a few of nature's treats that you'll get to know well in this book. A taste of any one of them — when perfectly ripe and freshly picked — explains why thousands of gardeners take special pride and pleasure in growing their own fruits, nuts, and berries.

For some, the sweet taste of success is at its best in fresh fruit pie or jam—or simply in a juicy peach, just off its branch and still warm from the sun.

For many gardeners, the sheer magnanimity of nature in fruit, nut, or berry harvests holds irresistible appeal. To own and cultivate even one dwarf plum tree is to partake directly of nature's seasonal cornucopia.

If you're a veteran gardener, though, you know that nature won't lavish much of a crop without careful planning and hard work from you. Luck counts, too: it's a plain truth of all gardening enterprises that some plants fail despite the most meticulous care, while others thrive under all-out mismanagement. Veteran gardeners have learned to shift their tactics with these vicissitudes until they strike a balance with nature.

This book offers a clear, detailed, and thoroughly researched guide to finding that balance in the cultivation of 34 fruits, nuts, and berries, plus their numerous varieties. Starting on the next page, the most popular of these are listed alphabetically — each with its concise encyclopedia entry of individual gardening advice. (You'll find the less familiar subtropicals listed separately, on pages 81–82.)

Suppose, for example, that you hunger to grow a pear tree. First, you will turn to its alphabetical listing and check its zone numbers to be sure your garden climate suits a pear's preferences; consulting, too, the climate maps on pages 84–87. If the pear looks promising for your zone, continue reading its encyclopedia entry for all the basics you'll need to know about its cultivation.

You'll also find all the important details of pear care, with such crucial aspects as fertilizing carefully spelled out. You'll learn about the pear's pest and disease enemies, and how to thwart them if necessary. Best of all, the entry tells you about how many pears you can hope to harvest, as well as when to expect them. And a chart within the entry lists dozens of varieties, along with information to help you choose between them.

A gardening primer follows these alphabetical listings. Written for the novice gardener, it covers the fundamentals of growing any fruit, nut, or berry plant. Beyond that, it answers such questions as what the nitrogen in fertilizer does for a tree's growth— and how to graft one type of fruit onto the stock of another.

If you'll be growing your pear in a small suburban garden, you'll welcome the primer's explanation of how to espalier fruit trees, along with other space-saving techniques. Should your pear happen to be aged and ailing, the primer can help you to keep it alive and kicking.

Our exemplary pear may or may not be your first preference. Either way, when you're deciding to grow any fruit, nut, or berry, it's smart to select from plants that have already proven themselves to be reliable in your immediate area. To do this, you'll want to supplement information from this book with advice from local experts. Usually, the county farm advisor can most fully explain local soils and climatic shifts, and tell you which plants are most likely to thrive. Take your questions to experienced neighbors, too, and to the staff of a good nearby nursery.

Finally, take encouragement from the fact that most trees and shrubs that bear fruits, nuts, and berries tend to be tough.

Sharing the rewards of growing a good crop

Almonds

O ne of the most familiar nuts in the kitchen, the almond is also one of the hardest to grow in any region outside an ideal one.

AT A GLANCE

Climate: Performs best in western regions with long, dry summers, especially inland valleys of California, Zones 6–9.

Soil: Needs deep, well-drained loam or sandy loam.

Trees bear: At four years.

Typical life span: 50 years.

Typical yield at maturity: 10 to 20 pounds per tree.

Self-pollenizer: No.

Semidwarfs and dwarfs available: No.

Harvest season: Late summer, after husks split.

Principal pests and diseases: Brown rot, mites.

Almonds

Where they grow

Because the immature nut in April is even more frost-prone than its tender blossom in March, and because the almond nut ripens well only after a long summer of dry heat, the growing range of reliably fruitful trees is limited to the great inland valley of California, to southern California, and a few other spots in the arid Southwest.

Parts of California's coastal valleys, where spring frosts are not severe or late, can do well for home gardeners (though not for commercial growers). A few gardeners in Washington and Oregon have had nearly annual crops from trees facing west toward large bodies of water (Puget Sound, the mid-Columbia, any of several sizable lakes), but most trees in humid areas bear poorly if at all.

Gardeners in Virginia, for example, have tried almonds with such meager success that farm advisors

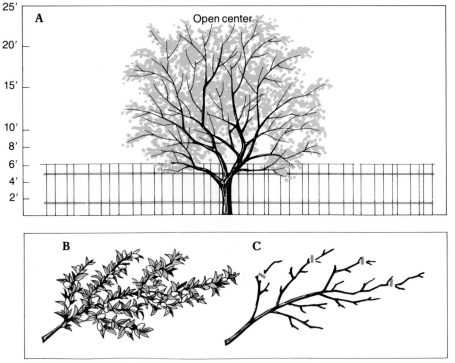

(A) *Most almond varieties grow to 40 feet, but can be kept at 25 by pruning. They are best trained to open center. If a young tree produces quantities of vegetation but few nuts, do not fertilize. Once a tree has its basic shape, most pruning is for wood renewal to ensure steady crops.*

(B) *Almonds bear along short fruiting spurs, which produce for about 5 years. They do not require thinning.* **(C)** *Each winter, remove about a fifth of the oldest fruiting wood, along with damaged or crossing branches.*

will not recommend planting them. On the other hand, one hardy variety, 'Hall', has grown well in Kansas and other Plains states.

In both areas, only the crops are at risk, not the trees—they are as hardy as their close botanic relatives, peaches. (Indeed, the almond has the diverting capacity of being able to bear peaches and plums on grafted branches. In this way, no few gardeners in marginal areas have assured themselves of some crop when the almonds fail.)

The focal points of varietal choice are blossom-time (late bloomers where spring frosts are a threat) and resistance to extreme heat. Because few almonds are self-pollenating and none is completely satisfactory as a self-pollenizer, gardeners should assume to plant two trees or, better, get a neighbor to plant one. Also, a second variety may be grafted onto the original stock, though this is less sure for anyone not skilled in the technique.

These are the most available varieties:

'Carmel' produces regular crops of small, flavorful nuts. It is a pollenizer for 'Nonpareil' and 'Texas'.

'Garden Prince' is a genetic dwarf to 10 feet tall. It also is a self-pollenizer, one of only two. The nuts resemble 'Nonpareil'.

'Hall' (or 'Hall's Hardy') blossoms late and is as hardy as a peach. Hard shelled nuts have good flavor. It is partially self fertile, but yields better with 'Jordanolo' or 'Texas' as pollenizer.

'Jordanolo' can give superior fruit, but is questionable in areas of intense summer heat. 'Ne Plus Ultra' and 'Nonpareil' are pollenizers.

'Kapareil' is much used as a pollenizer for 'Nonpareil'.

'Ne Plus Ultra' yields large nutmeats and has soft, easily cracked shells. It is a pollenizer for 'Nonpareil'.

'Nonpareil' is the best all-around variety. Fine nuts may be shelled easily by hand. It suffers some bud failure in regions of intense summer heat. Pollenize it with 'Jordanolo', 'Ne Plus Ultra', or 'Kapareil'.

'Texas' (or 'Mission'), a regular, heavy producer, is a late bloomer and hardy, a choice for cold-winter or late-frost regions. Pollenize with 'Nonpareil' or 'Hall'.

Blossoms need dry warmth to set fruit

Site & soil

Almonds adapt to almost any soil except heavy, slow-draining types. They will endure if a heavy soil is mixed half-and-half with peat moss or ground bark, and the planting hole is substantially larger than normal. The roots do best in soil at least 6 feet deep.

Like all other plants with tender blossoms, they should be planted on a slope with good air drainage in areas where spring frosts are a threat. Where summer heat is marginal, western exposures—especially ones facing water—may provide enough reflected warmth and light to ripen the fruit.

Propagating & planting

Almonds are propagated by grafting fruiting wood onto disease-resistant rootstock. Most gardeners buy bare-root plants from nurseries to assure healthy trees and trueness to type. The bare-root planting season in the West is February into March. It is prudent to whitewash the trunk to prevent sunscald. During the first growing season, a temporary screen to shield bark and foliage from wind and hot sun is good extra insurance.

Caring for the trees

Almonds are close to trouble-free.

Watering. Almonds require less water than most trees, but produce bigger crops if their root zones stay damp. Where there is some spring and summer rainfall, they may not need any irrigation; where there is little or no rainfall, they may need two or three waterings. If the top 2 to 3 inches of soil dries, run a slow stream for an hour or more.

Fertilizing. If trees make 8 to 15 inches of tip growth (the usual case), they need no fertilizer. If fertilizer is needed for a mature tree, apply 14 pounds of 10-10-10 per year, half before budbreak, half after harvest.

Pests and diseases. Brown rot, the principal disease, must be controlled by an annual spraying program (see page 108). Mites can be fatal, but control is required only when they appear (see page 110).

Apples

'Red Delicious'

Snappish aunts in the era of Booth Tarkington novels used to say "Applesauce!" to indicate they had just heard a batch of malarkey. It is hard to imagine how they got away with it.

The apple, after all, is pretty considerable—religiously, socially, and medically. Eve could not resist one in the Garden of Eden. Johnny Appleseed is a heavyweight in American folklore. Once the apple is in a pie, it shares a rung on our social ladder with Mom and the American flag. And the effect of an apple a day on medical doctors is well known.

Another sign of the importance of the apple is its ability to set off the kinds of debate otherwise reserved

'Granny Smith'   'Golden Delicious'

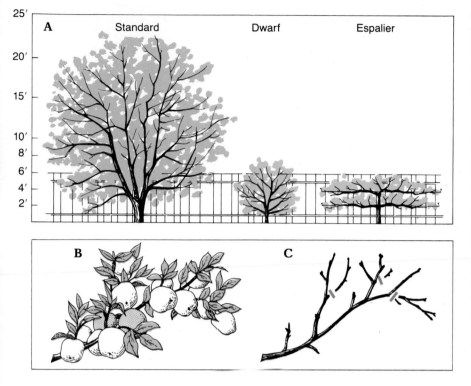

(A) *Standard varieties, particularly the vigorous and more erect ones, will grow to 35 feet unchecked. They can best be kept at 20 to 25 feet high with open-center training. Spur varieties and semi-dwarfs can be trained to open centers with three main branches, but respond well to central leader training.*

When central leader tree reaches desired height, prune leader back 2 to 3 feet, to a strong lateral. Repeat whenever tree exceeds desired height. Fully dwarfed varieties can be trained with central leaders, and also are best suited of all fruit trees to formal espaliers.

(B) *Fruit grows from stubby spurs that produce for as many as 20 years. Spurs have distinctive terminal buds. Healthy trees require little thinning to balance at one apple per 8 inches of branch.* (C) *Annual pruning removes crossing branches and weak, diseased, or damaged branches, and keeps center of tree open to sunlight. Side branches should not outgrow leader; secondary branches should not outstrip primary ones. Pinch out to inhibit; cut back to correct.*

for wine grapes. People get testy about which variety is best, and where it grows to perfection.

Where they grow

Many—perhaps most—home gardeners who plan to plant a new apple tree had a memory-haunting one in childhood. It may have been a spindly old tree that hung on for dear life in scant soil, producing never more than 60 apples in a year. Ah, but any of those 60 could engrave itself on the memory with incomparable flavors.

No matter that decades of breeding have produced scores of newer, more reliably good varieties. No matter that the new garden is hundreds of miles in a warmer or colder direction from the old one. If the goal is to recapture the exact flavors of those golden memories, and if memory says the old tree was a 'Yellow Transparent', then 'Yellow Transparent' cannot be forgotten lightly.

Nevertheless, the proper advice is to scout out a variety that produces its best flavors in the climate where it is to grow, that ripens when apples are in short supply in the market, and that gives a steady, sizable crop. Subparts of the suitability question

include disease resistance and how well the fruit serves its main purpose—eating fresh, baking whole or in pies, making applesauce or cider. A separate but important factor is tree size.

The consoling fact for anyone who abandons a sentimental favorite is that a good many of the 7,000 varieties of apple will grow and bear good fruit in almost every one of the United States and the Canadian provinces, and that one or another of those will taste much like the one of treasured memory.

Choosing a variety

The simple way out is to opt for a proven variety under local soil and climate conditions. If the choice is to be something rare, several questions about regional adaptation need answers. Because people tend to feel more strongly about the differences among apple varieties than they do about most other fruits, this is as good a place as any to go through the list of primary factors.

Climate considerations. The crucial limitations on varietal selection are how much cold the tree can stand, and how much cold it needs.

In simple summary, most commonly available apples grow well in nearly every part of USDA Zones 6 and 7. Several notably hardy ones will bear fruit in the warmer parts of Zone 5. A few of the very hardiest can give steady, large crops in cold Zone 5, even in Zone 4. Most regions in zones warmer than 7 can grow only a handful of select varieties needing little winter chill.

Like other temperate-zone fruits, most apples require four seasons to flourish. Unless the trees are chilled into full dormancy, crop levels and fruit quality suffer. The standard index is the annual number of hours of temperatures of 45°F/7°C or lower. Most apple varieties need 900 to 1,200 chilling hours, which is what limits many of them to areas no warmer than USDA Zone 7. Those able to produce fair to good fruit with fewer hours of chill—down to 200—are noted in the chart (pages 13–15), as are varieties needing especially long chilly seasons.

The other edge of the frame, freeze-hardiness, is at once more critical and a bit harder to pinpoint. A good many of the classic varieties are practical in Zone 5.

However, nothing is simple. There is Zone 5 and there is Zone 5. A long-time grower in Pennsylvania thinks that freeze-hardiness is easy

Tree at midseason

to plot on the Atlantic seaboard, but increasingly dicey with each mile inland. In his view, western Pennsylvania is a very difficult place to recommend planting apples, Ohio even more so unless the garden faces a large, warming body of water from a slope that provides good air drainage. Dry valleys and other air sinks in much of the upper Midwest will not yield rewarding crops of many varieties generally recommended for Zone 5.

At the other end of the climate scale east of the Rockies, few varieties produce crisp, juicy fruit in Zone 8, and hardly any can be close to their best in Zones 9 or 10.

West of the Rockies, Pacific Ocean-tempered air allows much USDA Zone 8 and parts of Zone 9 to be plausible apple country. (Zone 9 Sonoma County, 70 miles north of San Francisco, grows superior 'Gravensteins' around the town of Sebastopol, to give just one example.) Colder winters at high elevations in the mountainous deserts also permit apple growing in some of those parts of Zone 9. However, parts of the coast are too cool in summer to ripen many traditional varieties, and

much of the desert is too hot. These regions have their own short lists of growable apples. The western parts of Zone 10 are about as limited as the eastern ones, though their roster of suitable varieties is not the same.

There are a few surprising spots where apples are almost impossible to grow. One example is southern Georgia, which, in spite of being Zone 9, gets late frosts that kill the blossoms on those few trees able to withstand the summer heat there.

Georgia's blank spot brings up the last vital aspect of matching variety to climate: the growing season, from blossom time to harvest time. The trick in most of Zones 5, 6, and 7 is to find a variety that blooms just after the last killing spring frost, and ripens just ahead of the first freezes of autumn. Where the growing season is short, this mainly means midseason bloomers and ripeners. In longer-season areas with hot summers, the best hopes usually bloom early; areas with cool summers have the widest scope.

There is no sure-fire index. Local climates radically affect both blossom and harvest dates. Nursery staff and county farm advisors are

the most likely wellsprings of knowledge about local conditions and about the names of well-suited varieties.

Varietal character. Once the climatic needs of the tree have been met, choice of variety also should take into account how the greater part of the fruit will be used—for eating fresh, baking, applesauce, cider, whatever. Varietal character differs greatly. Here is an explanation of the qualities underlying top rankings in the chart:

A good dessert apple—for eating fresh—must have a pleasing aroma and a certain crispness of flesh.

Baking apples should retain their shape firmly after cooking. Pies demand the same qualities.

Any apple that tastes good cooked is good for sauce.

Cider apples need to be juicy, and their flesh must resist browning better than most (otherwise the cider may taste flat and heavy almost before it can be gotten out of the press).

The same two characteristics are desirable in apples for salads.

An apple that doesn't darken when cut is ideal for salad; however, brushing any cut apple with lemon juice will prevent darkening.

Nowhere do these notes on varietal character mention skin color. It does not matter. Though shoppers have been conditioned by the appealing red hue (and great symmetry) of 'Red Delicious', growers know that some of the greatest flavors in the world are locked inside lumpy, knobby apples with green skins and rusty patches.

One other set of varietal characteristics that does matter is disease resistance. Varieties notably prone or resistant to the major problems are noted in the chart.

Pollenization. Very few apple varieties are self-pollenizers. The main ones are, again, noted in the chart. With these exceptions, all varieties need another tree within 100 feet to fertilize blossoms.

A handful of varieties are pollen-sterile, requiring two other varieties to pollenize them and each other. The sterile group includes 'Gravenstein', 'Jonagold', 'Mutsu', 'Rhode Island Greening', 'Winesap', and 'Stayman' and all of its sports ('Stayman Winesap', 'Stayspur', and others). It is possible, and may be desirable in crowded gardens, to graft a second variety onto an existing tree as a pollenizer. Better, convince a neighbor to plant one.

Tree size. If varietal names pose some difficulties, at least the breeders have worked things out so apple trees come in every size one could hope for. A full-size tree is big enough for any farmyard. One of the smaller trees can be grown in a container on almost any sunny balcony, regardless of how cramped. As an example of what can be done, one inspired gardener in Portland, Oregon, has managed to pack 300 varieties on 140 cordon-trained trees into a 30 by 40-foot plot.

Two naturally small types of tree exist, spur strains and genetic dwarfs.

Spur apples are about ¾ normal size. A genetic quirk causes them to space their buds closer together than normal for their variety. In other words, these trees bear more apples per linear foot of branch than standard varieties.

Genetic dwarfs are the smallest of all apple trees, the tiniest of them maturing at 6 to 10 feet high, depending on pruning. Also the result of genetic quirks, they bear normal-size fruit, but much less of it than either a standard or spur variety.

The rest of the small apple trees are not genetic, but the result of grafting standard apple varieties onto abnormally small rootstock. There is a series of such rootstocks, indexed by size, that produce trees ranging from semidwarf to dwarf. The exact size varies, being in proportion to the original variety.

There are variations in rootstocks dictated by regional climates and varietal characteristics of the fruiting wood. The following are the commonest rootstocks. (Those identified as MM were developed at an English research station at Merton-Malling; those labeled EM come from nearby East Malling.)

MM104 produces ¾-size trees that do not bear quite so much fruit as a spur type. Trees on MM111 or EM2 reach about ⅔-normal size. Those on M7A, M26, or MM106 top out at ½-size; M9 is ⅓-size, and M27 at ¼-size. Trees identified with two numbers, such as M9/MM106, have a dwarfing rootstock *and* an "interstem"—that is to say, there is the rootstock, plus a second, connecting piece of wood grafted between the rootstock and the fruiting wood to reinforce the dwarfing, improve bud unions, or otherwise give the tree desired characteristics. For instance, coupling strong-growing MM106 roots with a strong-dwarfing M9 interstem produces a semidwarf tree of the same size as M26, but a better-anchored one. Or, M9/MM111 is the same size as M7 but better anchored and more drought-resistant.

For most urban and suburban gardeners, one or another of the small trees is imperative. Not only is the reduced size welcome on a standard lot, so is the reduced crop a relief to a typical family. Three bushels of apples from a standard tree may not sound like much, but three bushels of medium to large apples is enough to keep the doctor away from a family of four for 109 days.

Not incidentally, dwarfs, whether genetic or grafted, make the best candidates for espaliering.

Variety names. The naming of all the thousands of apple varieties seems designed to drive buyers daft. Not only is the poetry of old names ('Black Gilliflower', 'Winter Pearmain', 'Duchess of Oldenberg') disappearing, but the new crop of corporate-sounding, coined-word identities is a trackless desert. Standard strains of 'Red Delicious' are known, for example, as 'Classic', 'Early Red One', 'Nured Royal', and 'Starking Full Red' while spur strains of the same variety go by names as diverse as 'Spurred', 'Crimson Spur', 'Red King Oregon Spur', 'Spured Royal', and 'Wellspur'. All told, 'Red Delicious' is sold under some 200 names.

While complete sense cannot be made of the situation, there is some help in the fact that most varieties fall within one of a half-dozen main groupings. The heads of families other than 'Red Delicious' include 'Golden Delicious', 'Jonathan', 'McIntosh', 'Northern Spy', 'Rome', and 'Winesap'. The experts cited in a preceding paragraph can help locate other apples within the family groupings.

Crab apples are a subtribe unto themselves. Though of the same botanical family as all other apples, adapted to the same climates and responsive to the same cultural practices, they differ by producing tiny, tart fruits. Few varieties make good eating. Most are used for spiced apples, pickling, or jellies. A short list of the most usable varieties (many are only ornamental) concludes the chart of apple varieties.

Site & soil

The basic requirements of the apple are full sun and deep, fertile, well-drained soil.

Full sun means at least 4 hours a day with no shadows cast on the tree. In humid climates where there is regular morning dew, the best site for an apple allows morning sun to dry the leaves and the forming fruit before molds and mildews can advance.

In regions where a particular variety is only marginally freeze-hardy, the planting site should not be in a low spot where cold air stands. When a variety tends to bloom before the last hard frosts, planting the tree on a north exposure or otherwise sheltering it from the spring sun may slow budbreak enough to minimize damage. Apples do not do well at the crests of windy hills; the brittle fruiting spurs can snap off in a strong gust.

The ideal soil is fertile loam at least 4 feet deep, with a pH of 6.5. Some gardeners recommend adding lime to soil more acidic than pH 5.5. Others suggest no such change, on grounds that apples will more than get by in many imperfect situations. Notes on adding agricultural lime may be found on page 104.

Good drainage is more important than fertile soil, apples being susceptable to several root rots. Their frailty in face of cotton root rot is such that one Texan advises against planting any apple in any soil with any history of it. A number of southern authorities suggest raised beds for apples that have to be planted over slow-draining clay pan.

Because semidwarfs and still smaller apples have restricted root systems, with many feeder roots near the surface, the root zones should be protected by 4 to 6 inches of mulch in hot climates. Trees on M9, M26, M27, and MM206 rootstocks all should be staked or otherwise supported against uprooting by wind, especially when young.

Propagating & planting

Apples are propagated from hardwood cuttings if they grow on their own roots, by budding if on rootstock.

Few home gardeners attempt to graft a fruiting variety onto rootstock, but many will graft or bud a pollenizing branch onto a chosen fruiting variety.

The most economical method of buying and planting an apple is bare-root. Most authorities advise buying a second-year tree for the purpose.

The bare-root season varies slightly by region. In mild-winter regions, planting may be as early as January. In cold-winter, late-frost regions, the recommended time is late March through mid-April. No authority counsels planting bare-root apples after April 15 except in Zones

3 and 4. The basic idea is that the last killing frost should be past, and the ground just beginning to warm beneath the spring sun.

Apples also are sold in containers or balled and burlapped for planting in other seasons. In hot-summer, mild-winter regions, especially, autumn planting of a container or balled tree allows it to establish roots through the cool months, improving its chances of survival in the hot season. In Florida, most plants are sold in containers; dormancy is too short and shallow to allow bare root planting.

By whichever method of planting, be sure any grafted tree is set with its bud union 2 to 4 inches above ground level. If a grafted apple is planted with the bud union at or below ground level, the top variety will be able to send down roots, and a dwarf or semidwarf tree may—probably will—revert to a standard one. In the case of an interstem tree, the lower graft is below grade, the upper one 2 to 4 inches above ground.

Caring for the trees

Apples need unflagging across-the-board care to prosper.

Watering. Consistent watering is necessary throughout the growing season to deliver a full crop. In fact, one of the sure signs of underwatering is heavy premature fruit drop.

An apple on well-drained sand in dry country may need soaking as often as once a week. A tree in heavier soil and a cooler, moister climate may need to be irrigated only two or three times in a season, when rainfall falters. The best monitor of need is an indicator plant such as hydrangea. If it wilts, the apple will need water. The two must be watered together for the indicator to work.

Dwarfs need more careful attention to watering than standard trees because of their small, shallow root systems.

For all apples, the soil should be kept damp between growing seasons, a fact that may require some supplemental irrigation after harvest in the Southwest and some other regions where the dry season is prolonged well into autumn.

Fertilizing. A healthy apple will make 6 to 8 inches of tip growth per year and put out a healthy crop. If it does so without fertilizer, none is needed.

There are two basic regimes for apples needing fertilizer—a changing one for the sapling, a more rigid one for the mature tree. Added variations depend on tree size, from dwarf to standard.

Most programs call for gradually increasing amounts of a complete fertilizer over the first 3 to 6 years, then a leveling off as the tree matures. Too much growth promises too many leaves and not enough fruit, and increases the risk of fireblight.

A simple program calls for ¼ pound of 10-10-10 per tree at budbreak the first year, then an annual increase of ¼ pound until a maximum is reached. The specific recommended maximums are 2.5 pounds for a dwarf, 5 for a semidwarf, and 10 for a standard. An easily remembered variation for mature trees suggests 1 pound of 10-10-10 per inch of trunk diameter just before budbreak, between early March and mid-April. Both are only central figures, meant to be adjusted up or down as tip growth suggests.

From Pennsylvania State University, the program resembles closely those of many cold-winter, cool-summer regions.

A program recommended in the South calls for ½ pound of 12-12-12 per tree per year for the first 3 years, with that total divided among three applications. The first is to be done in winter, the second at budbreak, the third in early summer, each spread thinly to avoid burning roots.

For mature standard trees, the program, devised by the University of Georgia, calls only for nitrogen fertilizer applied in spring. Specifically, the amounts and fertilizer type are 4 cups of ammonium nitrate per tree 6 to 8 years old, 6 cups for those 9 years and older. Semidwarfs get 4 cups, dwarfs 2. In many regions, equivalent amounts of ammonium sulfate would have to replace the ammonium nitrate because of fire code restrictions.

In California, a long, dry autumn follows the harvest, so fertilizer can be applied immediately after a crop has been picked, when it can help develop fruit buds for the coming year. The University of California recommends 5 pounds of ammonium sulfate for mature standard trees, applied as soon as possible after harvest. In this region there is little worry that early frosts will harm tender new growth.

In every case, with young trees and old alike, the fertilizer should be spread in a circle extending to or just beyond the drip line, but leaving a gap of 1 foot between the trunk and the inner edge of the circle.

A mineral deficiency that looks like a disease is bitter pit. It begins with pitted skin and quickly rots the apple's flesh. Large-fruited varieties ('Buckley Giant', 'Tropic Beauty') are especially prone. To avoid the deficiency—of calcium—water faithfully and give the trees very little nitrogen. It also helps to minimize pruning of subject trees; one trick is to tie vertical branches down, forcing them to become lateral growth.

Pests and diseases. Codling moth—rather its larval form, the familiar little white worm—is the worst pest almost everywhere apples grow; see page 109 for treatment. Apple maggot is another familiar pest, one susceptible to the same controls as codling moth.

Of diseases, apple scab is a threat from fruit set until harvest, especially in wet climates. The best control is resistant varieties, but fungicides help inhibit formation of the hard, corky crust on apple skins. Apply a dormant spray of lime sulfur before buds open (repeating if rain washes it off), then spray regularly through the growing season with wettable sulfur, benomyl, or captan.

Lesser problems less specific to apples are mites (see page 110), curculio and fireblight (see page 109).

Rabbits and mice also can be something of a problem anywhere. In deep-snow country, rabbits can chew away bark all the way up to the first scaffold branches. For defenses, turn to page 111.

Apples

Variety	Tree					Fruit							Chart Key:
	USDA Climate Zones*	Minimum chill hours**	Ripens	Bears	Spur dwarf	Size	Color	Fresh	Baked	Sauce	Cider		**Ripens:** E/Early, M/Mid, L/Late, VE/Very early, VL/Very late **Bears:** L/Light, M/Medium, MH/Medium heavy, H/Heavy, VH/Very heavy, AI/Alternate years **Size:** S/Small, M/Medium, L/Large, VL/Very large **Color:** R/Red, D/Dark, Y/Yellow, G/Green, S/Striped, RU/Russet **Fruit quality:** O/Outstanding, E/Excellent, A/Average, P/Poor **Comments**
'Akane'	5–7	Avg	E	L		S	R	E	A	A	A		Annual bearer. Fruit holds better on tree than in storage.
'Anna'	8–9	400	E	H		L	R	A	A	A	A		Recommended from o TX to GA.
'Arkansas Black'	6	Avg	L	L/M	•	M	D/R	A	A	E	A		Hard, crisp flesh. Spur dwarf available.
'Astrachan' ('Red Astrachan')	4–9	Avg	E	L/M		M	R/S	E	E	A	A		Russian native adapted logically to NE, surprisingly to s CA.
'Baldwin Woodpecker'	5–7	Avg	L	M		S/M	Y/R/S	A	A	A	A		Old-timer still in demand in NE.
'Beverly Hills'	9	400	E	M		S/M	R/S	A	A	A	A		Will not take desert heat; at best near s CA, Gulf coasts.
'Buckley Giant'	8	Avg	M	H		VL	G	A	A	A	A		Single fruits weigh 1½ pounds! Proven in w WA.
'Chehalis'	6–8	Avg	E/M	H		L	Y	A	A	E	A		Pick firm; stores poorly. Proven in w WA.
'Cortland'	4–8	Avg	M/L	H		M/L	Y/R/S	E	E	A	E		Annual bearer in mountainous W, NE. Poor overripe.
'Cox Orange'	5–7	Avg	M/L	H		M	Y/R/S	E	A	E	E		Juicy, aromatic old-timer from England.
'Crimson Beauty'	4–6	Avg	M	M		M	R	A	A	A	A		Found primarily in Ontario.
'Criterion'	5–8	Avg	L	M		L	G/Y/R	O	A	A	A		Favored in Willamette Valley and east of Cascades where it gets plenty of warmth. Ripens consistently only in warmest parts of w WA. Susceptible to scab. Good keeper.
'Delicious' ('Red Delicious')	4–7	Avg	M/L	MH	•	M	R	O	P	P	P		Widely adapted in scores of strains, including dwarfs, spurs (see text).
'Dorsett Golden'	8–9	100	E	MH		M	Y	A	A	A	A		Bears in Bahamas; pollenizer for 'Anna'.
'Earliblaze'	4–8	Avg	E	M		M/L	G/R/S	A	E	E	E		Adapted to Plains, but okay in mild-winter W.

*See climate zone maps, pages 84–87.
**Average chilling hours 900–1200. For more information, see pages 84–87.

Apples

Variety	USDA Climate Zones*	Minimum chill hours**	Ripens	Bears	Spur dwarf	Size	Color	Fresh	Baked	Sauce	Cider	Comments
'Ein Shemer'	8–9	400	E	M		M	Y	A	A	A	A	Adapted to TX, s CA. Stores poorly.
'Empire'	5–7	Avg	M/L	H	•	M	R	E	E	E	E	Colors long before ripe. Stores well. Fine in NE.
'Fameuse'	4–5	Avg	M/L	AI		M	R	E	P	A	E	Very hardy; bears at high elevations. Needs good drainage.
'Gala'	5–8	Avg	M	M		M	Y/R/S	E	A	A	A	From New Zealand; has done well in w WA, MO.
'Golden Delicious'	5–9	Avg	M/L	H	•	M/L	Y	E	E	E	E	Widely adapted except in deserts. Does not store well.
'Golden Russet'	4–6	Avg	M/L	M		S	D/Y	E	A	A	E	Old-timer still admired in Ontario, NE.
'Gordon'	9–10	350	M	M		M/L	G/R	A	A	A	A	Adapted to s CA. Annual bearer with long flowering and fruiting season.
'Granny Smith'	7–8	Avg	VL	H		M/L	G/R	E	A	E	A	Needs long season. Mildew-prone. Good keeper.
'Gravenstein'	5–9	Avg	E/M	M		M/L	G/R/S	E	A	E	O	At best along central CA coast, in cool-summer NE.
'Grimes Golden'	7–8	Avg	L	M		S	Y	E	A	A	E	Popular old-timer from VA. Slow to bear.
'Holland'	9–10	Avg	M	M		VL	R	E	A	A	A	Bears in 2 years in s CA.
'Hubbardston Nonesuch'	5–6	Avg	M	H		L	R	E	P	P	A	Old variety still admired in NE. Reddest strains best.
'Idared'	6–8	Avg	L	H		M/L	R	E	E	E	E	Fine in NW, NE. Stores well. Mildew-prone.
'JerseyMac'	5–8	1000	E	H		M/L	R	E	A	A	A	Recommended in NE, s to mountainous GA.
'Jonagold'	5–8	Avg	L	H		L	Y/R/S	O	E	A	A	'Jonathan' x 'Golden Delicious'. Stores well.
'Jonamac'	5–8	Avg	M	H		M	G/R/S	E	A	A	A	Betters parents ('Jonathan' x 'McIntosh'), but disease prone.
'Jonathan'	5–8	Avg	M	H		M/L	R	E	A	A	E	Many strains; popular in MW.
'King' ('Tomkins King')	6–8	Avg	M/L	MH		M/L	Y/R/S	E	E	A	A	Weak grower. Recommended in NY, WA. Stores well.
'Liberty'	5–8	Avg	L	H		M/L	R/Y	E	A	A	A	Resistant to mildew, cedar apple rust, fireblight and apple scab.
'Lodi'	5–8	1000	VE	AI		L	Y	E	E	E	A	Crisper, more tart than 'Transparent'. Prone to fireblight.
'Macoun'	4–8	Avg	L	AI		M	G/R/S	E	E	A	A	Widely available. Disease-resistant. Bruises easily.
'McIntosh' ('Red McIntosh')	4–7	Avg	M/L	MH	•	M/L	R	E	E	E	E	Needs thinning in W, extra care everywhere.
'Melrose'	5–7	Avg	L	H		L	R	E	E	E	A	Trees produce young. Recommended in OH.
'Mutsu'	6–8	Avg	L	H		VL	Y	E	E	A	A	Japanese cross becoming widely available.
'Newtown Pippin'	5–9	Avg	L	M		M/L	Y	A	E	E	E	Widely available. Good keeper. Ripens in poor soil.
'Northern Spy'	4–6	1000	L	AI		L	Y/R/S	O	A	A	A	Slow to bear. Widely available, much prized.

*See climate zone maps, pages 84–87.
**Average chilling hours 900–1200. For more information, see pages 84–87.

Apples

Variety	Tree					Fruit		Quality				Comments
	USDA Climate Zones*	Minimum chill hours**	Ripens	Bears	Spur dwarf	Size	Color	Fresh	Baked	Sauce	Cider	
'Paulared'	7–8	Avg	E/M	H		M	R	E	A	A	A	Useful in w WA; recommended in MW, especially OH.
'Prima'	6–8	Avg	E/M	H		M/L	R	A	A	A	A	Fine in MW; good near NW coast. Resists disease.
'Priscilla'	6–8	Avg	M/L	M		M/L	R	E	E	A	A	Resists scab.
'Rome Beauty' ('Red Rome')	5–8	Avg	L	M/H		L	R	P	O	A	A	Stores well. Not for high elevations.
'Roxbury Russet'	6–7	Avg	L	M		M/L	RU	A	A	A	E	Most popular russet in NE. Stores well.
'Spartan'	6–9	Avg	M/L	H		S/M	R	E	A	A	A	Needs thinning. Good keeper.
'Spigold'	4–6	1200	L	M		VL	Y/R/S	E	A	A	A	'Northern Spy' x 'Golden Delicious'; fine in salads.
'Spitzenberg' ('Esopus Spitzenberg')	6	Avg	L	Al		M/L	R	E	P	E	A	Old favorite e of Rockies; parent of 'Jonathan'.
'Stayman Winesap'	5–8	Avg	VL	H	•	M/L	R	E	E	E	E	Popular, better-tasting offspring of 'Winesap'.
'Summer Rambo'	5–7	Avg	E/M	M/L		VL	Y/R/S	E	A	E	A	From France, one of the oldest apples.
'Summerred'	6–9	Avg	E	H		M/L	R	A	E	E	A	Needs thinning. Overripens in hot climates.
'Tolman Sweet'	5–6	Avg	E	M		M/L	Y	E	E	A	A	Tree is hardy, but fruit stores poorly, bruises easily.
'Transparent' ('Yellow Transparent')	6–9	Avg	VE	MH		M/L	Y	A	E	E	A	Will overripen; does not keep well.
'Tropical Beauty'	7–9	750	M	H		M/L	R	A	A	A	A	Mild to bland flavor.
'Twenty Ounce'	5–7	Avg	M	L		L/VL	Y	A	A	A	A	Good all-purpose apple; stores poorly.
'Tydeman's Red'	6–9	Avg	E	L/M		M/L	R	E	E	A	A	Best as semidwarf. Good keeper for early apple.
'Vista Bella'	6–8	Avg	VE	H		M	R	E	E	E	A	One of the best early varieties for eating.
'Wealthy'	5–6	Avg	M	Al		M/L	R	A	A	E	A	Requires heavy thinning. Tart as dessert apple.
'Westfield Seek No Further'	6–7	Avg	M/L	L		M	Y	E	P	P	A	Does not brown in salads.
'White Astrachan'	7–9	Avg	E	M		M	Y	E	E	E	A	Seven years to bearing.
'White Winter Pearmain'	5–10	400	M	M		S/M	Y	E	A	E	A	Seven years to bearing. Good in s CA.
'Winter Banana'	7–9	Avg	M/L	M	•	M/L	Y	A	A	A	A	Tasty mild-winter variety. Needs 'Astrachan' to pollenize.
'Wolf River'	5	Avg	M/L	M		V/L	Y/R/S	A	A	A	A	Primary virtue is hardiness in upper MW.
Crab Apples												
'Hyslop'	5–8	Avg	L	VH		M	Y/R	A	E	E	A	Fruit clusters produce ornamental effect in fall.
'Transcendant'	3–8	Avg	M/L	VH		L	Y/R	A	E	E	A	Beautiful tree; heavy bearer. Good for jelly.

Chart Key:

Ripens:
E/Early, M/Mid, L/Late, VE/Very early, VL/Very late

Bears:
L/Light, M/Medium, MH/Medium heavy, H/Heavy, VH/Very heavy, Al/Alternate years

Size:
S/Small, M/Medium, L/Large, VL/Very large

Color:
R/Red, D/Dark, Y/Yellow, G/Green, S/Striped, RU/Russet

Fruit quality:
O/Outstanding, E/Excellent, A/Average, P/Poor

*See climate zone maps, pages 84–87.
**Average chilling hours 900–1200. For more information, see pages 84–87.

Apricots

Ripe apricots

Climate: USDA Zones 5–9 west of the Rockies, 5–6 east of the Rockies. Fares poorly in humid regions.

Soil: Grows best in light loam, but fairly adaptable.

Trees bear: At 3 to 4 years.

Typical life span: 20 to 30 years.

Typical yield at maturity: 100 pounds per tree.

Self-pollenizer: Most varieties, yes.

Semidwarfs and dwarfs available: Yes.

Harvest season: May–June for most varieties; one in August–September.

Principal pests and diseases: Brown rot, canker (gummosis), gophers. Also scale, twig borers.

There is good news and bad news about the apricot.

The good news is its incomparable flavor, revealed at its peak in saucy, spicy Mediterranean cuisines, never better than in the Portuguese and Moroccan. Almost as good news is apricot's ability to be dried, canned, frozen, and otherwise preserved.

The bad news is that, in favorable places, apricot trees deliver heavy crops in a swift avalanche of ripe fruit, usually over a span of 10 (seldom more than 20) days, condemning tree owners to eat to surfeit while spending a good deal of extra time in the kitchen preserving the excess.

But varied use can spread out the harvest slightly. Fruit for canning or storing should be picked just before it ripens to full color. Fruit for fresh eating and drying can wait until fully ripe—and will taste the better for it.

If the bad news is not an avalanche of fruit, it is that the tree will

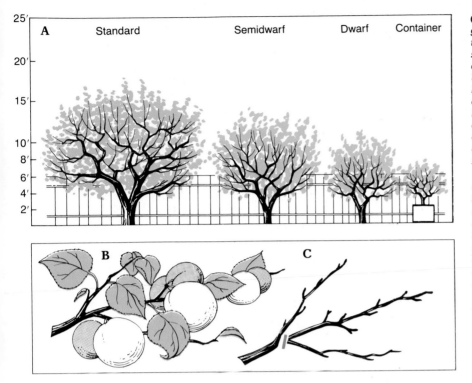

(A) *Because of apricot's tendency to grow too dense a canopy, open-center training method is preferred for both standard and semidwarf trees (on plum or 'Nemaguard' peach rootstocks). Usually there are three or four main branches. Semidwarfs and genetic dwarfs lend themselves to espaliering, better in informal shapes than rigid cordons. Branches should be about 14 inches apart. Genetic dwarfs will grow in containers, minimum size 3 feet by 3 feet, and 2½ feet deep.*

(B) *Fruit sets on spurs formed on second-year growth. Spurs remain fruitful 2 to 4 years. Remove doubles soon after fruit has set. For optimum size at harvest, thin to 4 to 6 inches apart when fruit is ¾ to 1 inch in diameter.* (C) *To sustain crop levels, annual pruning should trim out older fruiting wood, retain new growth. Fruiting branches should be about 14 inches apart. To avoid over-dense canopy, do not head back, but prune out whole branches.*

yield only a modest crop every second or third year. In addition to being generally more troublesome to grow than some other tree fruits, the individual varieties can be remarkably responsive to subtle changes in the climate.

Where they grow

Commercial orchards point to the most promising pattern of weather: chilly winters, an early end to frosts, and fairly warm, dry springs. A long growing season is not part of the profile—the name apricot meant "early ripener" in its original form.

California grows more than 90 percent of the market apricots in the country, mainly in the San Joaquin Valley, to a lesser extent in several coastal valleys south of San Francisco. (California also points up just how fine the shadings can be for apricots. While coastal valleys south of San Francisco are almost ideal, those north of the city grow apricots poorly if at all because the frost season lasts a few days longer there, and summers are a few degrees warmer. The early bloomers get

caught in the frost; the later ones cannot take the extra heat.)

Washington state's Yakima Valley and southern Idaho share most of the rest of the commercial orchards. There are smaller districts in similarly restricted parts of Utah, Colorado, and Michigan. In Canada, the counterpart districts are the Okanagan Valley of British Columbia and the Ste. Catherine's district of southern Ontario.

The middle ground, where home gardeners can hang on to hopes for some reasonable crops, includes the Plains states from northern Texas northward into the Great Lakes basin, and east into New York and parts of New England.

At the other end of the pole, the apricot sets poorly, ripens fruit uncertainly, and is disease-prone in cool, humid summer regions typified by the Pacific shoreline from San Francisco northward, and including Washington's Puget Sound basin. The hot, humid summer climate of the Gulf states is even less promising. Mild-winter climates may not do well by the apricot either; most varieties need 900 hours of chill weather to go properly dormant, though a few varieties require only 350 hours at 45°F/7°C or lower.

Because choice of variety weighs so importantly, the chart (see page 19) pays particular heed to specific climate adaptations.

Site & soil

Apricots grow best in deep, light loam, but will perform well in sandy soils if well fertilized. They do not adapt well to heavy soils with poor drainage.

Owing to their annual game of tag with spring frosts, it is well to plant them on slopes with good air drainage, risky to plant them on valley floors. They should not be crowded by other trees, nor should they be planted in soil where tomatoes, cotton, or other plants subject to verticilium wilt have grown in the preceding 3 years. (The same fungus causes "black heart" rot in apricots.)

Propagating & planting

Apricots are propagated by grafting scion wood onto seedling rootstocks. Most home gardeners purchase 1 or 2-year-old trees from nurs-

Apricots must blossom after last frost

eries to minimize diseases or other weakness and to guarantee trueness to type.

In most of their range (USDA Zones 5–9), apricots are set out as bare-root plants in spring after the last hard frosts. In mild-winter regions they can be planted from containers in autumn, a practice that is useful in developing a root system before the rainy season ends.

Caring for the trees

Apricots require careful, consistent programs of disease control.

Watering. Apricots ripen so early that winter rains usually carry the tree to harvest, but the same tree often needs irrigation to get it through the summer. As a practical measure for well-drained soils in dry areas, a tree can use an hour's soaking whenever the top 3 inches of soil goes dry.

In sandy soils, give the tree shorter soakings more frequently; in heavy soils, use as much water as for loam, or slightly more, but irrigate less often. Flood irrigation is the preferred way in any soil. Build a watering basin to keep the trunk dry at the ground line (see pages 89 and 107), minimizing risk of any fungus infection there.

Fertilizing. An almost perennial deficiency in apricots is nitrogen. Yellowed leaves and failure of fruit to reach proper size are symptoms; so is tip growth of less than 4 inches per year. (More than 6 inches of new growth is a sign of too much fertilizer.) If symptoms of deficiency occur, follow this maintenance program in cold-winter regions: in early spring apply ¼ pound of ammonium sulfate per first-year tree, increasing the amount by ¼ pound per year, to a maximum of 1¼ pounds as the tree matures. Experience may show more to be required by a mature tree, but approach this fertilizer cautiously—overuse can burn roots.

The most aggressive program is the University of California's, which recommends a maximum of 6 pounds of ammonium sulfate for a mature tree, half in late summer, half in early spring. The late summer feeding is meant to help form new fruit buds; it is inadvisable in regions of early autumn frosts and cold winters. The UC program also calls for a feeding of potassium sulfate every fourth autumn.

In the arid West, zinc, manganese, and iron are common soil deficiencies that hamper apricots. If a tree fruits or grows poorly in spite of a steady fertilizing program, check with a farm advisor for a corrective action.

Pests and diseases. Brown rot and canker (bacterial gummosis) are serious diseases. Other, less frequent disease problems are oak root fungus, shot hole fungus, and cytosporina. Gophers dote on apricot roots. Serious insect damage is rare, though codling moths and twig borers can produce heavy infestation of fruit in a few areas. Aphids, Japanese beetles, mites, the oriental fruit moth, curculio, and scales also can affect trees, though no control is needed until the pests appear.

Brown rot (see page 108) is almost certain to develop in humid weather. It and fungus can be guarded against with a spray program during dormant season, before and after flowering, and at red-bud stage. For exact dates, check with a local county farm advisor.

Canker (see page 110) must be treated firmly, and surgically. Cut off dead branches before leaf drop. As leaves begin to drop, spray with Bordeaux mixture; then spray again after all leaves have dropped. If the tree dies in spite of the surgery, it must be dug out and disposed of away from the garden.

Gophers can be held at bay. Just enclose the root zone in wire mesh at planting time.

Apricots

Variety	Tree						Fruit					Chart Key:
	USDA Climate Zones *	Minimum chill hours **	Ripens	Bears	Semidwarf	Dwarf	Size	Quality				**Ripens:** E/Early, M/Mid, L/Late, VL/Very late **Bears:** L/Light, M/Medium, H/Heavy, VH/Very heavy **Size:** S/Small, M/Medium, L/Large, VL/Very large **Fruit quality:** O/Outstanding, E/Excellent, A/Average, P/Poor
								Fresh	Frozen	Canned	Dried	**Comments**
'Autumn Royal'	5–8	Avg	VL	H			M	A	A	E	E	A sport of 'Royal', it is the latest ripening 'cot.
'Bryan'	5–6	Avg	L	M			M	A	A	A	A	Recommended for n TX.
'Chinese' ('Mormon')	5–6	Avg	M/L	H			M	A	A	A	A	One of the best in mountainous late-frost areas.
'Earligold'	6–9	600	E	H			M	E	A	E	A	Needs pollenizer. Good for s CA, AZ.
'Early Gold(en)'	5–6	Avg	E	VH			M	E	A	E	A	Grows well in Northeast.
'Flora Gold'	5–8	Avg	E	M/H	•		M	E	A	E	A	Genetic dwarf about half normal size.
'Garden Annie'	5–9	600	M	M		•	M/L	E	A	A	A	Smallest of the genetic dwarfs.
'Goldcot'	4–9	900	E/M	H			M/L	E	A	E	A	Tough-skinned but tasty fruit. Grows well in MW.
'Golden Amber'	5–9	Avg	L	H			L	A	A	A	A	Tree is healthy, hardy; fruit is versatile.
'Goldkist'	7–9	600	E	H			M	E	E	E	E	Mild-flavored fruit tends to crack. Large tree.
'Goldrich'	5–6	Avg	M	H			L	A	A	A	A	Recommended in PNW, intermountain basin.
'Hardy Iowa'	5–6	Avg	I	H			S	E	A	E	A	Recommended in n Plains states. Fruit very sweet.
'Jannes'	5–8	Avg	E	L/M			M	A	A	A	A	One of few for cool, humid regions such as w VA.
'Manchu'	5–6	Avg	M	H			L	A	A	A	A	Hardy; well suited to Plains, Great Lakes states.
'Moongold'	4–6	Avg	L	M		•	M/L	E	A	A	A	Good in Plains, Great Lakes states; must have 'Sungold' as pollenizer.
'Moorpark'	5–7	Avg	M	L		•	VL	A	A	A	A	Highly regarded flavor; most widely adapted variety.
'Newcastle'	7–9	350	M	H			S/M	A	A	A	A	Highly subject to brown rot, canker; okay in s CA.
'Perfection' ('Goldbeck Perfection')	6–8	600	E	H			VL	E	A	A	A	Needs pollenizer. Grows best in NW; does well in w WA.
'Riland'	5–6	Avg	E/M	L/M			L	E	A	A	A	Good flavor, coarse texture; needs pollenizer.
'Rival'	5–6	Avg	E/M	H			L	P	A	E	P	Leggy tree. Fruit tends to brown.
'Royal' ('Blenheim')	6–8	600	E/M	VH			M/L	E	E	E	E	Standard CA commercial variety.
'Royal Rosa'	6–8	Avg	M/L	H			M	O	A	A	A	Pleasingly tart. Tree is compact.
'Royalty'	5–7	Avg	E	E/M			VL	A	A	A	A	Fruit spurs especially wind-resistant.
'Scout'	4–6	1000	L	L			M	A	A	A	O	Hardy in Manitoba; grows best in W.
'Sungold'	4–6	Avg	E	M			M	E	A	E	A	Mainly pollenizer for 'Moongold'.
'Superb'	5–6	Avg	E/M	M/H			M	A	A	A	A	Recommended KA to MN.
'Tilton'	5–7	1000	M	H			L/VL	A	A	A	A	Resists brown rot, canker. Can be alternate bearer.
'Wenatchee' ('Wenatchee Moorpark')	5–6	Avg	M	H			L	E	A	A	A	For PNW; sometimes confused with 'Moorpark'.

*See climate zones maps, pages 84–87.
**Average chilling hours 600–900. For more information, see pages 84–87.

Avocados

How to harvest treetop avocados

Millions, from every corner of the North American continent, have amused themselves growing avocado shrubs from seeds in the kitchen window, but only Californians, Hawaiians, Floridians, and handfuls of Louisianans and Texans can hope to grow a fruiting tree in the garden.

Where they grow

These unsweet, least fruity of fruits perform only when they find warm (not desert-hot) summers, virtually frost-free winters, balmy springs, and well-drained, well-watered soil. Nearly all commercial orchards are in southern California from Santa Barbara County southward to San Diego, and in southern Florida. Home gardeners who want a crop can push the range only a bit beyond

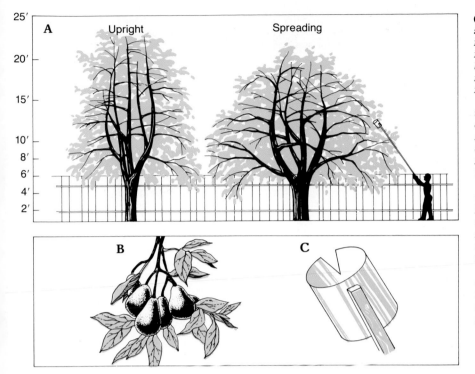

(A) *Though trees vary by variety from strongly upright to spreading, the modified central leader is an effective training method for all. Once the tree has its basic framework established, it will need episodic heading back to keep the fruit within reach.*

Many avocados keep an open center themselves through continuing dieback of internal branches, but may need occasional thinning. Otherwise pruning is done only to retain shape and to eliminate damaged or crossing branches. This may be done at any time.

(B) *There is no need to thin fruit, which grows at the tips of new branches. In removing branches, remember that avocado bark is sensitive to sunscald; if removal of a branch exposes previously shaded trunk to direct sun rays, coat the newly exposed bark with whitewash.*

(C) *As a substitute for manufactured picking devices like the one shown in the photo on page 20, nail a 2-pound coffee can or number 10 juice can to a pole. Use tin snips to cut the notch.*

those places—up the California coast into Santa Cruz County and the San Francisco Bay area, and throughout that state's great inland valley as far north as Colusa. In the Southeast, where lack of drainage can be a limitation, avocados grow in and around New Orleans and in the southern tip of Texas. Most of Hawaii is amenable.

Two strains of avocado grow in the U.S. The fruits of Guatemalan varieties are marked by thick, knobby skins of blackish green. Mexican varieties have thinner, shiny green or black hides and are much the cold-hardier of the two.

Hardiness is the key to correct selection of a variety, but if climate permits any latitude, give a thought to tree size. Some avocados demand large space; others, as the chart (see page 22) shows, are far more compact even though avocados are not classed as standard or dwarf.

Also, in considering size, remember harvest time. Tall avocados have to be harvested using a can (big enough to hold one or two pieces of fruit) with a sharp V-notch cut in one side (to snip the stems) and a long pole attached to the other (to reach up as much as 30 feet).

Site & soil

Not merely good but excellent drainage is a necessity. One winter of water table as high as the feeder root zone may be enough to kill a tree, so a site should be chosen with that in mind. The best sites are on slopes with good water *and* air drainage. Avocados should not be planted in lawns; they can't take as much water as grass needs. Given good drainage, the tree is adapted to a wide range of soils.

Propagating & planting

To get fruit, it is important to buy a nursery stock with a certified fruiting variety budded to rootstock. Most plants are sold balled and burlapped, or in containers, and are best set out in early autumn or spring in the West, the year around in Florida.

Avocados should be planted at the same depth as they grew in the container. Many growers build a temporary earthen collar equal to the diameter of the root ball around the trunk of a young tree to help steer

water to roots, which stay in the container zone for the first year. This can be especially important if a balled and burlapped tree has heavier soil around its roots than in the planting hole; in this situation, water may drain away too rapidly to soak the rootball unless applied with care.

Caring for the trees

Consistent, accurate watering is the key to success for avocados.

Watering. Avocado is more exacting about moisture than most trees. Too much and roots may rot (see "Pests and diseases," page 22). Too little or too erratic watering results in little or no crop and sickly trees.

During the first year, irrigate around the roots when the soil approaches dryness, usually every 7 to 12 days in summer. In following seasons, until the tree has a spread of 10 feet or more, build a 4 to 6-inch-deep watering basin to the drip line. Flood-irrigate every 2 to 4 weeks (lightly three times out of four, heavily the fourth to wash away accumulating salts). Mulch the basin surface with dropped leaves to keep

Ripe avocados

feeder roots cool. (In the rainy season, breach the low side of the basin wall so rainwater drains instead of standing.)

Because mature trees have deep tap roots, they may not require watering. However, they may bear more fruit in dry-summer climates if given a light irrigation every 4 weeks. If regular watering is not done, test during long dry spells to assure moisture in the top 15 inches of soil, where feeder roots concentrate. If this zone dries out, or if leaves begin to wilt, irrigate.

Fertilizing. In the West, avocados need only light fertilizing, if any. The University of California recommends 5 pounds of ammonium sulfate for a mature tree, broadcast in January or February and left for winter rains to soak into the root zone. Some growers use a 50-50 solution of fish emulsion, a quart for young trees, a gallon for ones 12 years old and older.

In Florida, the recommendation is for annual applications of balanced fertilizers in the 6-6-6 to 10-10-6 range. First-year trees are fed ¼ pound every other month; amounts increase by ¼ pound per year for 4 years. Thereafter, feedings are quarterly.

Mineral deficiencies are a separate problem. To correct chlorosis (iron deficiency revealed by yellowed leaves), apply chelated iron or iron sulfate. If leaves become narrow, curled, and concentrated toward branch tips, spray with zinc sulfate. Use volumes indicated on package.

Pests and diseases. Root rot is a prime disease of over-watered trees. The symptoms are dropping, yellowed leaves. No sure-fire cure exists. The most practical move is to give the tree only about a fourth as much water as a healthy tree uses, then wait and see. If root rot is known to have occurred in an area, it is best not to plant avocados at all. Anthracnose is a particular problem with Mexican varieties in the Southeast.

Avocados

Variety	Origin	Height	Frost hardiness	Bears	Ripens	Fruit size	Comments
	Tree						Chart Key: **Origin:** M/Mexico, G/Guatemala, X/Hybrid **Height:** S/Short, M/Medium, MT/Medium tall, T/Tall **Frost hardiness:** T/Tender, M/Medium, H/Hardy, VH/Very hardy **Bears:** M/Medium, H/Heavy **Fruit Size:** S/Small, M/Medium, L/Large
'Bacon'	M	M	H	H	Nov–Mar	M	Hardy; giving way to similar, hardier 'Jim'.
'Choquette'	X	M	T	M	Nov–Feb	L	Good FL variety. Resists scab.
'Duke'	M	T	H	H	Sep–Nov	M/L	Thin-skinned. Productive in home gardens. Somewhat resistant to root rot.
'Fuerte'	X	T	H	M	Nov–Jun	M	Best known, much grown. Not for spring frost areas.
'Hass'	G	MT	M	H	Apr–Oct	S/M	Fine commercial variety. Thick skin peels easily.
'Jim'	M	M	VH	H	Oct–Jan	M	Hardier seedling of 'Bacon'.
'Mexicola'	M	M	VH	H	Aug–Oct	S	Deliciously nutty fruit. Excellent for CA home gardens.
'Reed'	G	M	T	H	Jul–Sep	M/L	Excellent flavor. Limited range.
'Rincon'	G	S	T	M	Jan–Apr	S	Small fruit has large seed, resembles 'Fuerte'. Tree size an advantage.
'Tonnage'	X	M	M	M	Sep–Oct	M/L	One of the hardiest in FL; good fruit.
'Waldin'	X	M	T	M	Sep–Oct	M/L	Another solid, scab-resistant variety in FL.
'Wurtz'	G	S	T	M	Jul–Sep	M	So slow to grow to 12 feet, often sold as dwarf. Bears early.
'Zutano'	M	T	H	H	Oct–Feb	S/M	Flavorful. May suffer brown, scaly "end spot" in s CA.

Blueberries

Blueberries nearing ripeness

Two bushes per family member will yield all the fresh blueberries (swimming in milk, in compotes, or over ice cream or yogurt) the average soul can stand, plus enough for a wealth of blueberry cobblers, muffins, pies, and pancakes.

All varieties are at their crisp, flavorful best used fresh; all will freeze or can well. They also cook into delicious sauces for desserts, and make distinctive jams and jellies.

Where they grow

Two separate but similar and similarly flavored species of blueberries grow in North America. The highbush blueberry grows well from Michigan and Ontario eastward into New England, as far south along the Atlantic coast as Virginia (into North Carolina, with special care),

Green berries will be too tart to eat

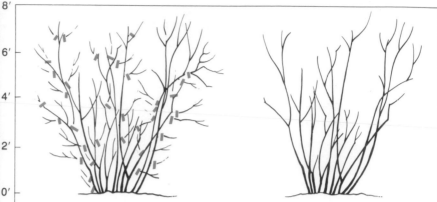

Most highbush varieties grow upright. A few sprawl. All can be planted 3 feet apart in informal hedges, but usually are spaced about 5 feet in home gardens. Rabbiteye bushes are slightly larger, requiring 5 feet of spacing in hedges, 8 feet in open plantings.

At planting, either species should be pruned to three or four strong canes 18 to 24 inches long, and stripped of plump fruit buds.

When canes reach desired height, tip them, leaving six to eight buds to promote side branching, on which most of the fruit will grow.

To keep mature plants strong and bearing well, each year cut out one or two weakened older canes (those with twiggy side branches) and cut away late-season growth near the base of the bush. If there is twiggy old growth at the base of an established plant, trim it away. For bigger berries, trim side branches to six to eight fruiting buds. Pruning can be done any time between harvest and the following March; the preferred season is January (in milder climates) to mid-March.

The illustration at left shows where to prune; at right is the finished product.

and along the Pacific Coast from northern California well into British Columbia. Highbush varieties require winter chill and do not take intense summer heat well.

The rabbiteye blueberry belongs exclusively to the U.S. South, from Georgia south into Florida, and—in spots—west into Texas. Rabbiteyes reverse the needs of their northern cousins, withstanding heat better, resisting cold less ably.

The territory of both species can be expanded by determined gardeners willing to create proper soils and manufacture tolerable imitations of correct weathers. At least one gardener in Los Angeles grows highbush blueberries in peat moss, in drip-irrigated containers, getting crops of about half normal volume.

Wherever they grow, blueberries ripen nearly all of their fruit at once, with the curious quirk that they do not sweeten until 3 days after full color.

Site & soil

Highbush blueberries thrive in frequently watered, well-drained, acid soil rich in organic matter—the kind that suits rhododendrons and azaleas, to which the berry is related. Bushes survive in soils ranging from pH 3.4 to 6.5; they prosper in the range 4.5 to 5.0. The water table

should be at least 14 inches below the surface during the growing season. In their normal territory, they need full light. (In the wild in New England, they grow mainly on small hummocks in open, swampy terrain.)

Recommendations for rabbiteye varieties are nearly identical: soil rich in organic matter, pH ideally between 4.5 and 5.2, and a water table about 20 inches below the surface during the growing season. The upper limit on pH has been given as 5.5 for rabbiteyes. They do not require full sun, having been cultivated from native plants that grow along stream banks in wooded areas.

Soils slightly high in pH can be corrected if you dig in peat moss just before planting, or fertilize with sulfur 6 months before planting. (Direct contact with raw sulfur will kill blueberry roots.) If garden soils have been limed or are naturally alkaline, it is best to plant blueberries in beds of pure peat moss. Both species need proper soils to a depth and width of 18 inches.

Propagating & planting

Few blueberry varieties self pollenate. Any two varieties of highbush will pollenate, as will any two rabbiteyes. Three varieties that ripen one after another will pollenate and prolong the harvest season profitably. Alternate varieties in (and across) rows for effective pollenation.

Blueberries are propagated from hardwood cuttings. Certified 2 or 3-year-old rooted cuttings in containers give the best guarantee of healthy plants and early crops.

Rooted cuttings of highbush blueberries should be planted in spring in cold-winter eastern areas, in autumn in much of the mild-winter West. Rabbiteye blueberries are planted in autumn.

Caring for the bushes

The commonest maintenance problem with these plants is lack of

Blueberries

Variety	USDA Climate Zones*	Plant			Fruit
		Comments	Ripens		Comments
Highbush blueberries					
'Atlantic'	6–7	Sprawling; best in E.	L		Pale, large. Flavorful dessert berry.
'Berkeley'	5–8	Tall, spreading, productive.	M/L		Pale, mild. Good in pies; middling as dessert.
'Bluecrop'	5–8	Tall; can overcrop; resists drought.	M		Mild, excellent flavor.
'Blueray'	5–7	Tall, upright, productive in NE.	M		Almost as flavorful as 'Berkeley'; more tart, crisp.
'Bluetta'	5–6	Compact. Resists spring frost.	E		Firm flesh. Fairly flavorful.
'Coville'	5–8	Vigorous, productive.	L		Tart, aromatic. Good dessert berry.
'Croatan'	7–8	Bears young. Standard in NC.	M		Aromatic, mild acidity. Good dessert berry.
'Darrow'	5–6	Vigorous, very productive.	L		Resembles 'Coville'; can be more tart.
'Dixi'	7–8	Straggly, but produces in W, especially PNW.	L		Big, tasty dessert berry. Easily bruised.
'Earliblue'	5–7	Hardy, shapely, upright.	E/M		Large berries, excellent flavor. Moderately acidic.
'Ivanhoe'	5–6	Erect, vigorous. Subject to canker.	E/M		Large, crisp berry of excellent flavor.
'Jersey'	5–6	Vigorous, hardy. Widely grown.	M/L		Large, bland berry. Keeps well.
'Late blue'	6	Productive. Ripens in short span.	L		Small, firm-fleshed, highly flavored.
'Pemberton'	5–6	Productive. Hard to pick.	L		Delicate flavor. Fair to good dessert berry.
'Rubel'	5–6	Needs consistent pruning.	E/L		Firm, tart berry.
'Stanley'	5–7	Erect, open. Easy to prune.	E/M		Firm, aromatic, spicy. Excellent dessert berry.
Rabbiteye blueberries					
'Bluebelle'	8	Moderately vigorous. Long season.	M		Soft skinned. Excellent flavor.
'Brightwell'	8	Vigorous. Ripens in short span.	E		Medium size. Good flavor.
'Briteblue'	9	Produces few new canes.	M/L		Fair flavor. Firm, sturdy berry.
'Climax'	8	Upright, open.	E		Medium size. Dark blue berry. Good flavor.
'Delite'	9	More vigorous than 'Briteblue'.	M/L		Excellent flavor; less tart than most.
'Powerblue'	7–8	Very similar to 'Tifblue'.	M		Excellent flavor; less tart than most.
'Tifblue'	7–8	Vigorous. Ripens well in TX.	M/L		Firm flesh, good flavor, tart until fully ripe.
'Woodard'	8–9	Short, spreading. Productive early.	E		Pale. Firm-fleshed. Slightly tart at full ripeness.

*See climate zone maps, pages 84–87.

watering. A web of fine roots grows close to the surface, a circumstance which, coupled with a lack of hair roots, makes frequent watering a critical need.

Watering. During the growing season, young plants need 1 to 2 inches of water a week to bear a full crop. Mature plants can use the equivalent of 5 to 7 gallons per day, especially toward harvest time; a weekly soak works well. Both species respond well to drip irrigation. A 6-inch-deep bark mulch conserves moisture.

Fertilizing. Blueberries in less than ideally acidic soils benefit most from a high-nitrogen, acidifying fertilizer such as ammonium sulfate (21-0-0) or one formulated for rhododendrons and azaleas (18-4-7, for example); the usual amounts for either are 2 ounces for a first-year plant, then 2-ounce increases each subsequent year to a maximum of 8 ounces. In good soil, a complete fertilizer such as 10-10-10 (from 4 ounces to a maximum of 16) works well and should replace any other fertilizer at least every third year. Fer-

tilize in spring. In alkaline soils typical of southern California and parts of the Southeast, it may be necessary to supplement fertilizers with iron sulfate or iron chelate to correct chlorosis.

Pests and diseases. Neither blueberry is so susceptible to pests or diseases as to require a regular program of spraying or other control except where powdery mildew is common. Netting will keep birds at bay in regions where they compete for ripe berries.

Brambleberries

Red raspberry vines

AT A GLANCE

Climate: Prospers along cool, humid coasts (northern California to British Columbia, the Northeast, Mid-Atlantic), in the Great Lakes basin, and in cool-night areas at moderate elevations in mountainous country. Selected varieties good in Gulf states. Not adapted to the Plains states or other regions of hot, dry summers and harsh winters.

Soil: Tolerant, but best in rich, well-drained sandy loam, pH 5.5 to 6.8. Poorly adapted to heavy, slow-draining soils.

Bushes bear: In second year.

Typical life span: 5 to 30 years (self-reproducing).

Typical yield at maturity: 2 to 4 pounds per bush.

Self-pollenizer: Yes, with rare exceptions.

Harvest season: Early summer; into autumn for everbearers.

Principal pests and diseases: Aphids, borers, leaf and cane spot, mites, strawberry root weevil, root rots.

Blackberries and raspberries taste a fair bit different—blackberries wilder, raspberries tamer—but the two botanical cousins are known together, poetically, as brambles. Their cultivation is not half so diverse as their flavors. Indeed, there is more variation in growing habits among blackberries than there is distance between some of them and raspberries, and so they are gathered here.

Where they grow

Blackberry varieties typical of the eastern half of the continent grow upright canes, while western varieties are trailing in habit. (Crosses

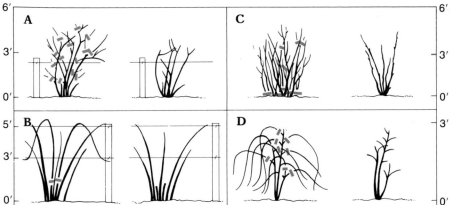

Roots and crowns of brambles are perennial, but canes live only 2 years, growing the first year (as primocanes), bearing fruit the second (as floricanes). Training varies sharply by type.

(A) Erect blackberries are planted 5 feet apart, and any canes are cut back to 6 inches. Best three to five canes of first year are cut back to 24 to 36 inches during first summer to force side growth, and tied to wire. Side branches are cut to 12 to 15 inches during dormancy. These bear fruit in second year. Directly after harvest, canes that bore fruit are cut to ground; newer canes, having been headed back to desired height during season, now are tied to wire in place of pruned canes (immediately in mild-winter regions; after over-winter mulching in hard-winter areas).

(B) Trailing blackberries are spaced 4 to 6 feet apart at planting (except for 'Evergreen', spaced 8 to 12 feet), and all canes are cut back to 6 inches. Train strongest first-year canes onto trellis to fruit the following season. Directly after they fruit, trim them to ground and replace them on trellis with (as plants mature) 12 to 16 strongest

canes of newer growth. Head these back to 6 to 8 feet to force side growth. During dormancy cut side branches back to 12 inches.

(C) Red (and yellow) raspberries are planted 3 feet apart. After being cut back to 6 inches at planting, they go unpruned during their first year. During second year, summer-bearing varieties are headed back to about 5 feet to fit trellis, and thinned to six to eight strong canes. After harvest, cut to ground all canes that fruited, and guide younger canes onto trellis. As plants mature, thin canes to 6 to 8 inches apart. Everbearing varieties fruit in their first autumn on top third of cane, in second summer on lower two-thirds. First-year canes go unpruned until they have fruited, then are cut back to lowest point that bore fruit. After fruiting on lower portion in second year, canes are cut to ground.

(D) Purple raspberries are planted and pruned exactly as erect blackberries. So are black raspberries, with the exception that side branches are cut back to 8 to 10 inches, substantially shorter than their cousins.

Although a few varieties of each are advertised as thornless, most of the highly desirable ones exact the price of thorns—longer or shorter, sharper or duller, but thorns. However many thorns, 15 plants will satisfy the needs of an average family.

Site & soil

All brambles fare best in deep, rich, well-drained soil and full sun. However, depth and drainage are more important than soil texture at the surface. Because of their susceptibility to verticillium wilt, brambles should not be planted where potatoes, tomatoes, eggplants, or peppers have grown within the previous 2 years, or within 500 feet of older brambles. The best edible plants to grow to rehabilitate soils with wilt include beans, cauliflower, peas, and summer squash.

To give new roots room to develop, work soil to a depth of 9 inches or more. Many veteran gardeners dig animal manure into new beds.

In hard-winter areas, brambles are best planted on slight slopes with good air drainage. North exposures help keep plants dormant until spring freezes are past. Wherever any bramble crowds its hardiness limitations, the bed should have a thick enough mulch for the first-year canes to be buried for protection against freezing. No bramble endures standing water during the dormant season.

between the two are held to be semi-upright or semitrailing, depending on the eye of the beholder.) Also, some varieties are so distinctive that they have separate identities, four of the best known being boysenberry, loganberry, marionberry, and ollalieberry.

In one or another of their many forms, blackberries are adapted to a broader range of weathers than raspberries, especially to hotter climates. They make incomparable pies, fine jams and jellies, tangy syrups, and, in skilled hands, very good wines. Excepting a few sweeter varieties, the tart, often seedy, always strongly flavored blackberry gives more pleasure in processed forms than it

does in fresh fruit desserts.

Raspberries, for their part, are subdivided by color—black, purple, red, and yellow—as a quick index of deeper distinctions. Red raspberries are erect and grow primarily in the West. Yellow varieties are identical to red raspberries in all but hue. Black raspberries have arched canes; they grow in much the same range as erect blackberries, and in the Pacific Northwest. Purple raspberries, crosses of red and black, grow in the same range as the black half of their parentage. Their blander flavors make them ready candidates for fresh desserts. They also yield fine pies, jams, jellies, and syrups.

Propagating & planting

Erect blackberries and red raspberries are propagated most readily by root cuttings. Trailing blackberries and black and purple raspberries are propagated by tip layering. Nurseries sell them all as bare-root plants or in containers.

In hard-winter regions, planting usually is done after the last hard freezes, when soil begins to warm. New bare-root plants should be set an inch deeper than they grew at the nursery, their crowns covered with an inch of soil. In mild-winter areas, gardeners can plant in spring, or gain half a season by transplanting growing plants.

Spacing and training methods differ for erect and trailing varieties, as noted in the caption accompanying the illustration on page 27.

Caring for the bushes

Brambles need regular maintenance on all counts.

Watering. It is better to underwater brambles than to overwater them, because of their susceptibility to root rots. In the coastal Northwest and much of the Northeast and Southeast, they may not need irrigation at all. In dry areas, water weekly or less often—not before the top 2 inches of soil has dried out.

Fertilizing. Use manure or a commercial type of fertilizer specified for berries (often 10-10-10, sometimes 5-10-10 or 5-10-5 for young plants). A middling course is 7 to 8 pounds per 100 square feet of vines per year. In most mild-winter regions, the recommended practice is to divide the total volume of fertilizer into thirds, for application first before new growth starts, again in midspring, and finally in midsummer just as the berries are ripening. In harsh-winter areas, feed only twice—never after June 15, because late growth cannot harden against freezes. In the Pacific Northwest,

Brambleberries (Blackberries)

Variety	Plant				Fruit			Chart Key:
	USDA Climate Zones*	Ripens	Habit	Bears	Fresh	Cooked	Frozen	**Ripens:** VE/Very early, E/Early, M/Mid, L/Late, VL/Very late **Habit:** U/Upright, T/Trailing, SU/Semiupright, ST/Semitrailing **Bears:** M/Medium, H/Heavy, VH/Very heavy **Fruit quality:** O/Outstanding, E/Excellent, A/Average Quality **Comments**
'Black Satin'	6–8	L	U	H	A	A	A	Thornfree. Hardy. Good in IL, OH, mid-Atlantic, NE.
'Boysen'	7–8	L	T	VH	A	A	A	Fine flavor, not as sweet as 'Young'.
'Brazos'	8–9	E	U	M	A	A	A	Adapted to TX, Gulf. Large berries over long season.
'Cascade'	7–8	E	T	H	O	O	E	Only in W. In pies, superb flavor reminiscent of wild blackberry.
'Chehalem'	7–8	L	T	H	A	A	E	Only in wet, rich soils of W. Small berries, excellent flavor.
'Cherokee'	6–8	E	U	M	A	A	A	For AK and nearby.
'Comanche'	6–8	E	U	M	A	A	A	For AK and nearby.
'Dallas'	6–8	E	ST	M	A	A	A	For TX, OK.
'Darrow'	5–7	E	U	H	A	A	A	Hardy, reliable in VA, KA, NY. Good flavor, a bit bland.
'Dirksen'	5–7	M/L	U	M	A	A	A	Disease-resistant in IL, OH, mid-Atlantic states.
'Ebony King'	5–7	E	U	M	A	A	A	Hardy in MI. Sweet, tangy.
'Eldorado'	5–7	E/M	U	M	E	A	A	One of best except in deep S. Large, firm, sweet berries.
'Evergreen'	8	VL	T	H	A	E	A	Only in W. Will run rampant. Exceptionally firm, sweet. Big seeds.
'Floridagrand'	9	VE	T	H	A	E	A	Adapted to hot, humid areas. Needs 'Oklawaha' as pollenizer.
'Gem'	8	E/M	T	M	A	A	A	Hardy in S. Firm flesh, good flavor in home gardens.
'Georgia Thornless'	9	M	SU	M	A	A	A	Firm flesh, good flavor in Gulf Coast home gardens only.
'Jerseyblack'	6–7	M	U	H	A	A	A	Rust-resistant. Resembles 'Eldorado'; a bit bland.
'Logan'	7–8	E	T	H	A	E	A	Very tart in jams, other cooking uses. Only for W.
'Marion'	8	L	T	VH	O	E	E	Only in coastal NW. Flavor superior to 'Boysen', 'Evergreen'.
'Mayes'	7–8	E	T	M	A	A	A	Much grown in TX. Subject to anthracnose. Berries very soft.
'Oklawaha'	9	VE	T	M	E	A	A	Largely self-fruitful. Delightful flavor. Berries soft.
'Olallie'	8	M	T	VH	E	A	A	Adapted OR to s CA, on Gulf Coast. Excellent flavor only if fully ripe.
'Raven'	6–7	E	U	M	A	E	E	Hardy from MD s and w. Attractive, richly flavored fruit.
'Smoothstem'	7–8	VL	SU	M	A	A	A	Hardy from MD s. For home gardens. Tart, good flavor.
'Thornfree'	6–8	L	SU	H	A	A	A	Productive in OR, from MD s to NC, w to AK. Pleasingly tart.
'Young' ('Lavaca')	6–8	M	T	M	A	E	E	Disease-prone in S, less so in W. Wine-colored fruit very sweet.

*See climate zone maps, pages 84–87.

many growers make one annual feeding at blossom time.

Pests and diseases. Brambles seldom need an annual spraying program to control pests, but they should be controlled as soon as they appear in any numbers. To control mites (see page 110)—and whiteflies—use a dormant spray containing lime sulfur in winter and again just before budbreak; then spray with malathion when leaves unfold, and again a month later. To control cane borers, which reveal their presence by pinhead-size holes in canes at or near ground level, spray with diazinon no more than twice during the dormant season, repeating for 2 years. Also, prune out and destroy all damaged canes (and, if necessary, crowns).

Anthracnose, a common fungus disease in humid regions is treated with annual applications of lime sulfur during the dormant season and again at the start of blossom. Most other fungus diseases are controlled primarily by pruning out and disposing of damaged canes.

Brambleberries (Raspberries)

| Variety | Plant | | | | Fruit | | | Chart Key: |
	USDA Climate Zones*	Type	Ripens	Bears	Quality Fresh	Cooked	Frozen	**Type:** B/Black or purple (trailing), R/Red or yellow (upright) **Ripens:** VE/Very early, E/Early, M/Mid, L/Late, Ev/Everbearing **Bears:** M/Medium, H/Heavy, VH/Very heavy **Fruit quality:** O/Outstanding, E/Excellent, A/Average, P/Poor Comments
'Allen'	5–7	B	M	H	A	A	A	Large, firm berries ripen all together. Adapted to Great Lakes, NE.
'Black Hawk'	5	B	L	H	E	E	E	Hardy from Iowa e. Widely grown.
'Brandywine'	4–8	B	M	H	A	A	A	Purple. Berries large, tart. Plant very hardy.
'Bristol'	5–8	B	M	H	A	A	A	Excellent flavor. Easily damaged by rain.
'Canby'	5–8	R	M	M	E	P	E	Red or yellow fruit. Fine in NW. Thornless, hardy; not for heavy soils.
'Clyde'	4–8	B	L	VH	A	A	A	Purple. Berries large, tart. Plant very hardy.
'Cumberland'	5–8	B	M	H	A	A	A	Widely grown in E; hardy but virus-prone.
'Dorman Red'	5–8	R	M	M	A	A	A	Mediocre fruit, but only hope in hot, humid SE.
'Durham'	5–7	R	E	M	A	A	A	Good quality. Ripens early in autumn.
'Fairview'	5–8	R	M	H	E	P	O	For coastal NW. More tolerant of heavy soils than most.
'Fallgold'	4–8	R	Ev	H	E	A	A	Among the hardiest.
'Fallred'	4–8	R	Ev	H	E	A	A	Main crop late summer. Fine in Great Lakes, NE. Mow instead of pruning.
'Heritage'	5–8	R	Ev	M	A	A	A	Small berries tasty, a bit dry. Hardy in NE, but broadly adapted.
'Huron'	5–7	B	M/L	H	A	A	A	Good all-around berry.
'Indian Summer'	4–8	R	Ev	H	A	E	A	Berries large, tasty. For home gardens; autumn crop often the heavier one.
'Latham'	4–8	R	L	H	A	E	E	Crumbly fruit. Hardy in intermountains. Mildews if summer is humid.
'Meeker'	5–8	R	M	H	A	E	E	Large, firm berries. Best suited to NW. Resists mildew.
'Milton'	5–7	R	L	H	A	A	A	Good flavor. Virus-resistant in E.
'Morrison'	5–7	B	L	M	A	A	A	Largest black berry. Grows in OH, PA, western NY.
'Munger'	5–8	B	M	M	A	A	A	Fine flavor. The only black variety widely grown in NW.
'Newburgh'	5–7	R	M/L	M	A	P	P	Hardy. More tolerant of heavy soils than most. Adapted to NE, NW.
'Reveille'	5–7	R	E	M	E	A	A	Soft-fleshed variety, best in home gardens.
'September'	4–7	R	Ev	M	A	A	A	Small, flavorful berries. Autumn crop the real one. Much planted in E.
'Sodus' ('Burgundy')	5–7	B	L	H	A	A	A	Hardy, drought-resistant. Susceptible to verticillium.
'Sumner'	5–8	R	E	M	E	E	E	Fine fruit. Hardy. Plant takes heavier soils. For NW.
'Sunrise'	4–8	R	VE	M	A	A	A	Surpasses 'Latham', one of its parents.
'Willamette'	5–8	R	M	H	A	E	E	Firm, dark red berries hold shape well. Much planted in NW.

*See climate zone maps, pages 84–87.

Cherries

A climber's cherry tree

Climate: Most varieties suited to USDA Zones 5–6 everywhere, and to cool-winter parts of Zones 7–9 west of the Rockies. Hardy varieties may bear in Zone 4.

Soil: Ideal is fertile loam at pH 6.5. Requires good drainage.

Trees bear: Early maturers at 3 years; late ones at 8.

Typical life span: 30 years.

Typical yield at maturity: 15 quarts (pie and sweet dwarfs) to 35 quarts (sweet standards).

Self-pollenizer: Sweet cherries no, with two exceptions. Sour cherries yes.

Semidwarfs and dwarfs available: Yes.

Harvest season: Mainly June. Earliest variety in May, latest in early July.

Principal pests and diseases: Birds, brown rot. Also aphids, bud moth, canker, cherry fruit fly, cherry leaf spot, curculio, fruit moth, Japanese beetle, pear slugs, scale.

'Bing'

A full-grown 'Bing' cherry tree towers high enough and has enough thick, gently angled limbs to provide a whole day of bird's-eye views for any agile child at any time of year.

As a harvest-time bonus, the mere gleanings will allow heedless youth to cultivate a heroic bellyache.

The most practical way to acquire such a tree is to inherit one with a property. Sweet cherries are such slow growers that the grandchildren of whoever plants a tree are the most likely first generation of climbers in it. Rate of growth aside, not every modern lot will hold a standard 'Bing', or any of the other vigorous varieties. Not only do they tower, they spread. That is to say, for most properties other than farms, a stan-

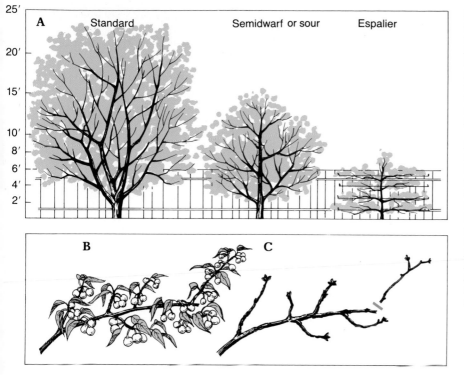

A — Standard / Semidwarf or sour / Espalier

25'
20'
15'
10'
8'
6'
4'
2'

B   C

(A) *The tall, upright sweet cherry is typically trained to the open-center system in all parts of the country save the Midwest, where the modified central leader system is preferred. In all regions, short and spreading sour cherry tree responds best to central leader system, as does Duke. Dwarfs and semidwarfs of both sweet and pie cherries make good formal espaliers.*

(B) *Cherries bear on long-lived fruiting spurs. Except for removing doubles, fruit seldom needs to be thinned.*

(C) *Aside from removing weak or damaged branches, cherries need pruning only to maintain shape, remove crossing branches. In cold-winter areas, trees may need no pruning from year to year. If tree becomes too crowded in center as it matures, thin lightly. To help young tree spread, head branches in crowded center back to an outward-facing bud. Do not create gaping holes in canopy; trunk and main branches are susceptible to sunburn.*

dard tree has to be the centerpiece in the landscaping.

Fortunately, all sweet cherry varieties bear fruit early enough to provide learning experiences in the bellyache department for young planters, let alone the first generation of small fry. Further, new but promising dwarf and spur varieties are small enough to be grown in cramped spaces, even in containers. They also are perfect candidates for espaliering. The dwarfs include some genetic varieties and a number of familiar varieties grafted onto dwarfing rootstocks.

In fact, the only real problems with sweet cherries are the limitations imposed by climate. They are less hardy than any other stone fruit, but need substantial winter chill to bear well. At the other end of the year, even modest summer rains can lead to splitting and spoilage of the ripening fruit.

In compensation there are sour cherries—more usefully known as pie cherries—and their near cousins, the Dukes. They expand the climatic range somewhat in both hotter and colder directions, and are not so prone to splitting. Besides, they hardly ever cause a bellyache, at least not directly.

Where they grow

Even more than apples, sweet cherries must have long hours of winter chill to grow and bear well, a fact that makes them much better adapted to the northern half of the country than the southern. Their minimum requirement is 800 hours at 45°F/7°C or lower; more chill—ideally 1200 hours—is better. The cherry's inability to withstand long hot spells pushes plantings in the same northerly direction. However, the northerly limits are strict, too. Cherries are not hardy in the severe winters of USDA Zone 3, and their ability to bear can be damaged by autumn freezes even in Zone 5.

The tendency of the ripening fruit to split during summer rains is yet another limitation on the range of most cherry varieties. Similarly, the diseases to which they are most susceptible are those commonest in humid climates.

As usual, ideal climates are revealed by the location of commercial orchards. The Willamette Valley of Oregon, the Yakima Valley of eastern Washington, and the Okanagan district of British Columbia—with their long, dry summers and chilly but

not bitter winters—are prominent sources of commercial sweet cherries in the West. (California's finest orchards, in the low-rainfall coastal valleys south of San Francisco, largely have been supplanted by housing, but the area remains among the most rewarding for home gardeners.)

East of the Rocky mountains, regions of greatest commercial importance for sweet cherries stretch along the southern side of the Great Lakes basin, including southern Ontario, and eastward as far as the Hudson River Valley of New York.

Sweet cherries grow fairly successfully in home gardens throughout the western states, except in southern California, the southwest desert, and in the higher mountains.

East of the Rockies, USDA Zone 6 is the natural home of sweet cherries. Home gardeners willing to settle for short crops, irregular ones, or both, grow sweet cherries in Zone 4. That is to say, in one fashion or another they will do well somewhere in nearly every state north and northeast of Texas, save for Minnesota and the Dakotas, but not everywhere in any of them. As with other fruit trees, the most promising sites are on air-draining slopes facing bodies of water large enough to temper extreme temperatures.

Sour cherries are a slightly hardier, more adaptable tribe. They are a much more reliable bet than sweet cherries in most of New England and in the colder parts of the Great Lakes basin and much of the Great Plains. The subtribe known as amarelles are hardiest. A second group, morellos, has greater ability to withstand summer heat, making them a better choice than sweet cherries in northern Texas, Oklahoma, and elsewhere in the Plains.

Duke cherries, hyrbids of sweet and sour varieties, taste better in pies than fresh, but grow most reliably where sweet cherries do.

Choosing a variety

Beyond climate adaptability and resistance to disease, the choice of type and variety of cherry depends mostly on which uses the fruit will serve. Other important factors are tree size and the need (or lack of need) for a pollenizer.

The basic choice, of course, is between sweet and pie cherries. But among sweet cherries there are better and worse varieties for fresh eating, and better and worse varieties for canning or freezing. Pie cherries, after years of selective breeding, now have a broader range of sweetness than they once did, and also have gotten meatier.

Pie cherries and Dukes are, without exception, self-pollenizers. Only two commonly available sweet cherry varieties are self-pollenizers, and three are sterile. 'Garden Bing' and 'Stella' are the self-fertile varieties. No combination of 'Bing', 'Lambert', and 'Royal Ann' will produce fruit, all three being sterile. Any other combination of varieties can pollenize each other, though pairing an early and late variety may not work well.

Pie cherries and Dukes take considerably less space than a standard sweet cherry (or a pair of them). Some nurseries sell trees with second (and third) varieties grafted on as pollenizers for the main selection, a way to have one big tree. (The skilled sometimes do their own grafting, but it is not a game for the uninitiated.) The other spacesavers—genetic dwarfs, spur varieties, and varieties grafted onto dwarfing rootstock—show great promise but remain unknowns in most regions because they are so recently introduced.

The smaller varieties train very well as espaliers to save space.

Site & soil

Cherries need deep, well-drained loams with pHs in the 5.5 to 6.5 range, preferably 6.0 to 6.5. Reliable drainage is more vital to a healthy tree than fertile soil.

Because cherries blossom early, gardeners who elect to control pests and diseases with sprays should not plant these trees close to later fruits; the spraying schedules are incompatible. Neither is it a good idea to plant cherries in lawns, because their fertilizing and watering requirements differ.

Varieties planted in regions where late frosts threaten blossoms may benefit from a north exposure that helps retard bloom.

Pollenizers must be within 200 feet of each other.

Propagating & planting

All cherry types grown on their own roots are propagated from hardwood cuttings, or from rooted suckers in the case of some shallow-rooted varieties. (The latter technique is sometimes used to replace age-worn trees on the spot.) Trees on dwarfing rootstock are propagated by budding.

As with most fruits, the least expensive new tree is a bare-root one planted in March or April. Trees can be bought in containers or balled and burlapped for planting in other seasons.

Grafted trees must be set with the bud union 4 to 6 inches above grade to prevent the top variety from rooting and reverting to standard size.

Caring for the trees

Cherry trees require especially watchful attention to pests—notably birds—and diseases.

Watering. Cherries are less drought-resistant than most trees, yet, curious as it may seem, they hardly ever need watering in their most productive ranges—the coastal Northwest and the Northeast from the Great Lakes eastward. Even in dry California, early varieties may bear without irrigation. However, all cherries will need water to get through the summer, be it rainfall or irrigation.

Water should be applied as soon as the top 3 inches of soil is dry, and should be run long enough to soak down 4 feet. In rich loam, this usually means a 2-hour soak from a trickling hose whenever a dry spell lasts longer than 2 weeks. In sandy soil, use less water more often. In clay loams, the interval is likely to be longer.

The needs of shallow-rooted dwarf cherries are an exaggerated version of the needs of standards.

Fertilizing. A healthy standard sweet cherry should produce between 6 and 12 inches of tip growth per year.

In the Northeast, the trees grow that well with no more than an annual mulch of straw or lawn clippings, according to the University of Massachusetts. In the coastal Northwest, they seldom need even that. More aggressive fertilizing programs differ sharply by region.

For mature trees, Pennsylvania State University recommends a maximum of 5 pounds of balanced fertilizer (10-10-10) between March 15 and April 1. Young trees get ½ pound per year of age. The school cautions against fertilizing later; tender new growth cannot harden before the first freezes of autumn. For regions with a long, warm autumn, the University of California suggests 4 pounds of ammonium sulfate per mature tree, applied directly after harvest in order to boost production of new fruit buds.

The same fertilizers work for dwarf sweet cherries, sour cherries, and Dukes. An easy rule of thumb for them is ½ pound of 10-10-10 per inch of trunk diameter measured at the ground. Penn State University recommends a different program for sour cherries: 1 ounce of ammonium nitrate per year of tree age to a maximum 8 ounces, plus 8 pounds of 0-20-10 every third or fourth year.

As with all fruits, distribution of any fertilizer should start 1 foot away from the trunk and extend outward to the drip line.

Pests and diseases. The long list of diseases to which cherries are prone includes bacterial gummosis, brown rot, cherry leaf spot, and leaf curl. Insect pests include aphids, bud moth, curculio, fruit moth, Japanese beetles, mites, pear slugs, and scale.

The dormant oil spray (*not* copper sulfate and lime) that controls leaf curl also will take care of mites and scales (see pages 110–111). The growing-season spray—usually benomyl—used for brown rot (see page 108) also inhibits curculio and the other moths and maggots. To this list, gardeners in the Northwest must add the cherry fruit fly (better known as apple maggot).

Cracked fruit after rain is not a disease but a characteristic of some varieties. The only solution is to plant a resistant variety. Some of the most and least resistant are noted in the comment section of the chart.

Troublesome as insects and diseases may be, it is birds that pose the surest threat. Given free reign in a tree, the most lovable of them will leave the short end of a crop anytime, and will open that remaining fraction to brown rot or other spoilage in the process. Nurseries sell a loose-woven netting designed to thwart birds. Dwarf trees can be covered from the ground; standard trees must be shrouded from ladders or by using long sapling poles, or both.

Cherries

Variety	Tree				Fruit					Comments
	USDA Climate Zones*	Ripens	Bears	Genetic dwarf	Size	Fresh	Juice	Dried	Canned	
Sweet cherries										
'Angela'	5–9	M/L	H		M/L	A	A	A	A	Among hardiest; good in Intermountain Basin.
'Berryessa'	5–9	E	M/H		L	A	A	A	A	Good hot-summer tree in CA. Like 'Royal Ann'.
'Bing'	5–9	M	H		L	O	O	E	O	To Zone 7 in E. Standard commercial variety.
'Black Tartarian'	5–9	E	H		M	A	A	E	A	Soft fruit prone to cracking, but good pollenizer.
'Emperor Francis'	5–7	M	H		L	E	A	A	E	Resists cracking better than similar 'Royal Ann'.
'Garden Bing'	6–9	M	L	•	M	A	A	A	A	Smallest dwarf at 6 feet, but branches will revert.
'Kansas Sweet' ('Hansen')	5–9	L	M		L	E	A	A	A	Similar to 'Bing'.
'Lambert'	5–9	M/L	M		L	O	A	E	A	Hard to prune. Only for W, where it can outperform 'Bing'.
'Rainier'	5–9	E/M	VH		M	A	A	A	A	Among hardiest. Fruit like 'Royal Ann'; resists cracking. For W.
'Republican'	5–9	L	VH		S	E	A	E	A	Hardy. Bears in marginal areas. Fruit keeps well.
'Royal Ann' ('Napoleon')	5–9	E/M	VH		VL	O	A	A	E	*The* yellow cherry. Not for hot areas.
'Sam'	5–9	M/L	H		L	E	A	A	A	Slow to bear. Resists cracking.
'Schmidt'	5–7	M	M		L	E	A	A	A	Tree hardy, blossoms not. Fine, tart fruit.
'Spur Bing'	NT	M	NT	•	M	A	A	A	A	To 10 feet. The first and only proven dwarf; needs a pollenizer.
'Stella'	5–9	M/L	M		L	A	A	A	A	Self-fertile. Bears young. Fruit resists cracking.
'Van'	5–9	M	VH		L	E	A	A	A	Bears in marginal areas. Not for humid areas.
'Windsor'	5–7	L	H		M	E	A	A	A	Cold-hardy; bears in borderline areas.
Sour cherries										
'Early Richmond'	5–9	E	M		S	A	A	A	A	To 20 feet. Tart fruit for pies, jellies, preserves.
'English Morello'	5–8	L	H		S	A	A	A	A	For pies or canning. Will take some heat.
'Meteor'	5–9	L	M		S	A	A	A	A	Very hardy amarelle. Meaty fruit best in preserves, jellies.
'Montmorency'	5–9	M/L	M	•	S	A	A	A	O	To 10 feet. Major canner; the standard amarelle.
'North Star'	5–9	M	M	•	S	A	A	A	A	To 8 feet. Hardiest morello. Resists cracking, brown rot.

Chart Key:
Ripens: E/Early, M/Mid, L/Late
Bears: L/Light, H/Heavy, VH/Very heavy, NT/Not fully tested
Size: S/Small, M/Medium, L/Large, VL/Very large
Fruit quality: O/Outstanding, E/Excellent, A/Average

Quality

*See climate zone maps, pages 84–87.

Chestnuts

Burrs open when chestnuts are ripe

AT A GLANCE

Climate: USDA Zones 5–8, wherever peaches grow well.

Soil: Well-drained acidic soils, pH 5.5. Intolerant of alkaline soils.

Trees bear: In third or fourth year.

Typical life span: 50 years.

Typical yield at maturity: 40 to 70 pounds per tree (Chinese chestnut).

Self-pollenizer: No.

Semidwarfs and dwarfs available: No.

Harvest season: September–November.

Principal pests and diseases: Chestnut bark blight, curculio, oak root fungus.

The chestnut is not a tree to plant casually on an average lot. As the scaled drawing indicates, a typical one will top out around 60 feet—and spread more than 40, though severe pruning can hold a tree to around half that size. One species can reach 100 feet. Chestnuts are not self-pollenizers, but must be planted in pairs, at least. At whatever size, they cast dense shade.

As if those were not enough reasons to give them ample space, the pollen has an aroma that led some *Sunset* garden editors to recommend planting the trees well away from the house on country estates. Finally, the trees produce memorable amounts of litter—catkins in early summer, the spiny burrs that hold the nuts in autumn, and leaves all winter.

The other side of the coin is chestnuts roasting by an open fire. It can be enough.

Chestnut meat is a rarity among nuts. It has a high proportion of car-

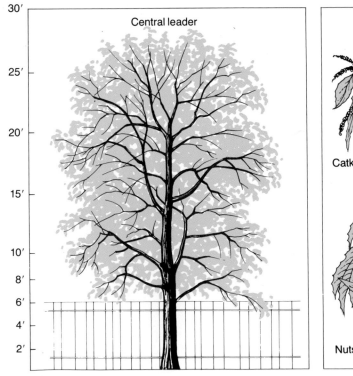

Central leader

Catkins

Nuts

Chestnuts are trained to the central leader system. Because of their height, they will need to be headed back to keep the crown within reach. At about the same interval they may need some lateral pruning to retain an attractive shape. Otherwise, the only need is to remove crossing and dead or damaged branches. Catkins in spring give way to burrs containing three to six nuts each in autumn.

bohydrates and a low percentage of protein and oil, resulting in a texture grainy and dry enough to be ground into meal. The nuts are ripe when the burrs split, revealing the brown skin of the one to three individual nuts inside.

There are two distinct choices for Westerners, only one for people east of the Rockies. The Spanish chestnut (also known as the European and Italian chestnut) has the larger, better-flavored nut, the familiar one of the marketplace. It is also the larger tree, and can be grown only in the West.

The wider alternative is the Chinese chestnut. Its nuts are more variable because most nursery plants are propagated from seed rather than cuttings. These variables include size (always smaller than the Spanish), texture (drier), and ripening time (earlier). The flavors tend to be consistent and agreeable, if not quite so distinctive as the Spanish cousin's. It is, not incidentally, a measure of familiarity that many citizens of the eastern states now prefer the Chinese to the European chestnut. Long exposure has made the Chinese species the norm rather than a substitute. Taste almost always works that way.

Chinese chestnuts sometimes are sold from nurseries by variety. The commonest names are 'Orrin', 'Crane', 'Nanking', 'Abundance', 'Kuling', and 'Meiling'. Plants sold by varietal name probably have been grafted onto native rootstock from an identified parent tree. However, because of the general habit of propagating from seed, even these distinctions by variety may be uncertain. Any tree sold only as Chinese chestnut probably has grown from seed.

'Colossal' is sometimes held to be a hybrid of the European and Chinese species, sometimes held to be purely of the European species, though developed in the United States. In any case, the variety is fairly well identifiable, and often sold in the West grafted onto European rootstock. For many of its familiars, it is the finest-flavored variety of them all.

Japanese chestnuts are available from nurseries, but best viewed as ornamentals. Their fruit is not as flavorful as any of the Chinese chestnuts.

A similarly textured and flavored nut to the chestnut is the chinkapin (also chinquapin and other variant spellings), which grows readily as a shrub in much of the eastern U.S. A native of the Southeast, ranging at least as far north as Virginia, it can be cultivated readily from wild seed.

The American chestnut is on the verge of extinction, victim of an intractable fungus disease that attacks the bark. It was not an eater's tree in any case. The nuts were so small that it took about 100 to make a pound, compared to two dozen for the Spanish chestnut.

Small nuts aside, it was the most impressive tree of the lot, the one with the spreading limbs under which the village smithy stood. A few specimens of each remain to be found.

Where they grow

The Chinese chestnut, almost immune to the bark fungus, grows across the American continent wherever peaches do, primarily in USDA Zones 5–8. The trees are generally hardy to −15°F/−26°C. Maryland and Georgia are centers of commercial production.

Natives of the Mediterranean basin, Spanish chestnuts grow only in the western U.S., where the chestnut blight has yet to appear. Within that limitation, their range, too, is similar to that of the peach, except that—being more heat tolerant—they fare a bit better in southern California.

The major areas of the West in which neither chestnut can do well are deserts and high mountains. Maximum elevations are about 3,500 feet in the north, 4,500 feet in the southern Sierra Nevada and southern Rockies.

Site & soil

Most of the considerations governing site have been noted already. Chestnuts' size and need of full sun mean they must have ample space for their own requirements; their messiness and unpleasant aromas may mean they must have even more

space for the comfort of their owners.

To pollenize, two trees must be within 200 feet of each other. Chestnuts prefer more acid soils than most nuts, pH 5.5 to a more usual 6.5. In general this means a high proportion of organic matter, though mineral soils can be fertilized to suit chestnuts. Fair to good drainage is another requirement.

Propagating & planting

Home gardeners often grow chestnuts from seed because they are not routinely stocked by many nurseries. Where they can be found in nurseries, the plants most likely have been grown from seed as well.

Nurseries usually sell chestnuts bare-root for planting in the dormant season—autumn in the mild-winter West, early spring in colder climates. They sometimes may be found as balled-and-burlapped or container plants for planting at other seasons.

Caring for the trees

Water is the crucial factor.

Watering. The rule of thumb for chestnuts during the growing season is an inch of water per week by rain or irrigation, applied just often enough to keep the soil damp. Dry soil will only inhibit the crop; soil that is too wet may kill a tree directly or by subjecting it to oak root fungus.

Fertilizing. It is almost never required in well-drained soil of correct pH in the West. Annual spring feedings of a balanced fertilizer (10-10-10 or similar) are useful in much of the East.

Pests and diseases. The chestnut is subject to very few pests or diseases other than the bark blight that has almost eradicated the American species. The blight can attack the Chinese chestnut, but usually can be controlled by pruning out weak and shaded branches and keeping all suckers trimmed. In some areas, chestnut weevils (curculio) may infest fruit; they can be controlled by sprays, as described on page 109.

Citrus

Climate: Most grow only in USDA Zones 9 and 10 because they are frost-prone and need hot weather to ripen. A few forms may bear in Zone 8. Grown indoors everywhere, though difficult to obtain fruit in that circumstance.

Soil: Tolerant of soil types, but must have good drainage.

Trees bear: Dwarfs at 2 years, standards at 3 in West; at 1 in Florida.

Typical life span: 30 years.

Typical yield at maturity: Wildly various, depending on fruit type and size, tree type and size.

Self-pollenizer: Yes.

Semidwarfs and dwarfs available: Yes, for all types.

Harvest season: Throughout year for several types; extended season for most.

Principal pests and diseases: Aphids, mites, scale, whiteflies. Also mealybugs, root rot, scab, canker.

Oranges bear most heavily on lower branches

The great kings of 17th century northern Europe built *orangeries*—vast sheltered courts—hoping to have the magical fruits at arm's length rather than depending on imports from the Mediterranean. A great many less ostentatious modern souls in the northern United States grow the whole spectrum of citrus—with the same general level of luck as their royal predecessors—in pots in the living room or, perhaps, in a greenhouse.

Citrus is so thoroughly the product of mild winters and hot summers that people in chillier places always have reveled in beating the odds, in cornering a healthy dose of sunshine of their own. At least as much to the point, citrus has such fascinating flavors that people in the murkiest climates want it, and will pay to have it.

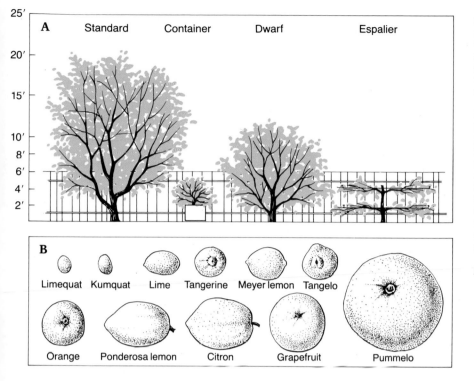

25'
20'
15'
10'
8'
6'
4'
2'

A   Standard   Container   Dwarf   Espalier

B

Limequat   Kumquat   Lime   Tangerine   Meyer lemon   Tangelo

Orange   Ponderosa lemon   Citron   Grapefruit   Pummelo

(A) *Regardless of their range in size, citrus can be trained either as single-trunked trees (putting more of the fruit of tall species out of reach), or as multi-trunked ones. Allow branches to grow up; later the weight of fruit will bend them outward.*

Once established, trees need very little pruning, though slender new branches should be kept short by pinching out or, later, by heading back. This is especially true of lemons and others that tend to bear fruit at the tips. Awkwardly long branches also can be headed back for shape. Old scaffold branches that lose vigor can be cut back to one-third their length; new sprouts will bloom in profusion; selected sprouts can replace the outworn limb(s).

(B) The various citrus fruits are ranked by size.

At first glance the object of all this attention seems simple enough. An orange is an orange, a grapefruit a grapefruit. But citrus is anything but simple. It is not only a question of what is a limequat or tangelo, but what, exactly, is an orange or a lime?

After centuries of hybridizing, the sex life of citrus is indescribable. However, one (possibly apocryphal) story from John McPhee's *Oranges* provides a start toward understanding: Two scientists in Florida needed Persian (a.k.a. Mexican) lime seeds to start a virus-free strain. They cut up 1,885 limes without finding a single seed. Then they went to a concentrate plant and filled two dump trucks with pulp from tens of thousands of Persian limes. In this they found 250 seeds, which they planted. From these lime seeds, up grew trees of sweet oranges, bitter oranges, grapefruit, lemons, tangerines, limequats, citrons, and two trees of Persian limes. The only surprise to their fellow scientists was that they found so many seeds.

Persian limes seem readier to misbehave in this way than some other citrus, but the primary point remains: anyone wanting a particular species or variety is well advised to choose asexual reproduction, and buy a nursery plant guaranteed as true to type.

Trueness to type is not the only argument for certified nursery plants. In their case, the right stuff comes grafted onto a disease-resistant rootstock—a dwarfing one if that is desired, or one that increases the frost-hardiness of the plant.

Disease plays another, more limiting role in plant selection. Because some viruses affecting oranges and their kin are intractable, nurseries in states with commercial citrus groves are not allowed to export or import citrus plant material across state lines of other citrus-growing regions. They may not even be able to ship between districts within a state.

In short, gardeners must buy plants from locally grown stocks in citrus states. Indoor gardeners in other states have wider options in compensation for smaller hopes.

What they are/Where they grow

The first job is to sort out the cast of players, and to get a line on who has a chance to grow them in the garden. The plain fact is that the limitations are USDA Zones 9 and 10. The hardiest citrus, the kumquat, suffers damage to its foliage at 18°F/−8°C, while the tenderest, the Mexican (or Persian) lime does not tolerate temperatures below 28°F/−2°C.

The fruits are even less frost-hardy. The toughest of them are damaged by temperatures between 26° and 28°F (−3°C and −2°C). Gardeners on the margins of these limitations try citrus anyway, because the trees will bounce back from slight freeze damage within a year.

The other side of the coin—heat requirement—can be just as troublesome, as underripe citrus is unlovely fruit. Rules on heat are harder to figure out for two reasons.

First, some citrus—oranges, for example—must become sweet-ripe; others—lemons—need not become sweet. The types that do not need to become sweet can get by with less heat than the ones that do. Second, some citrus fruits—grapefruit is one—will ripen in as little as 6 months, but can continue to ripen on the tree for a year, 14, even 18 months so long as they are not damaged by winter freezes, which means that the

'Eureka' lemon

Even grapefruit can prosper in a container

heat they need can come swiftly or slowly.

In alphabetical order:

• Citron. The primal citrus has a short life cycle and is extremely cold-sensitive. The large fruit has a thick skin that can be eaten fresh in salads, or candied. It grows well in southern California and southern Florida (where frosts seldom strike), but almost exclusively in home gardens. Because the fruit is frost-hardy and does not need to ripen sweet, it can be somewhat successful in carefully chosen sites in northern California and the Arizona deserts.

• Grapefruit. Grapefruit produces great juice by the glassful, and is delicious eaten fresh. Two favored locales are Florida, with its Indian River country, and the Rio Grande Valley of Texas. In California and Arizona, grapefruit needs desert heat to ripen well. (The trees will survive in California's Napa and other coastal valleys, but the fruit is intolerably bitter after one summer, and has the texture and taste of balsa wood after one frosty winter.)

• Kumquat. It reverses expectations for citrus by having a sweet skin and sour-bitter flesh. The small fruits can be enjoyed whole by people who favor tartness. Tenderer palates prefer theirs sliced into salads. The fruits candy well, too.

The tree is particularly frost-hardy among citrus, and needful of less heat than most to ripen well. (It bears and ripens well in many sunny parts of the San Francisco Bay area, as well as in most commercial citrus districts.) These facts, combined with the tree's small size, make it one of the best hopes for seasonal and year-round indoor container growers who want something to eat, as well as a handsome plant.

• Lemon. The lemon is several things, from the freakishly large 'Ponderosa' to the small 'Meyer'. The latter is the home gardener's favorite because its mildness is welcome in ades and pies, but is not a commercial variety because it does not store well. The relative frost-hardiness and low heat requirements make lemons the citrus of choice where oranges and grapefruits will not ripen.

• Lime. Limes are a poor choice for gardens anywhere except in USDA Zone 10. They tolerate almost no frost and demand high heat. Because they are best known sliced and stuck on the rim of a tall drink glass, they are not much missed by food gardeners. They do have hidden virtues as flavoring agents in cooking, as alternatives to lemons. Surprisingly, the leaves are almost as good as the fruits for this purpose.

• Limequat. The lime x kumquat hybrid grows with less heat and greater hardiness than the lime, and can substitute for lime in all of its roles. The other kumquat hybrids—citrangequat, orangequat, and calamondin—are largely ornamental, though the latter is the best producer of fruit indoors. Calamondin can make fine bitter marmalade.

• Orange. The widest variety of all citrus fruits is sheltered by the name. Most are classed as sweet oranges, including all of the navels and Valencias. Some sweet oranges belong to a subtribe known as blood oranges after the dark color of their flesh. A separate group is the sour orange, which covers a broad range of character within a short list of species—not varieties—and produces almost all of the marmalade worthy of the name. (For purists, marmalade is marmalade, and anything sweet is just citrus jam.)

One thing can be said of sweet oranges: For anyone who does not live near commercial orchards, trying to grow them produces more frustration than ripe fruit. No other fruit described in this book is as demanding of its environment as a sweet orange, and no other fruit tree puts on such a show of willingness when there is little or no hope of a ripe crop.

Sour oranges, hardier and less particular about heat, are no substitute. Tangerines are the edible alternative in country that will not quite suit a sweet orange.

• Pummelo. Pummelos are to grapefruit what 'Ponderosa' is to a regular lemon—a blander and outrageously bigger cousin. A pummelo is so big, in fact, that one breaks the fruit first into segments, and then segments of the segments in order to eat it. Climatic needs are almost identical to those of grapefruit.

• Tangerine. Small, loose-hided, traditional at Christmas, tangerines have a more intense perfume than oranges, and a wider tolerance of growing conditions. They will take more frost, and ripen with less heat.

In California, tangerines will sweeten nicely in most of the areas where lemons do well. Some varieties flourish along the Gulf Coast outside of traditional citrus regions. Most are well suited to fresh eating; some are so juicy they need to be squeezed into a glass just to keep them under control. Their other name is "mandarin orange."

• Tangelo. These tangerine x grapefruit hybrids have the strange—for citrus—habit of favoring one parent or the other almost entirely.

• Tangor. The tangerine x orange cross produces fruits leaning in the direction of tangerines. The best climate conditions for growing them, on the other hand, are about those favoring sweet oranges.

Site & soil

The first requirement is good drainage. The second is—almost always—the hottest microclimate on the property in any area cooler than regions having commercial citrus orchards. Sometimes the hottest spot is still the best one, even in commercial citrus country.

Because citrus trees need a good deal of water, their ideal soil in home gardens has a high percentage of organic matter. Humus keeps water where the roots can use it, and still drains enough for needed air to reach the roots. Both sands and clays can be improved by 4 to 6 inches of peat moss or ground bark dug into the top 12 inches of dirt; water retention is improved in the first case, drainage in the second.

Gardeners with persistently boggy soil can try citrus in slightly raised beds. In this case the bed should be surrounded by a berm to keep irrigation water in the root zone when it is needed.

Drainage needs satisfied, citrus appears to grow well in a wide range of loamy to sandy soils having a wide range of pH.

The purpose of hunting out the warmest spot in a garden is only partly to help ripen the fruit. As or more important, warm spots often offer the best frost protection as well. An espaliered tree under an eave and against the south wall of a white house is the ultimate example.

Propagating & planting

Evergreen citrus usually is planted from a container or as a balled-and-burlapped young tree, but sometimes can be obtained as a bare-root plant. In whichever of these three forms a new tree comes from the nursery, citrus should be planted in spring after the last danger of frost. For most types, the best months are April and May in the West. Some areas are safe in March.

All nursery citrus is sold on a rootstock. Standard trees grow on varieties that increase frost hardiness and are resistant to disease. The commonest ones are trifoliate orange, sour orange, and rough lemon.

Of all the trees gardeners are pleased to graft, citrus must lead the league. Sometimes it is to boost the crop of a flagging tree, sometimes to save space, sometimes because a tree gives too much of one fruit. More often it seems to be for the sheer joy of having as many as five different fruits on a single tree. The technique is T-budding (see page 101); the easiest timing is April into May, but budding can be done anytime between April and September. While citrus is fairly forgiving, not all types are compatible. The following are the most reliable combinations:

Orange: 'Lisbon' (but not 'Eureka') lemon, grapefruit, tangerine, tangelo.

Grapefruit: Orange, tangerine, tangelo.

Tangerine: Orange, grapefruit, tangelo.

Tangelo: Orange, grapefruit, tangerine.

Neither 'Eureka' nor 'Lisbon' lemons take budded branches well; they are best left as single-fruit trees. 'Meyer' lemons sometimes harbor quick-decline virus, so should be used neither as stock nor budwood.

Caring for the trees

Water is the key element in successful citrus growing, with fertilizing not far behind. Dwarfs need more careful attention than standard trees, container plants more than those in the ground. Pests and diseases exist, but there are ready means for dealing with most of them.

Watering. One rule of thumb says citrus soil should always be moist, but never have standing water.

Soil type governs the interval between soakings. Trees in clays may need at least 10-day intervals to allow enough air to get to the roots. Trees in sandy soils may need irrigation every third day; so may dwarfs. Container plants may require daily watering in hot weather. Newly planted trees benefit from water every other day, though the amounts are less than for mature trees by half to two-thirds.

The rules of thumb are relatively safe starting points, but are not the best answers. As usual, there is the possibility that individual plants may need double or half the amounts.

Growers of container plants in cold-winter regions should water very sparingly while their trees are in winter storage.

Fertilizing. Heavy feeders on the one hand, evergreens on the other, citrus trees prosper only with attentive fertilizing programs. The programs need not only to stimulate growth, but to induce an annual lull, which is as close as citrus can get to being dormant.

The basic formula for standard, 20-foot trees in California is 1½ pounds of elemental nitrogen per tree per year, divided among applications 6 weeks apart—the first early in February, the second in mid-March, the last in late April. Later feedings put late growth at risk of frost damage. For smaller trees, the amount should be diminished in proportion to tree size.

The recommended types are ammonium sulfate (21-0-0) or ammonium nitrate (34-0-0). Commercial citrus fertilizers (9-4-8 or similar) provide balanced feeding, though in normal soils trees seem to need much less phosphorus and potassium than nitrogen.

In Texas and Florida, feedings are about the same, but the recommended schedule is February, June and October.

(Continued on next page)

For most fruits, the feeding zone begins a foot from the trunk and extends to the drip line. For long-rooted citrus, it should extend to almost twice that diameter.

Citrus are somewhat subject to iron deficiency. If leaves pale, showing dark green veins, symptoms are advanced. Iron chelate should be applied and soaked in immediately; ⅓ to ½ pound is the amount. Preventive applications should be made in spring. The rarer zinc deficiency (betrayed by clusters of small leaves at the tips of branches, sparse foliage elsewhere) can be treated with an ounce of zinc oxide in a gallon of water, applied to the leaves as a spray.

Pests and diseases. The roster of citrus pests is short—aphids, mites (which cause bizarrely twisted fruit), scale, and sometimes mealybugs. All will yield to strong blasts of water from a hose. They also can be controlled by sprays, as noted in the section on pests and diseases (see pages 108–111). Florida gardeners may also have to spray for caterpillars of the orange dog butterfly, broad-winged katydids, and the citrus root weevil. Snails and slugs will get after citrus; the controls are the time-honored ones: stomping them underfoot, or baits.

Diseases are fewer yet, and strike mainly at trees in poorly drained soils. A root rot caused by water molds reveals itself in yellowed leaves and dropping foliage. The best control is a less frequent watering schedule. Gummosis occasionally occurs in older trees at the base of the trunk. To control it, trim and clean the oozing wounds, remove decayed bark to wood that is not discolored, and paint infected areas with Bordeaux mixture.

Not a disease, but a problem, is sunburn. New trees are susceptible. So is wood newly exposed by pruning on older trees. Nurseries sell commercial wrappers for the trunks of young trees. Whitewash or cold-water wall paint works well on trees of all ages. (Tan and pale brown paints work as well as white.)

Citrus

Variety	Tree					Fruit				Chart Key:
						Quality				Heat Requirement: H/Hot, M/Moderate, MH/Moderately hot, VH/Very hot Ripens: NT/Not fully tested, AY/All year Fruit quality: O/Outstanding, E/Excellent, A/Average, P/Poor
	Frost hardiness in F*	Heat requirement	Ripens	Tree size (standard)	Tree size (dwarf)	Fresh	Juice	Preserves	Flavoring	Comments
Grapefruit										
'Marsh'	26°	VH	Nov–Jun	30'	12'	O	O	A	A	Main variety in W. Ripe in 14–18 months if summer long, hot.
'Ruby' ('Redblush', 'Ruby Red')	26°	VH	Nov–Jun	30'	12'	O	O	A	A	Like 'Marsh', except pink with desert heat.
Kumquat										
'Nagami'	20°	MH	Dec–Mar	8'	3'	O	A	A	A	Will ripen where lemons do.
Lemon										
'Eureka'	25°	MH	AY	20'	12'	A	O	A	O	*The* market variety. At best in s CA.
'Improved Meyer'	25°	MH	AY	12'	6'	A	O	A	O	Thin-skinned. Juicier, less acid than 'Eureka'.
'Lisbon'	25°	MH	Oct–Dec	25'	12'	A	O	A	O	Vigorous tree; thorny. Takes heat, cold well. Fruit like 'Eureka'.
'Ponderosa'	25°	MH	Nov–Mar	10'	6'	A	O	A	A	Grows mild-flavored, elephant-hided fruit to 2 lbs.
Lime										
'Bearss'	32°	MH	Dec–May	25'	12'	A	A	A	O	Thorny tree drops leaves in winter. Fruit very juicy.
'Mexican'	32°	MH	AY	15'	8'	A	A	A	O	The bartender's lime.
Limequat (lime x kumquat)										
'Eustis'	20°	MH	Oct–Feb	15'	8'	A	A	A	A	Similar-flavored substitute for lime in frostier regions.
Mandarin orange (tangerine)										
'Clementine'	20°	H/VH	Nov–Dec	12'	6'	O	E	E	E	Bigger crops with pollenizer. Stores well on tree.
'Dancy'	20°	VH	Dec–Jan	12'	6'	O	E	E	E	The Christmas tangerine.
'Kara'	20°	H	Jan–May	20'	10'	E	E	E	E	Adapted widely. At 2½ inches, one of the largest.
'Kinnow'	20°	H	Jan–May	20'	10'	O	E	E	O	Adapted to all citrus regions. Richly flavored fruit.

*To convert Fahrenheit temperature to Celsius, use this formula: $(F° - 32) \times 5/9 = C°$.

Citrus

| Variety | Tree | | | | | Fruit | | | | Chart Key: |
	Frost hardiness in F*	Heat requirement	Ripens	Tree size (standard)	Tree size (dwarf)	Fresh	Juice	Preserves	Flavoring	**Heat Requirement:** H/Hot, M/Moderate, MH/Moderately hot, VH/Very hot **Ripens:** NT/Not fully tested, AY/All year **Fruit quality:** O/Outstanding, E/Excellent, A/Average, P/Poor **Comments**
Mandarin orange (tangerine) *(cont'd.)*										
'Owari'	20°	H	Oct–Dec	15'	6'	E	E	E	E	The commercially canned variety. Overripens on tree, but stores well. Not for desert.
'Satsuma'	20°	M	Oct	15'	6'	O	E	E	E	Widely recommended for Gulf Coast.
'Wilking'	20°	H	NT	15'	8'	O	E	E	E	Can be alternate bearer. Fruit stores well on tree.
Mandarin oranges (sour mandarin)										
'Calamondin'	20°	H	NT	20'	10'	P	P	E	P	For marmalades only. Bears hundreds of fruits.
'Otaheite'	20°	H	NT		5'	P	P	P	P	Mostly an indoor container plant, for decoration.
'Rangpur' lime	20°	H	AY	15'	8'	P	E	A	E	Not a lime botanically or in flavor. Good in ades.
Sweet orange										
'Diller'	25°	VH	Nov–Dec	25'	10'	E	O	A	E	Arizona Sweet variety. Tree is vigorous, dense.
'Hamlin'	25°	VH	Nov–Dec	25'	10'	E	O	A	E	Arizona Sweet similar to 'Diller'. Also for FL.
'Marrs'	25°	VH	Nov–Dec	15'	7'	O	E	A	E	Arizona Sweet. Bears young. Early ripener. Low-acid, tasty fruit.
'Moro'	25°	H	NT	20'	10'	O	A	A	A	Blood orange. Darkest flesh and juice of them all.
'Pineapple'	25°	VH	Nov–Dec	25'	10'	O	O	A	E	Early-ripening Arizona Sweet. A juice orange in FL.
'Robertson'	25°	H	Dec–Jan	25'	8'	O	A	A	E	Navel; very similar sport of 'Washington'; ripens 2–3 weeks earlier.
'Skaggs Bonanza'	25°	H	Dec–Jan	25'	8'	O	A	A	E	Navel; early-ripening. Bears young, heavily.
'Tarocco'	25°	MH	May–Jun	25'	10'	O	A	A	A	Blood orange; best color in cooler regions.
'Trovita'	25°	MH	Mar–Apr	25'	10'	O	A	A	E	Needs less heat than other sweet oranges, but passes as Arizona Sweet.
'Valencia'	25°	H	Summer	25'	10'	A	O	A	E	The standard juice orange in markets. Fine in FL, CA; poor bet in AZ.
'Washington'	25°	H	Dec–Feb	25'	8'	O	A	A	E	The standard navel. Widely adapted except in desert.
Sour orange										
'Bouquet' ('Bouquet des Fleurs')	20°	MH	Oct–Nov		10'	P	P	O	P	Cramped-space substitute for 'Seville'. Very hardy.
'Seville'	20°	MH	Oct–Nov	30'		P	P	O	P	Makes super-bitter marmalades.
Tangelo (tangerine x grapefruit)										
'Minneola'	25°	MH	Feb–Mar	25'	12'	E	E	E	E	Tangerinelike appearance, flavor.
'Orlando'	25°	MH	Feb–Mar	25'	12'	E	E	E	E	Tangerinelike; very juicy, mild. Early ripener.
'Sampson'	25°	MH	Feb–Apr	30'	15'	P	E	E	A	Grapefruit flavor in red-orange flesh. Tasty in marmalade. Sunburns in desert.
Tangor (tangerine x orange)										
'Dweet'	25°	MH	May–Aug		8'	A	O	A	E	Seedy but packed with juice. Poor in desert.
'Temple'	25°	MH	Mar–Apr	12'	6'	E	E	A	E	Distinctive flavor, low acid; easy to peel.

*To convert Fahrenheit temperature to Celsius, use this formula: $(F° - 32) \times 5/9 = C°$.

Currants & Gooseberries

Red currants

AT A GLANCE

Climate: Best adapted along cool, humid coasts (PNW, NE), in northern lake country, or in cool-night mountainous areas at 1,500 to 2,000-foot elevations. Not suited to hot-summer or mild-winter areas.

Soil: Best in fertile silt and clay loams, pH 5.5 to 6.8.

Bushes bear: In second year.

Typical life span: To 20 years.

Typical yield at maturity: 6 to 10 pounds per bush.

Self-pollenizer: Yes.

Harvest season: Late spring to summer.

Principal pests and diseases: Aphids, borers, mites; mice will chew bark. Plants may carry white pine blister rust, so are prohibited in many forested areas.

Red currants and their close relatives, gooseberries, earn their keep in the gardens of pastry eaters. Their tart, intensely flavored fruits make superior jellies and pies.

Both berries seem most at home from Oregon north into British Columbia, in the Great Lakes country (especially Michigan and Ontario), and along the Atlantic coast from New Jersey northward. In the western U.S., favored varieties of the only-for-cooking red currant are 'Red Lake', 'Perfection', and 'Cherry'. In The Great Lakes and New England, the hardy 'Wilder' is grown most, followed by 'Red Lake'.

'Oregon Champion' is the preferred gooseberry for cooking in the West. 'Poorman' has the best chance of becoming eating-ripe (and is less thorny than most). 'Pixwell' is hardier than others. In the East, 'Poorman' ranks first. 'Fredonia', a late variety, also is recommended as a sweet berry. Rarer and/or newer varieties include 'Clark' (delicious fresh, relatively thornless, proven in Ontario), 'Sylvia' (some say it has the finest fresh flavor), and 'Welcome' (pink cooking berry).

Would-be buyers should check in advance with the county farm advisor or a nursery; both fruits are prohibited where they might infect forest trees with white pine blister rust.

Any soil should be well drained. Sandy soils require the addition of peat moss or other organic matter before planting. Heavy clays also must be lightened with organic matter. In cool areas, plant in full sun; in sunnier regions, plant in partial shade. In warm, dry areas, protect shallow roots with a 6-inch layer of mulch.

For most families, two of either of these compact, easy-to-grow plants are enough. Put out rooted plants (often sold bare-root) early in spring. In light soils, set them 1 inch deeper than they grew at the nursery; in heavy soils, match the nursery depth.

Watering. Flood-irrigate weekly in warmer areas. Neither plant tolerates sodium in soil or water.

Fertilizing. If plants are not vigorous, feed them before growth begins with 2 ounces of ammonium sulfate per year of age, to a maximum of 8 ounces.

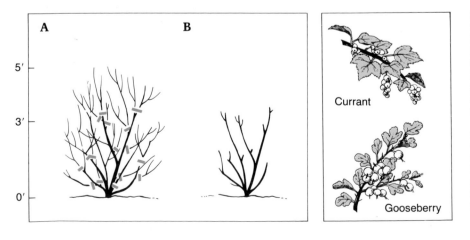

(A) *Plants 3 to 5-feet high do not require support. Fruit is borne on side branches of older stems, at base of first-year stems. In February of second winter, prune six to eight strongest stems to half their length (shorter if plant is frail); cut weaker stems to one or two buds. Make each cut above an outward-facing bud.*

(B) *Thereafter, keep a balance (three stems each) of 2 and 3-year-old wood, shortening side shoots of strong branches to 3 inches, of weaker branches to 1 inch. Keep five first-year stems for later choice. Gooseberries may need more thinning than currants at base and top.*

Currant

Gooseberry

Figs

AT A GLANCE

Climate: Most productive in hot-summer, mild-winter areas, especially USDA Zones 8–9. Will grow in Zones 6 and 7 with limitations.

Soil: Adaptable. Benefits from good drainage.

Trees bear: As early as first year.

Typical life span: Century.

Typical yield at maturity: About 30 pounds per tree.

Self-pollenizer: Yes (all recommended varieties).

Semidwarfs and dwarfs available: No (see pruning illustration).

Harvest season: June and July, again in September in California, in August elsewhere.

Principal pests and diseases: Dried fruit beetle, gophers, nematodes.

Mature fig at midseason

Accessible to gardeners across a broader swath of country than many suspect, figs are dramatic—if sometimes messy—contributors to landscaping, and their fruit is delicious fresh, frozen, canned, or dried.

Figs may be finest dried, when their subtle flavors are enriched and their soft flesh keeps a moist, almost jellied quality that makes them a perfect snack or dessert. Those joys are pretty much reserved for gardeners in near-desert climates; the varieties that dry well need unusual heat. The flavors of fresh and canned figs are hardly to be scorned. A bowl of either, alone or swimming in milk, makes breakfast something to sing about.

In the most favored growing conditions, fig trees bear a first crop on the previous year's new wood, and a second on the current year's growth. Heavy pruning and/or spring frosts can do away with much or all of the first crop.

(Continued on next page)

Figs meant for canning should be picked just before ripeness. Those meant to be eaten fresh should be allowed to ripen fully, or their flavor will be less rich than it might be. (Figs give a sign when they are ripe: the narrow neck softens, allowing the fruit to droop slightly.)

Figs for drying can be allowed to fall off the tree. Once they begin tumbling to the ground, they should be gathered daily and put on racks for the sun to finish the job. Surpluses need to be policed regularly, or they will attract legions of insects.

Where they grow

Because of their dramatic foliage, figs are too often assumed to be suited only to subtropical climates. Indeed, on the North American continent the trees grow tallest and bear most heavily in California's hot interior valleys, where most of the country's commercial orchards are to be found.

However, a few varieties ripen well in the cool summers of Washington's Puget Sound basin, and several withstand winter temperatures to 15°F/ − 9°C, the milder parts of USDA Zone 8, without serious winter damage.

In the coastal Northeast and mountainous Southeast, gardeners in colder parts of Zone 8 and even Zone 7 can harvest modest crops from a fig shrub every year. (In these regions, much or all of a plant may die back to the ground in winter cold, but it will spring up anew year after year.)

Because some varieties do not require great heat to ripen, figs can even be grown in winter climates as harsh as Zone 5 by anyone willing to go an extra mile. Container plants that can be moved into shelter during the depth of winter will yield small crops. A container plant can be happy in a pot or box as small as 18 inches in diameter and 18 inches deep, if its roots are given an annual trimming.

Another approach that yields more fruit requires outfitting a tree with a winter overcoat. More specifically, the tree has to be wrapped with burlap (or, better, fiberglass insulation), then a layer of plastic or other lightweight, waterproof material. The top must form a cap to prohibit cold air sinking inside the wrap. Once the tree has its coat, the root zone must be covered with a thick mulch. The wrapping should not come off until after the last frost is safely past.

Where lack of heat makes ripening difficult, plants can be espaliered or simply set close to a south wall to gain reflected heat.

The choice of variety in the Southeast is limited by a curious fact: the fig is not a true fruit, but rather a fleshy flower. All varieties have an opening, called the "eye," opposite the stem end. Only the most tightly closed eyes can resist invasion by the dried fruit beetle, a regional pest.

The main varieties:

'Brown Turkey' (also sold as 'Black Spanish' or 'San Piero'; large, purple brown fruit, best fresh; small tree does well from California deserts to Puget Sound basin and in Southeast; one of the hardiest).

'Celeste' (small, violet brown fruit is favorite in Southeast; fine for fresh eating; the hardiest tree; it also does well in the Southwest).

'Kadota' (tough-skinned, greenish yellow fruit favored for canning or drying; needs heat). The standard variety of commercial canners, it grows well in the California desert and will ripen in the Midwest.

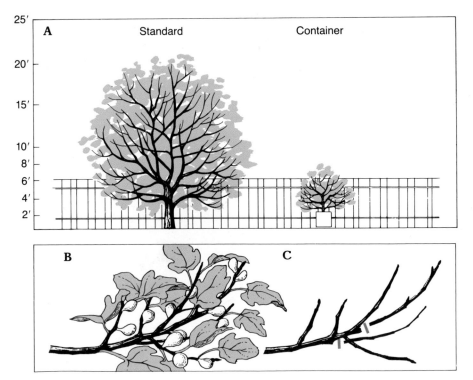

(A) *All-too-willing-to-grow figs usually are trained to open centers beginning nearly at ground. After main framework is formed, prune regularly to restrain natural height (to 40 feet) and spread (to 60 feet); usual size is 15 feet. Also prune to encourage new wood, because fruit forms near tips of branches and laterals.*

Where hardiness is marginal, allow to grow as multibranched shrub to facilitate recovery from dieback, or accept penalty of small crops and grow as south-wall informal espalier. In harsh-winter areas, try it as a shrub in a movable container.

(B) *Figs bear in early summer, again in late summer or early autumn. Some heading back may be needed between crops, at some cost of later crop size.* (C) *After picking autumn crop, cut out all weak and damaged branches; thin selectively if still crowded. Selective pruning of tips can help force laterals.*

'Mission' (also called 'Black Mission'; purple black fruit is fine fresh or dried; needs heat). One of the most-grown varieties in California gardens. Recommended for fresh fruit in the Midwest as well.

Others of interest: 'Adriatic' (grows well for drying in California); 'Conadria' (takes extreme desert heat without fruit splitting); 'Desert King' (ripens best in Washington, name notwithstanding); 'Green Ischia' (does well in Southeast); 'Latterula' (best for Oregon, good in Washington); 'Osborne Prolific' (good for coastal California and recommended in Midwest).

The primary commercial eating varieties, the imported 'Smyrna' and California-grown 'Calimyrna', cannot be recommended for home gardens because they require a pollenizer and a specific wasp to carry the pollen.

Figs droop at stem when fully ripe

Site & soil

Figs tolerate a wide range of soils, including mildly saline and alkaline ones. (Figs betray excessively salty or alkaline soil by tip dieback.) They may grow too exuberantly in rich soils.

Where plants are marginally hardy against frost, they benefit from a sloping site with good air and soil drainage, and from a thick winter mulch around the trunk to the drip line. Many gardeners in all regions keep mulch the year around to help control weeds and conserve moisture for the fig's shallow roots.

Once trees are established, the ground around them should not be tilled deeply because of their unusually shallow roots.

Propagating & planting

Figs can be propagated readily from 4 to 5-inch dormant hardwood cuttings, though hardwood is a relative term for the curiously rubbery first-year growth of this tree. Because the tree is so pest-free and cuttings root so readily, gardeners with access to an existing tree often grow a plant from a cutting of their own (taken from a branch well up the tree, not a sucker, to minimize risk of fungus or other infection).

Figs are available from nurseries both as bare-root and container plants. Bare-root plants should be set out after the last hard frost of spring. Container plants can be set out in autumn or winter in mild-winter regions.

Caring for the trees

Tender as they look, figs are easy trees to care for.

Watering. For the first 2 years, figs should be flood-irrigated weekly in dry regions through the growing season. Though an established tree is rather drought-resistant, a sizable crop of figs depends on regular deep watering from bloom to harvest—weekly in sandy soils in dry areas, every third week in heavier soils or wetter climates. The basic amount is an inch per application. Container plants require frequent soaking everywhere.

For figs planted in a lawn, wilted grass only under the tree signals lack of water. Another signal is wilting leaves in midday heat. Advanced symptoms of both under and overwatering are yellowed and dropping leaves. In colder areas, stop water after harvest to encourage early dormancy.

Fertilizing. None is required if a tree makes 1 foot of tip growth per year.

In soils with known nitrogen deficiency in dry, mild-winter California, the University of California recommendation is 2 to 3 pounds of ammonium sulfate applied in late winter or early spring. For its wetter climate, the University of Georgia suggests 12 pounds of 8-8-8 for mature bushes (15 feet), divided among late winter, early June, and late July feedings.

In Florida, with year-round rains, the university recommendation is light monthly feedings of a complete fertilizer such as 8-8-8. In colder-winter regions, the recommendation is an annual spring feedings of a balanced fertilizer.

Take care not to overuse nitrogen; it promotes lush foliage but no fruit.

Pests and diseases. Figs are immune to most problems. Their roots are subject to attack by microscopic worms called nematodes. This problem must be identified and the soil treated before planting; a county farm advisor can test the soil and recommend the most effective local program.

Roots are a favored food of pocket gophers in California, where many sadly experienced gardeners have learned to plant trees in "baskets" of chicken wire as a defense against the burrowing rodents. The control for dried fruit beetle in the Southeast is, as noted, proper selection of variety.

Grapes

'Tokay'

AT A GLANCE

Climate: European varieties best suited to USDA Zones 7–9 in the West; can be hardy to 6, but few varieties get enough summer heat to ripen. Concord-related American varieties well suited to Zones 6 and 7, sometimes 5; native Muscadines best in the Southeast, in Zones 8–9.

Soil: Well-drained sandy or gravelly loams, pH 5.5 to 6.5, suit all; some tolerant of heavier soils.

Vines bear: Partial crop in third year, full crop after fourth.

Typical life span: 40 years.

Typical yield at maturity: 7 pounds (European wine grapes) to 28 pounds (Muscadines) per conventionally trained vine; much more from arbors.

Self-pollenizer: Yes, except some Muscadines.

Harvest season: Late June into November, according to variety, climate.

Principal pests and diseases: Phylloxera, nematodes, mildew, leafhoppers, birds.

Grapes are unique among all the fruits in all the world for the fact that it still is possible to taste something pleasurable of the summer of 1929, or 1875, or 1864 in one of the great wines. Grapes are extremely distinctive for the fact that skilled tasters often can identify the source of wines from them, sometimes down to the exact patch of ground, by flavor alone.

These abilities of the preserved fruit to outlive any human alive in the year of harvest and to betray the place of origin make wines and their grapes the subjects of furious debates about the superiority of one region versus another, or one variety versus another. The stimulation of such emotion causes people to plant

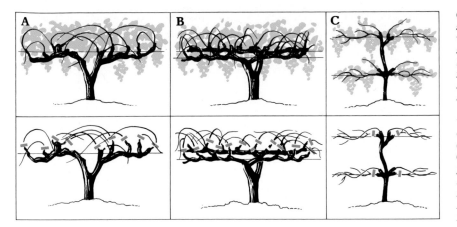

Grapes must be pruned annually to spurs (short stubs of year-old wood with two or three buds), or canes (long shoots of year-old wood with 12 to 18 buds). The chart on page 49 shows preferred methods by variety for European and American vines except Muscadines, all of which are spur-pruned.

Vines can be trained in scores of ways. Shown are **(A)** spur-pruned cordon, **(B)** spur-pruned double curtain (especially used for Muscadines), and **(C)** cane-pruned Kniffen. For arbors, expand on spur-pruned double curtain system to fit structure. Space vines 12 feet apart in rows 8 feet apart; space Muscadines 20 feet apart in rows 12 feet apart.

vines in crazy places in the hope that the local climate has been overlooked unjustly. Such hopes are dashed a million times for every modest success.

But grapes serve the rest of their many purposes—as fresh fruit, raisins, or jams or jellies—without exciting much debate, and with far more consistent rewards to grower and eater alike. Only the latter uses are to be covered here.

Grapes number into the thousands by variety. Some one of them will grow, in some fashion or another, on most of the North American continent, save the regions of harshest winter. They can be planted a thousand to an acre, or trellised so a single vine covers an acre. A fuller sense of the cultural possibilities can be gained from noticing that the standard text on grape growing, A. J. Winkler's *General Viticulture*, runs to 710 pages in its current edition.

Where they grow

Three principal strains come together on the North American continent—or, more to the point, stay apart on it. A native species, *Vitis labrusca*, dominates in the northeastern quarter of the United States, ranges into the central plains, and has a foothold in Washington and British Columbia. A second native, *Vitis rotundifolia*, grows only in the Southeast. The classic wine grape of Europe, *Vitis vinifera*, has dominated in the West since its importation into California in the late 1700s. A fourth group of vines, hybrids of

vinifera and labrusca, grow where labruscas do.

Vitis vinifera is, by a wide margin, the most diverse of the species. Among its several thousand varieties are the finest for table use and winemaking, and the only sources of raisins.

For home gardeners outside commercial vineyard districts, the family of Muscats are the best-adapted and most versatile hope among the viniferas. The vines bear heavily; the grapes have superior flavors fresh, and can be made into excellent wine if that urge becomes uncontrollable.

Even where the best known of the other table and raisin varieties ('Perlette', 'Thompson Seedless', 'Tokay', et al) are hardy enough to survive outside the Southwest, they are not suitable because they need more heat than most other regions can provide. The Southeast has enough heat, but its climate is favorable to downy mildew and Pierce's disease, to which viniferas are extremely susceptible.

No vinifera, incidentally, is adapted for use in jellies or jams, for lack of natural pectins. The native American species are much better equipped by nature for that job.

'Concord' is the most familiar name and flavor among the labruscas. It is the heart and soul of grape juice, grape soda, grape popsicles, grape jelly, and whatever other processed items are called just plain "grape."

Nearly all black labrusca grapes taste much like Concord. The white varieties, from the subtle 'Niagara' to

the bold 'Delaware', show a wider range of flavor and fit the same purposes. (Though tasty fresh, labruscas do not keep at all well compared to vinifera grapes.) Major commercial plantings of this hardy tribe are in New York, Ohio, and Washington states. However, home gardeners grow 'Concord' and its siblings in almost every state in the union and province in Canada where there is a 140-day growing season.

Most of what Americans call French-American hybrids (and French call *producteurs directs*) have been selected for their capacities as wine grapes. Crosses of classic vinifera varieties with labruscas, they were one solution to a pest, phylloxera, that threatened the extinction of vinifera vines during the 19th century.

If *Vitis vinifera* and *Vitis labrusca* are cousins, *Vitis rotundifolia*—the Muscadine—is well off among the nephews thrice removed. Some scholars hold that the fruits are not true grapes. Botanical fine points aside, the vines can be trained in much the same way as the others, and the fruit used in some of the same ways, especially for jams, jellies, and other preserves. (Muscadine is not much as fresh table fruit.)

Native to the American South, it is the only grape that will prosper in the warm, humid conditions there. On the other side of the coin, lack of hardiness has limited the vine to its native range in the southeastern quarter of the continent. It is not as well adapted as viniferas, labruscas, or their hybrids in the drier West.

Half a dozen varieties dominate in home gardens, 'Scuppernong' foremost among them by name but not always in fact, since many gardeners call any and every Muscadine "Scuppernong." A point to consider in choosing is that single plants of most Muscadine varieties bear only male or female flowers. When this is the case, plantings must include both male and female plants. One male plant will pollenize a dozen females. The chart specifies this characteristic for each Muscadine variety; it is not a factor for other grapes.

Of the several qualities that separate Muscadines from other grape species, the most functional is Muscadines' habit of dropping individual berries at ripeness. Rather than harvesting whole clusters with scissors or knives, one shakes the vines to drop berries onto cloths spread on the ground beneath.

Site & soil

In general, grapes do best in deep, well-drained, moderately fertile loams. Their extensive root systems find more water and nourishment when they can go deep. However, grapes do well in a wide range of soils. (Not all varieties are the same. Some tolerate heavy clays; some thrive in coarse gravels.) As a rule of thumb, vines meant to provide fruit for the table will yield bigger, more flavorful crops from fairly rich soil.

Preparation is simplicity itself: soil may be loosened to a depth of at least 12 inches, preferably 24, to give roots a good chance to head down. If soil is compacted, it should be loosened. (For a row, or several rows, of vines, a mechanical tiller is most useful. For one or two vines, dig planting holes out to a diameter of 30 inches or so.) Amending the soil is not suggested, for reasons given on page 104, except when drainage must be improved. To correct high pH, add sulfur and work into soil thoroughly. Muscadine growers sometimes add a half-cup of agricultural limestone to high pH soils.

Propagating & planting

Grapes are propagated from hardwood cuttings. European grapes almost always benefit by being grafted onto American rootstock because of their extreme susceptibility to two soil-borne insects, a root louse called *Phylloxera vastatrix*, and microscopic worms called nematodes. American and American hybrid grapes, with natural resistance to these pests, are planted on their own roots.

To minimize risks of vine-weakening virus infections, buy certified stock from nurseries. (Most nursery stock also is grafted to the appropriate rootstock when that is wanted.)

Bare-root cuttings are set out in early spring. In mild-winter regions, rooted cuttings can be set out from containers during the growing season. In the latter case, young plants will need careful watering throughout the dry season.

If a garden slopes, plant grapes well up the slope to avoid both frost and mildew damage that can come from planting in low spots where air stands. If hardiness is questionable, plant against a south wall. (Labruscas and viniferas can be mulched in winter; Muscadines should not be in any season.) All varieties need full sun.

Caring for the vines

Grapes demand a watchful eye over mildew and other molds.

Watering. Mature vines seldom need watering unless planted in extremely sandy soils or in near-desert conditions. Regions with 30 inches of annual rainfall usually get enough rain to sustain the plants, unless summer dry spells stretch out past 60 days.

Regions with less than that total may require supplemental watering. In such areas, drip irrigation is economical and satisfactory. Vines take overhead sprinkling well until the fruit begins to show ripening colors. Flood irrigation is workable so long as water does not stand around crowns.

In regions of dry summers, young vines may need watering during their first two to four growing seasons to help establish root systems. Again, drip irrigation is economical and helps roots push deep.

Fertilizing. Vines meant to provide grapes for the table or preserving often are fertilized to get the biggest possible crop. A basic program for European and labrusca varieties: After growth starts the first spring, spread ½ cup per vine of complete fertilizer (5 to 10 percent nitrogen) in parallel bands about 12 to 18 inches from the trunk; in the second year, use 1 cup per vine when the buds swell; in the third year 1½ to 2 cups; thereafter 1 to 2 cups per vine each spring, in a band 2 to 3 feet from the trunk.

A basic program for muscadines: In the first year apply ½ pound of a complete fertilizer (10 percent nitrogen) after planting, then ⅛ pound of ammonium nitrate in late May and again in early July. Spread fertilizer in two parallel bands 12 to 14 inches from the trunk. Repeat in the second year, doubling amounts and lengthening the bands to 48 inches. Thereafter, apply 2 to 4 pounds of the complete fertilizer each March, and ½ pound of ammonium nitrate each June, in a 6-foot-long band beginning 1 foot away from the trunk.

Pests and diseases. Phylloxera and nematodes must be dealt with *before* planting. Fumigation, the first defense of commercial growers, is seldom practical in home gardens. The best bet is correct choice of rootstock after consultation with a farm advisor or knowledgeable nursery staffer.

To control mildew in European grapes, dust vines with sulfur when shoots are 6 inches long, again when they are 12 to 15 inches long, and thereafter every 2 weeks or whenever damp weather ends. Control bunch rots in American grapes, hybrids, and muscadines, by using benomyl or captan at 7 to 10-day intervals until 10 days before harvest.

To control leafhopper in California, add diazinon dust to sulfur at third dusting. Grape mealybugs (especially in the Pacific Northwest) can be controlled by the use of dormant oil spray in late winter and malathion in June. Malathion is also a recommended insecticide for American and hybrid grapes in the East and Southeast.

Where birds compete for fruit, cover vines with netting soon after coloring of berries begins.

Grapes

Variety	Plant				Fruit				Comments
	USDA Climate Zones*	Ripens or Self-pollenizer	Bears	Pruning	Color	Fresh	Cooked	Wine	
						Quality			

Chart Key:
Ripens: VE/Very early, E/Early, M/Mid, L/Late, NT/Not fully tested
Self-pollenizer: Y/Yes, N/No
Bears: L/Light, M/Medium, H/Heavy
Pruning: C/Cane, S/Spur
Color: Bl/Blue, R/Red, G/Green, Br/Bronze
Fruit quality: O/Outstanding, E/Excellent, A/Average, P/Poor

Variety	Zones	Ripens	Bears	Pruning	Color	Fresh	Cooked	Wine	Comments
American									
'Catawba'	6–8	L	M	C	R	E	A	E	Distinctive native flavor. Makes naturally pink wine.
'Champanel'	8	NT	H	C	Bl	A	A	A	Adapted to heavy soils, summer heat of Gulf Coast.
'Concord'	5–7	M/L	M	C	Bl	E	E	A	Strong native flavor. Not adapted to dry heat.
'Delaware'	5–8	E/M	L	C	R	E	A	E	Vinous. Needs fertile soil to bear well. Mildew-prone.
'Fredonia'	5–8	E	M/H	C	Bl	E	A	A	Less flavorful than 'Concord', more widely adapted.
'Golden Muscat'	6–7	M/L	M	C	G	E	A	A	Slipskin, but 'Muscat' aroma. Good in S.
'Himrod'	5–8	VE	H	C	G	O	A	A	Sweet, seedless berries among most delicious for dessert.
'Interlaken Seedless'	5–6	VE	L	C	G	E	A	A	Sweet, seedless berries. Only moderately hardy in Zone 5.
'Niagara'	6–7	M	H	C	G	E	A	E	Strong native flavor. Good on arbors. Marginal in Zone 5.
'Seneca'	5–7	VE	L	C	G	O	A	A	Sweet, aromatic; not strong native flavor. Tender skin.
'Steuben'	4–7	M/L	H	C	Bl	E	E	A	Distinct native flavor akin to 'Concord'. Moderately hardy in Zone 4.
'Van Buren'	6	VE	H	C	Bl	O	E	A	Flavors much akin to 'Concord'. Blooms late.
European									
'Blackrose'	8–9	E/M	M	C/S	Bl	E	A	A	Bigger, tastier than 'Ribier'.
'Csaba'	6–9	VE	M	S	G	E	A	A	Some 'Muscat' flavor. Hardy; prospers in Yakima Valley.
'Italia'	8–9	M	M	S	G	A	A	A	Sweet, distinct 'Muscat' flavor.
'Muscat of Alexandria'	8–9	M/L	M	S	G	E	A	E	Rich, sweet 'Muscat' flavor in grapes and wine.
'Olivette Blanche'	8–9	M/L	M	C	G	A	A	A	Long berries often sold as 'Ladyfinger'.
'Perlette'	8–9	E	M	S	G	A	A	A	Needs less heat than most European varieties. Less sweet than 'Thompson'.
'Ruby Seedless'	8–9	M/L	M	C/S	R	E	A	A	Small, sweet berries; crisp, delicious.
'Thompson Seedless'	8–9	E/M	H	C	G	A	A	A	Standard dessert grape and raisin in CA.
'Tokay'	8–9	M/L	M/H	S	R	E	A	A	Crackling crisp, with distinct, winy flavor. Not for hottest areas.
Muscadine									
'Carlos'	7–8	Y	H	S	Br	A	A	A	Relatively hardy, disease-resistant.
'Dearing'	8	Y	M	S	G	A	A	A	Medium-size, sweet berries.
'Hunt'	7–8	N	H	S	Bl	E	E	E	Unusually even ripener. Berries very tart. Tops in home gardens.
'Jumbo'	8	N	M	S	Bl	A	E	A	Big berries ripen over long span, so good in home gardens.
'Scuppernong'	7–8	N	L	S	Br	A	A	A	The original and still most distinctly flavored.
'Southland'	8	Y	L	S	Bl	A	A	A	Does well near Gulf Coast.
'Topsail'	7–8	N	L	S	G/Br	A	O	A	Sweetest of them all. Marginal in Zone 7.
'Yuga'	8	N	L	S	R/Br	A	A	A	Too late, irregular for commercial use, but tasty for home growers.

*See climate zone maps, pages 84–87.

Hazelnuts

Hazelnuts about ready to drop

Climate: For European varieties, USDA Zones 6–7 east of Rockies, 6–8 west of them. European-American hybrids hardy to Zone 5, native Americans to Zone 4.

Soil: Best in deep, well-drained loam.

Trees bear: Begin at 4 years; mature at 7.

Typical life span: 50 years.

Typical yield at maturity: 5 to 8 pounds per tree.

Self-pollenizer: No.

Semidwarfs and dwarfs available: No; naturally small.

Harvest season: October to early winter.

Principal pests and diseases: Eastern filbert blight, bacterial blight (limit interstate shipment). Also filbertworm, aphids, bud mites.

In their natural range, hazelnuts are the sort of easy, undemanding plants that will crop up unbidden as shrubs on a vacant suburban lot, to the considerable pleasure of passers-by who recognize the sweet-meated nut.

A good many of those passers-by, especially in the West, will think of them by their other name, filbert, as they savor the gift.

In addition to producing tasty nuts, the plants are virtuous for being almost as easy to care for in the form of garden shrubs as they seem growing wild. With more effort they can be trained as small trees, should that fit a landscaping scheme.

The nuts drop when they are ripe, except for 'Du Chilly', which may have to be coaxed to give up its fruit. They should be gathered often to prevent spoiling on the ground, but will keep for months at cool cellar temperatures, waiting to be ground and toasted for topping on

(A) *For extra yield in West (but reduced yield elsewhere), train hazelnuts as small trees, using central leader system. Establish three to six scaffold branches on a tree.*

(B) *Hazelnuts grow suckers persistently; these must be trimmed or grubbed off two to four times a year, before they're 10 inches high. A simpler, less time-consuming approach is to let the plant grow as a shrub, with many trunks. In this case trim out a few old trunks and limit the number of new shoots to about as many trunks as were removed. In either case, the goal of annual dormant-season pruning should be to retain a substantial number of 6-inch to 9-inch shoots of year-old wood, the most fruitful kind.*

A — Central leader — Shrub

25'
20'
15'
10'
8'
6'
4'
2'

B — Nuts

cheesecake, or baked into cakes, or eaten for their own distinct flavor.

Where they grow

America's great commercial orchards of hazelnuts grow in the Willamette Valley of Oregon, from Hillsboro south as far as Eugene, where they are surrounded by their wild cousins. The species also has grown admirably in western Washington, California's Sierra Nevada foothills, and across much of the Great Lakes basin and into New England. Washington state has joined the country east of the Rockies as an area subject to eastern filbert blight. Where it is strongly developed, the incurable blight can make growing hazelnuts a poor bet.

Though not notably frost-hardy, hazelnuts require 800 hours a year at temperatures below 45°F/7°C to prosper, which rules them out of all mild-winter regions. Because their blossoms are damaged at 15°F/ −9°C, they are poor candidates for gardens in most mountainous areas.

Three strains of hazelnuts grow on the North American continent— native Americans, Europeans, and hybrids of the two. The prospects for individual varieties are not the same on the opposite sides of the Rockies because of eastern filbert blight. Primarily the differences are a matter of resistance to the blight, but also because of embargoes on interstate shipment designed to keep it from spreading. Oregon, with its commercial orchards, is particularly restrictive.

The biggest and best-flavored nuts are those of European varieties.

'Barcelona' is the standard commercial variety in Oregon, and the one commonly planted in gardens from California to British Columbia. It trains readily into a handsome small tree. A sure grower, it can reach 18 feet, with slightly greater spread. The nuts are considered the most flavorful of all.

'Ennis', more productive and with bigger nuts, is gradually replacing 'Barcelona'.

'Du Chilly' also produces excellent nuts in all western states. They are slow to drop and hard to free from the characteristic frilled husk. The tree is slightly smaller than 'Barcelona', which will pollinate it, and almost as slow growing. When it is trained as a tree, its limbs are strikingly horizontal.

'Royal' produces large, flavorful nuts earlier in the season than the preceding varieties. It can be a pollenizer to any of them.

'Daviana' and 'White Aveline', light croppers, are planted mainly as effective pollenizers for 'Barcelona'. 'Daviana' has fragile shells and is more susceptible to blight than the others, but is the best pollenizer for 'Barcelona'. The relatively new 'Butler' crops better than either of these, but otherwise resembles 'Daviana'.

The nuts of the hybrid types are smaller and less flavorful, but the trees resist eastern filbert blight better. 'Bixby', 'Buchanan', 'Potomac', and 'Reed' are the principal hybrid varieties available. A bit cold-hardier than the European varieties, they will bear in Zone 5. Any two varieties will pollenize each other.

The fruit of the native American hazelnut is smaller and less flavorful still, but the tree is hardy in Zones 4 into 7, and even in some sheltered parts of Zone 3. It is not sold by variety. Any two natives plants will pollenize each other.

Site & soil

The small size and general adaptability of hazelnuts give gardeners freedom to choose a spot in most gardens. One limitation, their lack of frost hardiness, suggests that European hazelnuts should not be planted in cold valleys, even in Zone 6.

For maximum yields, all hazelnuts need deep, well-drained soil with a high nutrient content; they will get by in shallow ground, though. They must be planted in full sun to prosper. As a practical matter, they should be placed where the ground within the drip zone can be kept firm and bare of grass or weeds. This allows nuts to be raked quickly into piles at harvesting, rather than picked up one at a time.

Propagating & planting

Hazelnuts can be propagated by layering in summer for readiness in late autumn. Most plants sold in nurseries are for bare-root planting from January through March, whenever the ground is warm enough to work. Planting holes are about 18 inches across, and as deep as required for the tree to be set at the same level as it grew in the nursery.

Caring for the shrub

Eastern filbert blight and filbert-worm are the chief concerns for most hazelnut growers.

Watering. From western Oregon north into British Columbia, supplemental watering seldom is required. East of the Rockies, irrigation usually is required only in periods of drought. In California, hazelnuts must be watered when the ground shows signs of drying.

Fertilizing. If growth stays vigorous, and leaves stay dark green, no fertilizer is needed. To reinvigorate a slow plant or to boost the crop of a healthy one, make annual applications of 1½ to 2½ pounds of ammonium sulfate or equivalent amounts of another nitrogen fertilizer. Compost or leaf mold can be substituted for a chemical fertilizer. The most effective time to fertilize in the West is mid-February, in the East during early March.

Pests and diseases. Neither eastern filbert blight nor bacterial blight has a known cure. Bordeaux 12-12-100 is a helpful control in regions where eastern filbert blight is known to exist. (Symptoms are darkened bark and girdled twigs and branches, leading to withered leaves. Finally pustules emerge through the diseased bark.)

Fungicides applied at leaf drop help control bacterial blight (marked by burned-looking leaves). Pruning away diseased wood helps restrain either blight—if pruning tools are sterilized with household bleach after each cut.

The pinkish caterpillar called filbertworm infests the nuts themselves. It should be sprayed or dusted (sevin is commonest) early and late in July to catch both early and late-emerging moths. Gathering the nuts early minimizes damage.

Peaches & Nectarines

Peaches ready for picking

AT A GLANCE

Climate: Most varieties bear in USDA Zones 6–8. Hardy ones can succeed in Zone 5. Some with low chill requirements bear in Zones 9 and 10.

Soil: Loam or sandy loam, pH 5.5 to 6.5 is best. Higher pH, heavy clays difficult but possible. Must have good drainage.

Trees bear: At 3 years. Some dwarfs bear at 2.

Typical life span: 15–20 years.

Typical yield at maturity: To 3 bushels for standards. Most dwarfs range around 1 bushel.

Self-pollenizer: Yes, except for pollen-sterile 'J. H. Hale'.

Semidwarfs and dwarfs available: Most popular varieties have a genetic dwarf strain.

Harvest season: Mostly June, July, and August. Some early varieties ripen in May in mild-winter regions. A few late varieties do not ripen until September.

Principal pests and diseases: Borers, brown rot, canker, curculio, leaf spot, mildew, peach leaf curl, scab.

S ome expert gardeners have recommended against planting a peach or nectarine as the only fruit tree in a garden, on the grounds that it looks ungainly. Real eaters—the kind who do not mind the juice of a just-picked, sun-warmed peach dribbling down their chins while they eat it in the shade of the branch that bore it—will pay no attention to such advice. A gangling solitary tree is no price to pay for the incomparable flavor.

Beyond this most basic way of enjoying the fruit, there are bonuses—jams and chutneys and cobblers and pies, and all the other ways peaches and nectarines taste fine.

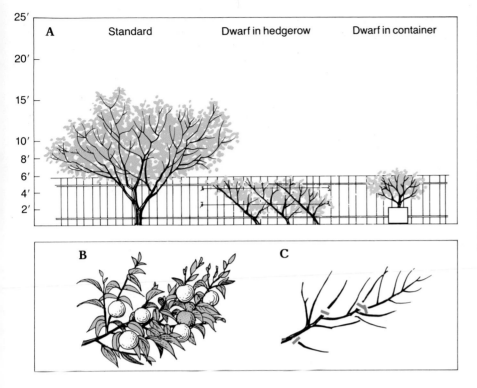

More separates the two than the fuzzy skin of the peach and the waxy-smooth skin of the nectarine, but the similarities far outweigh the differences. Both, botanically speaking, are peaches. Both have freestone and clingstone varieties. Both come in a staggeringly wide selection of standard *and* genetic dwarf trees (while neither takes to dwarfing rootstock at all well). Nectarines seem an atom or two more aromatic, and a bit firmer of flesh. Peaches are a shade juicier. The most practical distinction is that peaches adapt to a slightly wider range of climates.

Where they grow

Peaches grow best in USDA Zones 7 and 8 east of the Rockies, and 7, 8 and 9 west of them. A great majority of all commercial orchards are in these zones. Still, diligent commercial growers and home gardeners can grow fruitful trees in Zones 5 and 6. One needs especially favorable locations in Zone 5.

The trees need warm, dry springs to set a good crop, and considerable summer heat to ripen fruit properly. The drier that heat, the less trouble with pests and diseases. Slightly more than half of the commercially grown peaches in the United States, for example, come from California's interior valleys, virtually free of summer rains. Nevertheless, important orchard acreages are to be found in such diverse climates as eastern Washington, southern Ontario, southeastern Pennsylvania, and the Atlantic seaboard from New Jersey south to Georgia.

Most peaches need considerable winter chill—600 to 900 hours—but are not notably hardy. Fruit buds may be killed by winter temperatures of 0°F/−18°C. The trees themselves are not much more resistant to winter damage.

More explicitly on the subject of resistance to cold, experts at Pennsylvania State University recommend peaches freely only for the southeast corner of that state (the area shown on the map on pages 84–85 as Zone 7, plus some adjacent parts of Zone 6). But they encourage gardeners in colder districts to try a peach if their location has climate-moderating influences—the most promising being a southern exposure sloping down to a large lake. Major Canadian orchards are among those that fill that bill. They lie south of Toronto on the bridge of land separating Lakes Erie and Ontario.

The University of Massachusetts suggests 20 hardy varieties of peach for home gardens in coastal areas (as against 144 varieties thought suitable for southern Pennsylvania). The University of Missouri recommends only a few hardy varieties for the northern part of that state (Zone 5) and is cautious about low spots where cold air can settle even in the South (Zone 6). In short, most of the mid and upper plains and New England's inland are considered inhospitable, but hardly impossible.

In the West, commercial peach orchards can be found in eastern Washington around Yakima and in the Okanagan Valley of British Columbia (both Zone 6). In both regions, nearby rivers and lakes temper winter cold.

East of the Rockies, only the Gulf states so lack winter chill that peaches cannot perform well. There, mild winters combine with rot-producing high summer humidity to rule out peaches for all but the most

Dwarfs grow well in containers

determined. Southern California, especially its beach towns, suffers the same problems.

Western Washington and British Columbia, coastal Oregon, and California's north coast offer restricted opportunity. Only a few varieties will ripen in the cool summers, and the humidity invites brown rot and other disease problems.

Most of what can be said about peaches applies to nectarines as well, perhaps more strictly. Nectarines are less hardy than peaches, and more susceptible to the rots and other diseases of humid climates. As a measure of hardiness, Pennsylvania recommends several varieties for its southeast corner; Massachusetts does not suggest growing nectarines, nor does Missouri. At the other end of the scale, a handful of nectarine varieties are recommended for Georgia, but not for the warm, wet southern fifth of the state.

Site & soil

Peaches and nectarines thrive in deep loam or sandy loam of pH 6.0 to 6.5. They do not grow as well in clays. Excellent drainage is essential—they cannot survive with wet roots. Raised beds can save the day for gardeners with chronically wet soil. An effective system of drain tiles is better.

Acid soils can be corrected with preplanting additions of lime, as noted on page 104.

Like all other fruits, peaches and nectarines planted where they

Peach at blossom time

Nectarines approaching ripeness

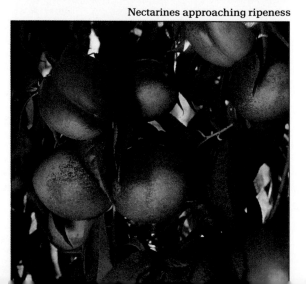

are only marginally freeze-hardy should be sited on slopes with good air drainage. Eroded or rocky slopes will not do.

The trees must have full sun—at least 4 hours a day without cast shadows in warm climates, 6 hours in cool ones. The more humid the area, the more important morning sun becomes, to help dry fruit and foliage—thus minimizing development of molds and rots.

Propagating & planting

Nearly all nursery peaches are grafts of fruiting wood onto a disease-resistant rootstock, usually 'Nemaguard' for sandy soils, but sometimes another. (A reminder: peaches grafted onto dwarfing rootstock are hard to keep healthy.)

Though all varieties save 'J. H. Hale' are self-pollenizers, most will set better crops if a second variety is nearby. If space-saving is a consideration, graft a second variety onto the first one, or train two trees as espaliers.

In mild-winter areas, the bare-root planting season is late autumn. For most districts (Zone 7 and cooler), spring is the time. Where spring comes early, March is the preferred month. In cool regions with late frosts, most authorities recommend April; the 15th is the latest date.

Container or balled-and-burlapped trees can be planted throughout the growing season, but the summer months are risky in hot regions.

Because peaches grow vigorously, many veteran gardeners use a nitrogen fertilizer at planting (usually 1 to 2 ounces of ammonium sulfate dissolved in 2 to 3 gallons of water, poured in when the planting hole is about three-fourths filled with dirt; the fertilizer *never* should be added dry).

Caring for the trees

More than most fruits, peaches and nectarines respond to environment. They are not troublesome in gardens where summers are dry and winters chilly. On the other hand, they take a good deal of care in humid, mild-winter climates where some of their commonest diseases flourish.

Watering. Both fruits are modestly drought-resistant. Standard trees can benefit from programs that allow the top 3 to 4 inches of soil to dry out, and they should not be watered so often that their root zones remain close to saturated all through the growing season. This may mean only one or two irrigations per season in moderately warm, moderately dry summer regions *and* loam or clay-loam soils.

In very dry areas and sandy soils, water may be needed as often as every 7 to 10 days. A useful trick in sandy soils is to grow a shallow-rooted "indicator" plant (hydrangea is a favorite) near the tree; it will show signs of wilt before the tree begins to suffer water stress. Irrigation should be planned to soak to a depth of 4 feet (see page 107).

Dwarf varieties should be watered as soon as the top 2 inches of soil is dry. Irrigation should penetrate to a depth of 2 to 3 feet.

The wetter the summer climate, on the other hand, the more care should be taken to assure steady drainage for a peach.

Fertilizing. Peaches and nectarines feed heavily, so need regular supplies of nitrogen to bear full crops. They may bear well for a few years without fertilizing, but will deplete the soil supply in time. In addition to nitrogen, they may need feedings of zinc, boron, magnesium, or potassium from time to time. A soil test is the only sure determinant.

The schedule and amounts of nitrogen feeding vary from region to region.

A modest, middle-of-the-road fertilizing program for standard trees is recommended by Pennsylvania State University. It calls for a maximum of 5 pounds of 10-10-10 per tree each year during the last half of March (at budbreak), to be spread evenly starting a foot away from the trunk and extending to or just beyond the drip line. (Give young trees ½ pound per year of age.) Recommendations in much of the Northeast and Midwest are about the same. In no cold-winter area should there be a post-harvest feeding; late growth is too subject to freeze injury.

The University of Georgia offers a similarly moderate program for its region of year-round leaching rains and mild winters, but calls for two applications of fertilizer per year, the second designed to help correct low pH soils. The recommendation for mature trees is 2 to 4 pounds of 10-10-10 each March, and 1 pound of calcium nitrate (15-0-0) or equivalent in August. New trees 1 to 3 years old get ¼ pound of 10-10-10.

The University of California has a more aggressive program for the sandy soils, dry summers, and mild winters common to its peach-growing areas. It calls for 6 pounds of ammonium sulfate per year, also divided between two feedings—one just after harvest in August, the other in March.

If the symptoms of zinc deficiency—small leaves clustered at the tips of bare branches—show up, the California recommendation is ⅔ ounce of basic zinc sulfate per gallon of water, applied as a spray in April. Three to four gallons of spray will cover a standard peach.

Any program using a complete fertilizer should provide more than enough potassium. Programs calling only for nitrogen may need to be supplemented each fourth year or so by a complete fertilizer, or by about 15 pounds of potassium sulfate per standard tree.

Pests and diseases. Peaches are like roses—they can't be healthy without regular spraying. Of the host of troubles that might afflict a peach or nectarine, the two most important are treated in the section on pests and diseases—brown rot on page 108, and peach leaf curl on page 111. Also covered there are aphids (page 108), curculio (page 109), leaf spot (page 110), mites (page 110), and scales (page 111).

The remaining possibly lethal pest is the peach tree borer, which attacks at or just below the crown. As the name suggests, the wormlike larval form of any of several moths burrows into the trunk. Enough borers can girdle a tree, killing it.

The usual first symptom is wilt during the heat of the day. A surer symptom is a mass of gummy, sawdustlike material at the base of the tree.

To inspect for borers, dig away the soil to a depth of 3 inches. If they are present, kill them by ramming a wire or other sharp object into each hole. (Take care not to extend horizontal damage in doing so; holes can be enlarged vertically, though, without damaging more cambium.) Paint the damaged area with tree seal, then use gravel rather than soil to refill the excavated area.

You can minimize chances of damage to a new tree by putting a gravel collar around the base and building a small dike to keep irrigation water away from the crown.

The Caribbean fruitfly is a serious pests in Florida. Unfortunately it is one without a practical control at present.

Other pests are the so-called catfacing insects, which scar fruit. Corrective sprays for these should be locally recommended.

Peaches

| Variety | Tree | | | | | Fruit | | | | | | | Chart Key: |
	USDA Climate Zones*	Minimum chill hours**	Ripens	Bears	Dwarf	Stone	Size	Fresh	Cooked	Canned	Frozen	Comments
'August Pride'	6–9	Avg	M	M		F	L	E	A	A	A	Blossoms early. Fine texture and flavor. Superior low-chill variety in CA.
'Autumn Gold'	6–8	Avg	L	M		F	M/L	A	A	A	A	Keeps well if picked when firm-ripe.
'Babcock'	7–10	400	E	M		SF	S/M	E	A	A	A	Not fuzzy; peels easily. White flesh, very sweet, some apple or honey tang; juicy. Requires heavy thinning. Recommended low to intermediate desert, s CA.
'Belle' ('Belle of Georgia')	6–8	850	M/L	H		F	M/L	E	A	P	A	Susceptible to brown rot. Hardy. Highly recommended in PA, MO.
'Bonanza'	6–9	500	E	M	•	F	M	A	A	A	A	Original genetic dwarf for home gardeners. Recommended for W and S.
'Bonanza II'	6–10	Avg	M	M	•	F	L	E	A	A	A	Melting texture. Flavor improved over 'Bonanza'. Grows to 5–6 feet.
'Bonita'	7–10	350	M	H		F	M/L	A	A	A	A	Performs well in coastal areas in s CA, FL.
'Cardinal'	7–9	950	E/M	M		C	M	A	A	A	A	Reliable fruit set in cool, rainy spring weather—ripens in w WA. Superior early variety.
'Cresthaven'	6–8	Avg	L	M		F	M/L	A	A	A	E	Flesh slow to brown. Self-fertile. Hardy.
'Desertgold'	8–10	Avg	E/M	H		SC	M	A	A	A	A	Early bloomer subject to late frosts in some areas. Recommended in FL.
'Dixired'	5–8	1000	E/M	H		SF	M	A	A	A	A	Hardy. Tolerant of peach leaf curl. Pits tend to split. Peaches mature gradually, not all at once.
'Early Amber'	6–10	350	E	M/H		SC	M	A	A	A	A	Fruit only so-so, but tree produces reliably in FL, s CA interior.
'Early Crawford'	6–8	Avg	M	M		F	M	E	A	A	A	Fruit irregular in shape and ripening, but an old favorite.
'Early Elberta' ('Gleason')	5–9	850	M	M		F	L	A	A	A	A	Thin heavily. Hardy. Resists fruit drop. Generally better quality than 'Elberta'; better growth than 'Elberta' in moderate climates.
'Elberta'	5–9	900	M/L	M		F	M/L	A	A	A	A	Fruit tends to drop when mature. Favored by many; good in all peach zones. Thrives in hot summers. Resistant to brown rot.
'Fairhaven'	5–9	850	M	H		F	M/L	A	A	E	E	Flesh slow to brown. Hardy. Showy flowers.
'Fay Elberta' ('Gold Medal')	6–8	Avg	M/L	M		F	M/L	A	A	A	E	Showy flowers. Thin for large fruit. One of the most popular freestones.
'Flavorcrest'	6–9	Avg	M	M		SC	M/L	E	A	A	A	Fruit firm, with fine texture and flavor.

Chart Key:
Ripens: E/Early, M/Mid, L/Late
Bears: L/Light, M/Medium, H/Heavy
Stone: F/Free, SF/Semifree, C/Cling, SC/Semicling
Size: S/Small, M/Medium, L/Large, VL/Very large
Fruit quality: O/Outstanding, E/Excellent, A/Average, P/Poor

*See climate zone maps, pages 84–87.
**Average chilling hours 600–700. For more information, see pages 84–87.

Peaches

Variety	USDA Climate Zones*	Minimum chill hours**	Ripens	Bears	Dwarf	Stone	Size	Fresh	Cooked	Canned	Frozen	Comments
'Flordasun'	7–10	300	E	M/H		SC	S	A	A	A	A	Needs thinning. Becomes freestone when fully ripe. Adapted to FL, s CA.
'Giant Elberta'	6–7	Avg	E/M	H		F	L	E	A	E	A	Similar to 'July Elberta'.
'Gold Dust'	5–9	500	E	H		F	S/M	A	A	A	A	Hardy, but needs summer heat. Produces well in s CA and in inland valleys of CA.
'Golden Jubilee'	5–8	850	M	H		F	M	A	A	A	A	Fair flavor. Good early peach in cold regions. Mature fruit falls. Recommended for mountain areas of w MO.
'Halberta; ('Hal-Berta Giant')	5–8	850	M	L		F	VL	A	A	A	A	Firm. Needs pollenizing—any peach except 'J. H. Hale' or 'Indian Free'.
'Halehaven'	5–8	850	M	M/H		F	M/L	E	A	E	A	Very sweet; firm and flavorful. Susceptible to brown rot. Hardy. Recommended for high desert.
'Halford'	6–8	Avg	L	H		C	L	A	A	E	E	Important commercial canning variety.
'Halloween'	6–8	Avg	L	M/H		F	L	A	A	A	A	Important late-maturing variety.
'Harbrite'	5–7	850	L	M/H		F	M	A	A	A	A	One of the hardiest all-around peaches.
'Indian Blood Cling' ('Indian Cling')	6–9	500	L	M		C	M	A	E	A	A	Old variety much admired in preserves. Pollenizer required.
'Indian Free'	6–9	Avg	L	M		F	L	A	A	A	A	Tart until completely ripe. Resists peach leaf curl. Requires pollenizer—any peach except 'J. H. Hale'. Recommended in high desert.
'J. H. Hale'	6–9	900	M/L	M		F	VL	E	A	A	A	Juicy fruits keep well. Pollenizer required—any midseason peach except 'Indian Blood Cling' or 'Halberta'.
'Jim Bowie'	5–8	900	L	M		F	L	A	A	A	A	Sweet, very juicy. Hardy, vigorous, spreading tree; resists bacterial spot.
'July Elberta' ('Kim Elberta')	6–9	750	E/M	H		F	M/L	E	A	E	A	Often requires heavy thinning to get fruit size. Good in Willamette Valley.
'Loring'	6–8	800	M	M/H		F	L	A	A	P	P	Reliable fruit set even where spring weather is erratic, but may not color well.
'Madison'	5–8	Avg	L	H		F	M/L	A	A	A	A	Flesh resists browning. Late flowering, so recommended for areas with frequent late frosts. Recommended in colder Zone 5 of PA and MO.
'Meadowe Lark'	7–8	Avg	E	M		F	M	A	A	A	A	Developed for medium and intermediate desert areas of SW and inland regions of s CA.
'Melba'	5–8	500	M	M		F	L	A	A	A	A	Flesh white, sweet, and juicy. Reliable fruit set in erratic spring weather. Fruits mature over long period.
'Nectar'	6–8	1050	E/M	M		F	M/L	E	A	E	A	White flesh tinged with red. Excellent flavor and aroma. Some consider it the best white peach. Recommended in GA.
'Orange Cling' ('Miller Cling')	5–8	800	M/L	M		C	L	A	A	E	A	Favorite for home canning.
'Pacific Gold' ('Rochester')	6–8	Avg	E/M	M/H		F	S	E	A	A	A	Long ripening season. One of best in w WA and OR for fresh use. Dependable producer.

Chart Key:
Ripens: E/Early, M/Mid, L/Late
Bears: L/Light, M/Medium, H/Heavy
Stone: F/Free, SF/Semifree, C/Cling, SC/Semicling
Size: S/Small, M/Medium, L/Large, VL/Very large
Fruit quality: O/Outstanding, E/Excellent, A/Average, P/Poor

*See climate zone maps, pages 84–87.
**Average chilling hours 600–700. For more information, see pages 84–87.

Peaches

Variety	Tree					Fruit						Chart Key:
	USDA Climate Zones*	Minimum chill hours**	Ripens	Bears	Dwarf	Stone	Size	Fresh	Cooked	Canned	Frozen	**Ripens:** E/Early, M/Mid, L/Late **Bears:** L/Light, M/Medium, H/Heavy **Stone:** F/Free, SF/Semifree, C/Cling, SC/Semicling **Size:** S/Small, M/Medium, L/Large, VL/Very large **Fruit quality:** O/Outstanding, E/Excellent, A/Average, P/Poor **Comments**
'Polly'	5–8	1000	M/L	M		F	M	E	A	A	A	Flesh white, juicy; excellent flavor. Good home orchard variety for cold areas; tree and buds both hardy. Recommended in IA.
'Ranger'	5–8	950	E/M	H		F	M/L	A	A	E	E	Medium to fine texture. Ripens in w WA. Excellent early canner. Resists bacterial spot.
'Redglobe'	6–8	Avg	E/M	M		F	M/L	E	E	E	A	Firm, fine texture. Adaptable. Highly colored, firm-fleshed peach of good flavor. Recommended GA, ID, e WA. Not always productive in cool Zone 6.
'Redhaven'	5–9	950	E/M	H		SF	M/L	E	A	A	A	Among best of all early peaches. Thin heavily. Recommended GA, MA.
'Redskin'	5–8	650	M	H		F	L	E	A	A	A	Flesh nonbrowning. Fruits keep well. Showy flowers. Tree resistant to bacterial spot. Recommended GA, PA, MO.
'Redtop'	6–9	450	M	M		F	L	A	A	A	A	Flesh very firm. Showy flowers. Productive in s CA. Sometimes susceptible to bacterial spot.
'Redwing'	6–9	500	E	H		F	S/M	A	A	A	A	Similar to 'Babcock' but needs more winter cold. Recommended for coolest s CA climates.
'Reliance'	4–8	1000	E/M	M	•	F	M	A	A	A	A	Flesh somewhat stringy. Hardy—tolerates −25°F/−32°C. Self-fertile. Recommended MA. Hard to find.
'Rio Grande'	7–9	450	E	M/H		F	M/L	A	A	A	A	Firm, medium-fine texture. Juicy.
'Rio Oso Gem'	6–9	900	M/L	H		F	VL	A	A	A	O	Small tree. Fruit of fine texture, excellent flavor. Recommended for S and W. Self-fruitful; also popular pollenizer for 'J. H. Hale'.
'Sam Houston'	6–9	500	E/M	H		F	M/L	A	A	A	A	Sets heavy crop; needs thinning. Susceptible to bacterial spot.
'Springtime'	8–9	500	E	M		SC	S/M	A	A	A	A	White flesh; good flavor. One of the earliest. Good in S, W.
'Strawberry Cling'	6–8	500	E/M	M		C	L	A	A	E	A	Flesh white, juicy; excellent flavor.
'Strawberry Free'	6–8	500	E	M		F	M	E	A	A	A	Excellent flavor. Old favorite of admirers of white peaches.
'Summerset'	6–8	Avg	L	M/H		F	L	P	A	A	A	Excellent late peach. Origin CA.
'Sunhaven'	5–8	900	E/M	H		SC	M/L	E	A	A	A	Very juicy, sweet. Resists browning.
'Tejon'	6–10	400	E	H		SF	S/M	A	A	A	A	Very juicy. Recommended for s CA, FL.
'Triogem'	5–7	850	L	M/H		F	M/L	A	A	E	A	Hardy, reliable producer in poor spring weather. Fruit resists browning.
'Tropi-berta'	6–10	400	M/L	M		F	L	A	A	A	A	Juicy; good flavor. Performs well in mild-winter coastal regions of CA, FL.
'Ventura'	9–10	400	M	M/H		F	S/M	A	A	A	A	Flesh firm; good flavor. Developed especially for coastal and mild-winter climates of s CA.
'Veteran'	6–8	1100	M	H		F	M/L	E	A	A	A	Easy to peel; low acid. Reliable fruit set in adverse conditions. Slightly soft when canned. Proven in w OR and WA.
'White Heath Cling'	6–9	Avg	L	M		C	M/L	A	A	E	A	Flesh white, juicy; excellent flavor. Hardy.

*See climate zone maps, pages 84–87.
**Average chilling hours 600–700. For more information, see pages 84–87.

Nectarines

Variety	USDA Climate Zones*	Minimum chill hours**	Ripens	Bears	Dwarf	Stone	Size	Fresh	Cooked	Canned	Frozen	Comments
'Armking'	6–10	Avg	E	M		SF	L	A	A	A	A	Tree medium-sized. Fruit fragrant. Recommended GA, central and s CA.
'Desert Dawn'	6–10	400	E	H		SF	S/M	A	A	A	A	Juicy, sweet, firm, fragrant. Heavy thinning required. Well adapted to desert W.
'Fairlane'	5–9	Avg	L	H		C	L	A	A	A	A	Vigorous tree bears regularly.
'Fantasia'	5–9	550	M	H		F	L	A	A	A	A	Flesh high quality, firm. Hardy. Susceptible to bacterial spot, brown rot. Recommended GA to PA, inland in central CA.
'Firebright'	5–9	Avg	M	M/H		SF	L	E	A	A	A	Firm, smooth-textured fruit. Hardy in e WA.
'Flaming Gold'	6–9	Avg	E/M	M/H		F	L	A	A	A	A	Showy fruit. At best in inland CA.
'Flavortop'	6–9	550	M	H		F	L	E	A	A	A	Flesh smooth, firm, juicy. Susceptible to bacterial spot, brown rot. Recommended PA, along Columbia River, in inland CA.
'Garden Delight'	5–10	450	L	M	•	F	M/L	A	A	A	A	Dense foliage. Grows to 5–6 feet.
'Garden King'	5–10	450	M	M	•	C	M/L	A	A	A	A	Dense foliage. Grows to 6 feet.
'Garden State'	5–9	Avg	M	M		F	L	A	A	A	A	Vigorous, spreading tree. Fruit firm, juicy. Recommended PA, NJ. Susceptible to bacterial spot and cytosphora canker.
'Golden Prolific'	5–8	1100	L	H	•	F	L	E	A	A	A	Hardiest genetic dwarf and one of the lastest. Grows to 6 feet. Recommended for colder Zone 5 in W.
'Gold Mine'	5–9	500	L	H		F	L	A	A	A	A	Flesh white, juicy. Favored, old-time variety.
'Gower'	7–8	Avg	M/L	M		F	M	A	A	A	A	Flesh white. Good flavor.
'Independence'	6–9	500	E/M	M/H		F	M/L	A	A	A	A	Flesh firm. Tolerates warm winters. Recommended PA, inland CA.
'Nectarina'	5–10	550	M	M	•	F	M	A	A	A	A	Sprightly flavor. Tree grows to 6 feet—original true dwarf nectarine.
'Panamint'	6–10	350	M	M/H		F	M/L	A	A	A	A	Well adapted to s CA.
'Pioneer'	6–10	400	M	M		F	S/M	E	A	A	A	Rich, distinctive flavor.
'Red Sunset'	6–9	Avg	E	M/H	•	F	L	A	A	A	A	Firm texture, juicy. Self-fertile.
'Silver Lode'	6–9	450	E/M	M		F	M	A	A	A	A	Flesh white, juicy; good texture, sweet flavor. Fruit ripens over a long period. Good in s CA.
'Southern Belle'	5–10	350	M/L	H	•	F	L	A	A	A	A	Blooms early. Grows to 5 feet.
'Stanwick'	6–9	Avg	L	M/H		SF	M/L	E	A	A	A	Flesh white, juicy. Fruits tend to drop before fully ripe. An old variety.
'Stribling White Free'	6–9	Avg	E	M		F	L	A	A	A	A	Flesh white, sweet, juicy with creamy texture. Good home orchard tree.
'Sunbonnet'	5–10	450	M	H	•	C	M/L	A	A	A	A	Firm, crisp, slightly acid. Blooms early. Grows to 5 feet.
'Sun Grand'	5–9	Avg	M	H		F	L	A	A	A	A	Firm with melting texture. Recommended in PA.
'Sunred'	8–10	450	E	M		SF	S/M	A	A	A	A	Firm with good flavor. Low chilling requirement; best in warm-winter areas.

*See climate zone maps, pages 84–87.
**Average chilling hours 600–700. For more information, see pages 84–87.

Pears

Climate: European varieties suited to USDA Zones 5–7 everywhere, and to Zones 8–9 west of the Rockies; Asian varieties suited to Zones 5–9 everywhere.

Soil: Best in well-drained loam, pH 5.5 to 6.5, but more tolerant of heavy, wet soils than most deciduous fruit trees.

Trees bear: Dwarf trees by 5 years, standards by 8. Some varieties 2 years earlier.

Typical life span: 60 (dwarf) to 75 years.

Typical yield at maturity: Dwarf trees 2 to 4 bushels, standards 4 to 5.

Self-pollenizer: In a few regions, yes; mostly no.

Semidwarfs and dwarfs available: Many varieties as semidwarfs, though rootstocks are not completely satisfactory.

Harvest season: July to late October; most varieties in August and September.

Principal pests and diseases: Fireblight, pear psylla, scab. Also codling moth, curculio, fruit spot, leaf spot, mites, scale.

'Red Bartlett'

No other temperate-zone fruit has a more distinctive flavor than a pear, yet few fruits have its subtle capacity to blend with other flavors and textures into memorable desserts.

A pear is a natural companion to Fontina cheese. After a light poaching in any of dozens of liquids from red wine to lemon-sugar syrup, a pear can be eaten just as it comes from the pan. Or a fresh pear can be cored and stuffed with a creamy cheese and just a hint of slivered ginger, or almonds. And with a properly sweet and juicy 'Anjou' or 'Bartlett', or a delicate 'Comice', these are but the beginnings.

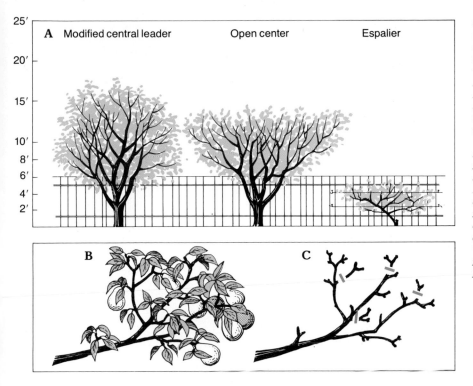

(A) Pears, which tend to be extremely upright, respond well to open-center training. Where a taller tree is desired, the modified central leader system also works well, but having several main limbs helps spread risk of fireblight. Because any tree can be held to as little as 10 feet by pruning, all pears can be trained as espaliers, better informal than rigidly horizontal.

(B) Fruit forms on long-lived spurs; thinning is needed only when much heavier than normal crops set, and then just before harvest. (C) Annual pruning should aim at keeping center of tree open, and at preserving fruiting spurs. Many commercial orchardists give their trees flattop haircuts, preferably to outward-facing buds. To avoid heavy new growth, with resultant risk of fireblight, do not prune heavily in any one dormant season.

A fair part of the art of the European pear has to do not with the tree, but with how the fruit is ripened after it is picked.

Cherries, peaches, and figs must be ripe before they are picked. Apples, apricots, and persimmons will ripen on the tree or off. But the European pear, and only the European pear, must be picked before it is ripe, then kept in the right surroundings so it can become buttery rich instead of dry and gritty, as it will if picked too soon or too late, or ripened wrongly.

The formula is simple. As soon as a full-size, healthy, mature fruit drops from the tree, choose another fruit as a test. If a black ring marks the joint between stem and spur, and the stem separates from the spur readily when the pear is lifted to horizontal and twisted gently, harvest the rest of the mature pears. Another test is a subtle shift in color from green to pale green or golden green. (The flesh should still be hard.) If the fruit does not meet both tests, wait a few days. Fruit picked too early will wither rather than ripen.

For most varieties, store harvested fruit in a covered box or closed bag in a dark, draft-free place, ideally at a temperature range of 65° to 70°F/18° to 20°C. The pears will ripen in about 10 days. The signal is a slight softening at the blossom end.

To slow ripening of some or all of the fruit, store it in a paper bag in a refrigerator before ripening it. The perishable 'Bartlett' will hold under refrigeration for 4 to 8 weeks; the durable 'Winter Nelis' may keep all winter long.

Two varieties, 'Anjou' and 'Comice', must be kept refrigerated for 4 to 6 weeks while they ripen.

Asian pears, on the other hand, ripen best on the tree, and seem better eaten fresh than poached, though they can be baked in tarts to elegant effect. Many varieties are good canned. Some gardeners and a good many produce clerks call them "pear apples," a term not true botanically and not true to their distinctive flavor, but evocative of both their plump shape and the crisp, grainy texture of their flesh.

Where they grow

The Europeans, the Asians, and their hybrids grow in most parts of the country as warm as or warmer than Zone 5, but each group has different limitations.

The European varieties are easiest to grow in such warm, dry parts of the West as Hood River and the Willamette Valley in Oregon, or the Ukiah Valley and Lake County in California—all regions of commercial orchards. East of the Rockies they can produce lovely fruit in Zones 5, 6, and the least humid parts of 7, but are troublesome to grow in all humid climates because of their extreme susceptibility to fireblight. Indeed, almost all commercial growing has ended east of the Rockies because fireblight makes commercial orchards uneconomical where climates are otherwise most favorable.

All European pear varieties need at least 600 hours of winter chill (temperatures of 45°F/7°C or below); most do better yet with 900, a circumstance that makes them poor bets in Zone 8 and warmer, including warm, dry southern California. The trees are hardy to −20°F/ −29°C. Their habit of blooming a week to a month earlier than apples puts them at unusually high risk of blossom damage where spring frosts occur most years.

Asian pears, more resistant to fireblight and needing fewer hours of winter chill (as few as 400), are the automatic choice all across the southern third of the United States. They also are popular in much of the West, not as alternatives to Europeans, but as an added choice. Asian pears apparently can be grown from the Great Lakes country east into Connecticut, but they have not been tried widely in that region to date.

Site & soil

Though pears perform at their best in deep, well-drained loams, the trees of both the European and Asian species are more tolerant of damp clays than most fruits are. This does not mean they can be grown in poorly drained sites; like all other trees, they will drown if their roots are constantly in saturated soil.

Asian pears, in particular, also will grow well in sandy soils.

Soils can be too fertile for pears, especially in humid climates, because new growth is the most vulnerable to ever-worrisome fireblight, above all when the new growth is lush. Asian pears accept too-fertile soils better than European ones.

All pears need to be planted in full sun. In humid climates, morning sun is most valuable because it helps to dry leaves and fruits quickly, inhibiting fungus and other diseases.

Because pears blossom so early—a week to a month ahead of apples—they are more subject to damage from spring frost than many other fruits. Planting sites in frost-prone areas should have good air drainage. In addition, planting on a north exposure can retard budbreak somewhat.

Propagating & planting

Most pears are propagated by budding. Asian pears, especially in the South, are budded on a fireblight-resistant rootstock, *Pyrus calleryana*. Though dwarfing attempts have had only modest success, it is possible to limit pear trees' size by grafting them on quince rootstock. Some varieties, incompatible with quince, must have an interstem of a pear variety called 'Old Home'. No few gardeners prefer to keep the trees at an elected size through pruning, though this must be consistent rather than drastic (see caption with drawings on previous page).

The least expensive way to buy pears is bare-root. In most parts of the continent, the planting season is after the last hard frosts of spring. In mild-winter Zones 8 and 9, pears can be planted in autumn as soon as the nurseries stock them.

Caring for the trees

Guarding against pests and diseases is vital to a consistent pear crop.

Watering. In most areas where pears do well, watering may mean only one or two deep soakings after rains have dwindled to light showers that are more than a week apart. In dry areas, irrigation should supplement rain whenever the top 3 inches of soil dries out; expect this condition when there is no rain for 10 days.

Fertilizing. Because of their extreme susceptibility to fireblight, pears cannot take much nitrogen, unlike most other fruit trees.

The goal should be tip growth of 12 to 18 inches per year, and a crop in the neighborhood of 5 bushels per tree. If the tree performs within this range, it probably need not be fertilized at all. When a tree does not do this well, a frequently suggested program in fireblight-prone humid regions is 5 pounds of a 5 or 10 percent nitrogen fertilizer every third or fourth year for a mature tree, applied before buds open. (In most areas this means mid to late March.) Trees younger than 10 years can be fed ½ pound of the same fertilizer per year of tree age. In dry regions, 10-10-10 is the typical choice.

An easy guideline for dwarf trees is ½ pound of 5-10-10 or 10-10-10 per inch of trunk diameter, measured at the ground.

Pests and diseases. Fireblight is the most serious potential disease, followed by scab; leaf and fruit spot are others. Pear psylla, which transmits pear decline, is the most damaging

Pear trained as formal espalier

pest. Codling moth, curculio, mites, and scales can be troublesome.

In addition to minimizing the chances of fireblight through choice and use of fertilizer—and through foregoing other susceptible plants, including pyracantha—a spray of copper sulfate and lime at bloom will help control it. Another choice is agricultural streptomycin.

Timing is crucial. The spray should be applied only when the daily mean temperature reaches 60°F/16°C; the bacteria are not susceptible to the spray at cooler temperatures. If a blighted branch does appear, cut it off 6 to 8 inches below the blighted leaf nearest the trunk and immediately dispose of it away from the garden. Clean the cutting tool with a 10 percent chlorine bleach or a 25 percent household bleach solution; if there is more than one infected branch, clean the tool after *each* cut.

A few varieties are notably resistant to fireblight, and might be chosen in areas where it is prevalent. Asian pears are generally less susceptible than Europeans. The most resistant single variety is 'Kieffer'; some others are noted on the chart.

Pear psylla sucks sap from the tree, then excretes the excess on leaves and fruit as a honeydew. The latter becomes a perfect breeding ground for sooty mold and fruit rot.

Control begins with a dormant oil spray (which kills wintering adults and inhibits breeding); it continues with soap sprays at pink bud and petal fall. In some regions, additional sprays may be required throughout the season to harvest time. In areas where psylla is common, an annual spray program is the only way to keep populations from building up to overwhelming levels.

These controls for psylla take care of several other pests.

Pears

Variety	Plant					Fruit						Chart Key:
	USDA Climate Zones*	Ripens	Bears	Dwarf	Origin	Size	Fresh	Cooked	Canned	Dried	Frozen	**Ripens:** E/Early, M/Mid, L/Late **Bears:** L/Light, M/Medium, H/Heavy, VH/Very heavy **Origin:** A/Asia, E/Europe, X/Hybrid **Size:** S/Small, M/Medium, L/Large **Fruit quality:** O/Outstanding, E/Excellent, A/Average, P/Poor **Comments**
'Anjou' ('Beurre d'Anjou')	5–9	M/L	M		E	L	A	A	A	A	A	Excellent late pear for all uses. Not for hot-summer areas.
'Bartlett'	5–8	E/M	M		E	M/L	A	A	A	A	A	Familiar summer pear in markets. Susceptible to fireblight.
'Bosc' ('Beurre Bosc', 'Golden Russet')	5–9	L/M	M		E	M/L	E	A	A	A	A	Young trees require training. Very susceptible to fireblight. Best in PNW.
'Colette'	5–9	M/L	M		E	M/L	E	A	E	A	A	Tree broad, short. Fruit firm, without grit cells.
'Comice' ('Doyenne du Comice', 'Royal Riviera')	5–10	L	M	•	E	L	O	A	P	A	A	Usually highest-quality winter pear. Cold storage required for ripening.
'Douglas'	5–9	M	M		X	S/M	A	A	A	A	A	Hardy hybrid; good fireblight resistance.
'Fan Still'	5–10	M	M		X	M	A	A	A	A	A	Tolerates heat and cold, requires little chilling. Resists fireblight. Grown in high desert. Hybrid.
'Flemish Beauty'	5–9	E/M	H		E	M/L	A	A	A	A	A	Susceptible to pear scab. Best ripened off tree.
'Kieffer'	5–10	L	M		X	M/L	P	E	E	A	A	Resists fireblight. Pick; then ripen at 65°F/18°C. Good pear for extreme climates.
'Le Conte'	5–10	L	M		X	M/L	A	A	A	A	A	Resists fireblight; good for extreme climates. Pick; then ripen at 65°F/18°C.
'Magness'	5–8	M	L		E	M	E	A	A	A	A	Pollenizers: 'Moonglow' or 'Orient'. Good fireblight resistance.
'Maxine' ('Starking Delicious')	5–10	L	M		X	L	A	A	E	A	A	Good fireblight resistance. Quality superior to most hybrid pears.
'Max-Red Bartlett'	5–9	E/M	M		E	M	E	A	A	A	A	Pollenizer required—in cool climates.
'Monterrey'	5–10	M/L	M		X	L	A	A	A	A	A	Very resistant to fireblight. Recommended for mild-winter areas.
'Moonglow'	5–9	M	VH		E	L	A	A	A	A	A	Good fireblight resistance. Best quality after 2½ weeks of storage.
'Nijisseiki' ('20th Century')	5–9	M	M		A	M	A	A	A	A	A	Use 'Chojuro' or 'Shinseiki' to pollenize.
'Orient'	5–10	L	H		X	L	A	A	A	A	A	Good fireblight resistance.
'Pineapple'	5–10	M	H		X	L	A	A	A	A	A	Flavor of pineapple. Vigorous.
'Seckel'	5–9	M	H	•	E	S	E	E	A	A	A	Good fireblight resistance. Alternate bearing. Use any pollenizer but 'Bartlett'.
'Seigyoku'	5–7	M	M		A	L	E	A	A	A	A	Tender, juicy, sweet fruit.
'Shinseiki'	5–7	E	M		A	M	E	A	A	A	A	The earliest-ripening Asian pear.
'Sure Crop'	5–9	L	M		E	L	A	A	A	A	A	Good fireblight resistance; recommended for areas with late spring frosts.
'Winter Bartlett'	5–8	M/L	M		E	M	A	A	A	A	A	Slightly smaller, matures later than 'Bartlett'. Ripens without cold storage.
'Winter Nelis'	5–8	L	H		E	S/M	A	E	A	A	A	Needs cold winters but tolerates hot summers. Requires another pear nearby for pollen.
'Yali'	5–9	M	H		A	M/L	E	A	A	A	A	Pollenizer required. Relatively low chilling requirement.

*See climate zone maps, pages 84–87.

Pecans

The pecan is *the* fancy nut of the South. Like the almond, it is good fresh off the tree, but so fine as to have spawned a whole processing industry. Pecans come spiced, toasted, and in or on pralines and several other confections.

Unlike the almond, it is not a tree to toss casually into a landscape. In fact it is so big that photographers have to think hard about how to take its picture on any property smaller than a farm. A 90-foot specimen of this member of the hickory family is nothing to turn the head.

Where they grow

All pecans like simmering summer heat, and most like a lot of moisture. They are best adapted from Texas east across the Gulf states, and north into Oklahoma, Arkansas, Tennessee, and the Carolinas—in essence, their native range. They will prosper in desert from west Texas to California if given enough irrigation. Selected varieties will grow well as far north as Iowa, Illinois, and Virginia, although the nuts are unlikely to be as good or as plentiful as farther south.

Papershell pecans

AT A GLANCE

Climate: Papershell pecans in USDA Zones 7–10; hardy northern pecans in Zones 6–7. Need summer heat to ripen.

Soil: Deep, rich loam of pH 6 to 7 is ideal. Must have good drainage. Intolerant of salt.

Trees bear: At 5 to 8 years.

Typical life span: 75 years.

Typical yield at maturity: 50 to 100 pounds (3,000 to 9,000 nuts).

Self-pollenizer: Variable; best to have two trees.

Semidwarfs and dwarfs available: No.

Harvest season: Mid-September through November.

Principal pests and diseases: Pecan scab, pecan weevil, pecan nut casebearer, sticky shuck, aphids.

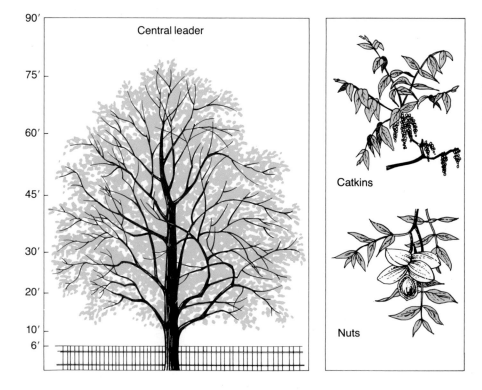

Pecans are best trained to the central leader system, selecting widely angled scaffold branches at 5 feet and higher. Pinch out early laterals to force growth of central leader. Here's how to develop laterals: in early years, prune outer 2 inches from scaffolds that grow 24 inches or more. Once tree is shaped, only pruning is to remove crossing, damaged, and shaded branches.

Central leader

Catkins

Nuts

Papershell pecans—the best-known ones—grow in hot country; they need a 210-day growing season to ripen. The papershells are divided into eastern and western subgroups. The disease-resistant eastern group can grow in the West, but most westerners, prone to scab, cannot do well in the humid East. Hardy northern pecans grow where their name suggests; they will ripen in 180 days.

Because individual trees usually fail to pollenize themselves well, in spite of having both male and female flowers, pecans need to be planted in pairs to yield substantial crops. For full crops there must be a tree from each of the two pollenizing groups noted as I or II in the following descriptions of the individual varieties.

These papershells are eastern varieties:

'Desirable' (I), an old variety, yields heavy crops of flavorful nuts, and its disease resistance is above average. Its drawback is brittler wood than most. It is recommended from Texas to eastern (but not mountainous) Virginia.

'Choctaw' (II) yields well, is extremely disease-resistant, and is a strong tree.

'Cheyenne' (I) is one of the smaller pecans, a heavy cropper yielding high-quality nuts.

'Mohawk' (II), a producer of very large thin-shelled nuts, is highly disease-resistant (therefore well regarded as a lawn tree), but it must have deep soil to produce consistently.

'Elliott' (II), an old variety, produces extremely small nuts by current standards, but the tree is strong and extremely disease-resistant. The last factor makes it a good lawn tree where spraying is impossible.

'Sioux' (II) is one of the smallest pecan trees and one of the easiest to train. The yield is moderate, and the nuts are of excellent flavor.

The next two varieties are western papershells:

'Western' or 'Western Schley' (I) is prone to pecan scab, a problem in humid areas, but not enough to keep it from being recommended for eastern Virginia. The variety is most planted in drier regions—from west Texas west—where it produces heavy crops of excellent nuts. It is the best bet as a self-pollenizer in home gardens.

'Wichita' (II) shares susceptibility to pecan scab with 'Western'. It has brittle wood, a tendency to form weak crotches, and blossoms that are less frost-hardy than many others. But the nuts are so flavorful it is commercially important in Arizona. It also is grown in the Southeast.

The hardy northern pecans able to bear in the Midwest include these four:

'Fritz' (II), the hardiest, is the best hope toward the northerly limits of the pecan's range.

'Greenriver' (II) produces flavorful nuts, but the flowers are susceptible to spring frosts.

'Major' (I) is a good producer. Aphids will infest it, though.

'Peruque' (I) is much the same as 'Major'. It has grown well in mountainous Virginia, along with the Group II variety 'Posey'.

Site & soil

Pecans growing wild in the Southeast and Midwest tend to be along river courses, a strong sign of their need for ample, consistent moisture. The sign should not be misread: pecans do not like soggy root zones. They must grow in well-drained soil; they cannot survive in low, boggy spots.

Propagating & planting

Gardeners in the humid Southeast can propagate pecans by whip-grafting the fruiting variety onto 2-year-old seedling rootstock. Patch-budding is commoner in the arid Southwest, where whip grafts are subject to excessive drying.

Caring for the trees

Pecans must have regular watering and watchful attention to pests.

Watering. The native range of these trees has annual rainfall of 60 to 90 inches, exactly the comfortable amount. The application must be systematic; any lapse that allows the soil to dry will result in under-developed nuts. The interval between deep soakings—whether from rain or irrigation—should not exceed 14 days. In areas with saline water, use only drip or slow flood irrigation, not sprinklers; the trees are intolerant of even a small build-up of salts.

Fertilizing. Pecans need regular feedings of zinc, and can use nitrogen.

Zinc is an absolute requirement for pecans, especially where soils are of pH 7.0 or higher. A deficiency leads to a condition called rosette. The early symptom is yellowed leaves, especially toward the top of the tree. Advanced symptoms are stunted growth and clustered leaves at the tips of shoots.

In humid areas, zinc sulphate or zinc chelate is applied to mature trees as a spray three times each spring. In drier climates, trees may need five sprays. Check with a farm advisor for the best local program. Trees not yet at bearing age should be sprayed fortnightly from mid-April through July. The heavy zinc requirement, not incidentally, makes pecans incompatible neighbors with many other fruit trees. For example, too much zinc will kill peaches.

The zinc spray can be mixed with one of the pest controls.

A nitrogen fertilizer may not be needed, but can be applied as often as twice a year to trees 5 years and older, oftener to young ones.

Pests and diseases. Pecan scab is a prevalent disease in high-rainfall areas, and a problem everywhere. It begins as black spots on leaves, and ends by turning the whole shuck black. The spray and its timing are local matters.

Pecan weevil is at least as destructive, but fortunately appears only in well-defined areas. The soil-borne insect lays an egg in the nut in August, and the egg becomes a red-headed grub that eats all of the nut kernels before boring a hole in the shell and going underground. A specifically formulated control is the only one that works; check with nurseries for commercial names.

Pecan nut casebearer and hickory shuckworm, two other insects peculiar to pecans, also must be controlled by sprays when adult form is present.

Persimmons

Persimmon fruits outlast the foliage

AT A GLANCE

Climate: American persimmons bear in USDA Zones 6–9, and are better adapted east of the Rockies; Asian persimmons produce in Zones 7–10 all across the South and Southwest.

Soil: Most productive in loams, but tolerant of sand and clay.

Trees bear: At 4 or 5 years.

Typical life span: 60 years.

Typical yield at maturity: 3 to 6 bushels.

Self-pollenizer: Asians yes, though a pollenizer improves yield; Americans no.

Semidwarfs and dwarfs available: No.

Harvest season: Late autumn into winter.

Principal pests and diseases: No major problems.

Two renowned palates are at odds over the persimmon.

Raymond Sokolov, a New Yorker who has written affectionately of many of America's disappearing native foods, says of American persimmons, "Small, about the size of walnuts or cherry tomatoes, they resembled the much larger, heart-shaped oriental persimmon . . . only in color and in the gooey texture of their inner flesh. In flavor, these American persimmons far surpass their imported cousins. They are powerfully fragrant, sweet and luscious, and taste like dates. . . . They are wonderful fruits."

Hugh Johnson, the Englishman who writes as movingly of gardening as he does of wine-drinking, thinks otherwise: "The Chinese tree . . . gives the edible persimmon, a succulent yellow fruit the size and shape of an apple. The American tree, . . . which is much more impressive, has fruit that is edible only late in the season, after a frost (when it is soft and sweet, but still without flavor)."

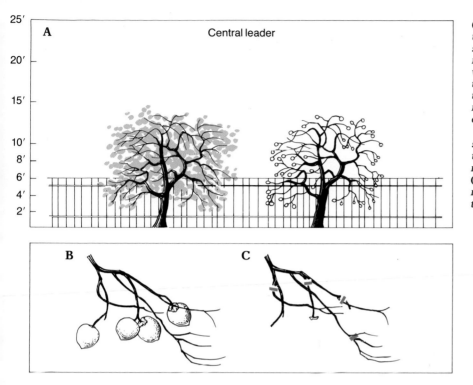

(A) *Tree will naturally grow with a central leader, and should be allowed to do so. In training it, establish at least three major scaffold branches with strong, wide crotches. Episodically, head the tree back and prune back any limbs that become overlong. Asian persimmons adapt well to training as formal espaliers.*

(B) *Pinch back shoots to keep them strong enough to bear fruit, which tends to form at outer ends. Thin fruit if necessary to relieve weight on shoots.*
(C) *Annual pruning is mainly for maintenance, but also should keep center of tree open, small branches short.*

Whichever side one comes down on, there are two distinct lines of persimmon. Right now, the Asian strain is in the ascendant in garden and kitchen alike, as even Sokolov admits, while the American one hangs on by a thread. Incidentally, the Asian tree is native to China but is now bred mainly in Japan, so "Asian" will be its shorthand name here.

The objects of these contrasting views are not the easiest fruits to use. The prime characteristic of most persimmons—a few Asian varieties excepted—is remarkable tannic astringency until they are mushy ripe. But then . . . ah, then!

Persimmons can be frozen whole, then the flesh dipped out of its skin with a spoon as it begins to thaw. Only a world-class sorbet can taste as good or feel as cool. The fruit can be dried, like a fig or date, and will taste much the same—in fact, an alternate name for the persimmon is date-plum. Not least, persimmons can be eaten fresh from the tree, with or without such fancy touches as a daub of yogurt.

The ripe, squishy pulp cooks into an extraordinary fudge or a cakelike pudding, or it flavors ice cream. If there is too much at hand for now, the pulp will keep, frozen, for making the same range of desserts in other seasons.

Knowing when and how to pick persimmons is a large part of the trick. Old tales have it that, to be edible, the American fruit has to fall from the tree after a frost. It is true that a frost helps do away with lingering astringency, but it is not a necessity, nor is it true that the fruit must drop. The flesh must, indeed, be soft to be edible, but the fruit can be picked from the tree once it has reached its ripe color—a dark orange—then ripened in storage. This saves a lot of bruised fruit and a squashy mess underfoot. If the flesh is not soft at picking, bag the persimmons and wait. Putting an apple in the paper sack with them will hurry the ripening.

To be storable, the fruit must be cut from the tree, with part of the stem plus the leathery green collar around it kept intact.

The same rules apply to the astringent varieties of Asian persimmon. A few Asian varieties are sweet when the flesh is firm, and can be eaten like apples. The sweet varieties, too, can be frozen or pulped for cooking.

For anyone who wishes to pick in easy stages, it is good news that persimmons store well on the tree. One of the beguiling habits of these fruits is their ability to hang on long after the leaves have dropped, creating an oddly decorative element in the wintry landscape.

Where they grow

The debate that divides Sokolov and Johnson does not matter much to gardeners in a region running from Kansas east to Indiana and onward to Connecticut—in essence, USDA Zone 6. In these chill-winter territories only the native American persimmon can survive. The native tree is not hardy enough for the northern Plains or for upper New England, though it can grow and bear a light crop in sheltered spots in Zone 5.

Though few nurseries carry native persimmons now, and more trees survive in abandoned gardens than flourish in tended ones, several specialist nurseries carry several cultivars that remain from the days when this fruit was more widely appreciated.

The Asian persimmon is hardy only to 0°F/−18°C, Zone 7. One ex-

Deep orange hue signals ripeness

pert puts its northerly limit at 1,000 chilling hours (at temperatures of 45°F/7°C and below) everywhere east of the Rockies. It needs only 100 to 400 chilling hours to bear consistent crops. However, most trees fruit poorly in southern Florida.

In the West it grows and bears well in nearly all of California's coastal and interior valleys, and into the Rogue River Valley of Oregon. It is borderline in the Willamette Valley of Oregon and in all of western Washington, where it can be expected to ripen a good crop only in warm microclimates. At the hotter end of the scale, the tree will grow in the western deserts, but it rarely fruits there.

The major varieties of Asian persimmon now available in the West are equally adapted within their range. The choice between them has to do mainly with the flavors and textures of the fruit. Principal varieties include the following:

'Chocolate', so named for brown streaks in the flesh, is one of the varieties that is edible while firm-fleshed. The variety sometimes is sold as 'Maru'.

'Fuyu' is small, flattened, and one of the nonastringent varieties; it can be eaten while it is as firm and crisp as an apple. A strain called 'Giant Fuyu' looks more like 'Hachiya'. 'Fuyu' is short-lived in hot climates and tends to be chlorotic.

'Hachiya', the standard commercial variety at present, is large, rounded, and astringent until soft-ripe. It should be picked as soon as it is color-ripe, then stored indoors until soft-ripe to avoid bird damage. 'Hachiya' is more likely than other varieties to fruit in desert gardens.

'Tamopan' is a blander flavored alternative to 'Hachiya'. A curious wavering indentation makes the fruit look as if it is wearing a beret.

'Tanehashi' is an astringent variety particularly well adapted to Florida.

A good many other varieties are being tested at university experiment stations for adaptability to American growing conditions.

Gardeners in Zones 7 to 9, coast to coast, have a choice between the American and Asian strains.

Site & soil

In keeping with their general ease of use, persimmons require little of the soil beyond fair to good drainage. They are most at home in loam of 5.8 to 6.5 pH, but will grow almost as well in clayish or sandy soils of greater or lesser acidity.

The native persimmon can fend for itself in getting adequate light, habituated as it is to competing in forest conditions. The Asian persimmon, no more than four-fifths the size of its American counterpart, and more attuned to heat, grows more steadily if given full sun in its early years.

For Asian persimmons to grow to full size, the trees should be spaced about 25 feet apart. If full size is not a goal, they can be pruned to fit much closer together. They also will perform well in hedges or as formal espaliers.

Propagating & planting

American persimmons can be grown readily from seed or from hardwood cuttings. Either should be taken in autumn, held in chilled conditions through the winter, and planted after the last frost of spring. As noted earlier, native trees can be found in specialist nurseries.

All American trees must have a second tree as a pollenizer. The Asian persimmon will bear without a pollenizer, but will produce more and tastier fruit with one. The exception is 'Chocolate', which alone has both male and female flowers on a single tree. (In its case, the sweet fruit from pollenated flowers has

seeds; the bitter fruit from unpollenated ones does not.)

Asian persimmons are propagated by grafting fruiting varieties onto native American persimmon rootstock. The grafted trees are available least expensively as bare-root plants from November through the winter; they can be planted from autumn (in the warmer, drier parts of their range) through early March (toward the colder end of their territory). Some nurseries carry container plants the year around.

All persimmons quickly develop long taproots, which may require a deeper planting hole than usual. (The taproot should have freedom to grow straight down in loosened soil.) Otherwise, plant the trees at the same depth at which they grew in the nursery, taking care to keep the bud union of a grafted tree 2 to 4 inches above the soil level.

Caring for the trees

There is not much trouble to be had with a persimmon.

Watering. Though more drought-resistant than most trees, they will yield larger, healthier crops if deep-watered at intervals far enough apart to let the soil dry out somewhat—but not completely. The minimum interval is 10 days. They will drop fruit if watered too much, or not enough.

Fertilizing. If tip growth is near 12 inches per season and foliage is a healthy, dark green, the tree needs no fertilizer. Few do.

The only element persimmons seem to need is nitrogen; the other elements in complete fertilizers have no apparent effect, whether applied in gross volumes or withheld altogether. However, because excess nitrogen causes fruit drop, experienced gardeners tend to use a slow-acting complete fertilizer when one is called for. A safe course is 1 pound of a 10 percent nitrogen fertilizer per inch of trunk diameter measured at the ground. The timing is late winter or early spring.

Pests and diseases. An insect-chewed or diseased leaf is a rare thing to see on one of these trees. They need no regular spraying program.

Plums & Prunes

Ripening plums

Thanks to their many forms, plums offer the one sure bet for gardeners anywhere on the American continent save for Florida and a few other spots along the Gulf of Mexico.

The names—'Yellow Egg', 'Green Gage', 'Blue Damson', 'Burgundy', and 'Redheart'—promise a rainbow of colors and flavors, and the fruits deliver. They are delicious fresh, canned, cooked, jellied, or dried.

The trade-offs are not exactly even among the European, Japanese, and native American plum species that provide so sweeping a guarantee of success. The broad rule of thumb is that the Japanese varieties are best fresh, the Europeans best cooked or dried, the Americans at their peak in jams, sauces, and other

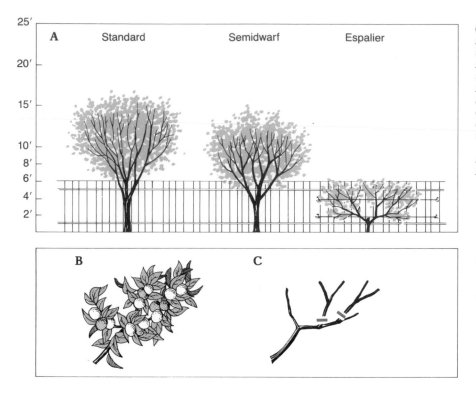

(A) *Upright growth habits make plums natural candidates for open-center training. Japanese plums will offer many more potential scaffold branches than Europeans do. In selecting scaffolds, take care to avoid V-crotches. Standard trees will grow to 30 feet, but can be kept to 15 by pruning. Semidwarfs also train well as open-center trees, topping out at 8 to 10 feet.*

Semidwarfs, especially, lend themselves to informal espaliers, and can be kept in containers.

(B) *Fruit forms on 4 to 6-inch spurs that bear for many years. Japanese varieties tend to overbear; fruit must be thinned to 4 to 6 inches apart. Europeans bear less but should be thinned similarly.* (C) *Annual pruning is mainly a matter of thinning out and heading back the yearly overabundance of shoots, taking care to keep a large number of fruiting spurs.*

preserves. Like all generalities, this one delivers no better than a glancing blow at the truth.

One other point about what's what among plums: All prunes are from the main species of European plums, set aside from the others only by an extra degree of natural sugar that allows them to dry before fermentation sets in around the pit.

The Europeans are without doubt the sweetest of the lot. A few varieties are superb straight off the tree, but not many are meaty enough to enjoy fresh. On the other hand, all of them cook or dry to perfection. It was one of their number that little Jack Horner pulled from a pie with his thumb, a 'Queen Ann' if the cook was in top form.

Two plums, 'Damson' (also called 'Blue Damson') and 'Shropshire', are European, but from a different species than the majority. Mainly desirable for cooking or jellies, they are among the hardiest European plums, and can be crossed freely with the others.

All Japanese plum varieties are fleshier, softer and juicier than the Europeans. Nearly all are tart by comparison, and all but the most tart are delicious for fresh eating. (Quite a few of the truly tart ones seem sweeter and milder if peeled.) Only a few cook as well as their European cousins, though some varieties make splendid sauces and jams. None will dry properly.

The Americans (most presently recognized varieties are not natives, but rather hybrids with a Japanese plum) are tart, usually tough-hided, better in jams or preserves than fresh. Their greater virtue is that the trees are so hardy, people can grow them where no other tree will bear much of a crop, if any.

Some purely native plums—known as either bush or cherry plums—come from bushes rather than trees. Some quite sour ones are adapted to the hot, humid Southeast (but not competitive with Japanese varieties), others to the coldest parts of the upper Midwest and the Canadian prairies. Like their hybrid cousins, the northerners are best in jams and preserves. Their other virtue is the ability to snuggle into tight spaces.

Where they grow

The territories of the three groups of plums do not separate neatly; nei-ther do they overlap in good order. The opposite poles of heat and cold require gardeners in large parts of the continent to make thoughtful choices—variety by variety, rather than species by species.

The grand generality about growing plums, such as it is, says Japanese plums are best in the West, Europeans best in the East, and American hybrids best in the upper Midwest. But the exceptions leave very little of the rule.

Japanese plums are least hardy of the three. Their fruit buds are killed at 0°F/−18°C, and their requirement for winter chilling hours (temperatures at or below 45°F/7°C) is slight, ranging from 400 to 1000 hours. At the other end of the scale, they need the most heat to ripen well.

In such warm, dry summer regions of the West as California's coastal and interior valleys, they ripen well with little or no care. The only general problem is their tendency to set a larger crop than they can ripen. They may grow in sheltered parts of eastern Washington and in the Okanagan country of British Columbia, but their early blossom time can make them a risky bet in any region of late spring frosts.

(Continued on page 72)

Plums & Prunes

Variety	USDA Climate Zones*	Minimum chill hours**	Ripens	Bears	Origin	Size	Fresh	Cooked	Canned	Dried	Frozen	Comments
'Burbank'	5–10	Avg	M	M	J	L	A	A	A	A	A	Good in cold-winter areas. Pollenizers: 'Beauty', 'Santa Rosa'.
'Casselman'	5–10	Avg	L	M	J	L	A	A	A	A	A	Slow to ripen. Somewhat self-fertile; better with 'Santa Rosa'.
'Damson' ('Blue Damson')	5–10	Avg	L	M	E	S	A	A	A	A	A	Tree small, fruit slightly tart. Virtually identical to 'Shropshire'.
'Duarte'	5–9	1200	M	M	J	M/L	A	A	A	A	A	Hardy. Pollenizers: 'Beauty', 'Santa Rosa', 'Wickson'.
'Elephant Heart'	5–9	Avg	M/L	M	J	VL	E	A	A	A	A	Highly flavored, tart-skinned. Pollenizer: 'Santa Rosa'.
'French Prune'	5–9	Avg	L	M	E	S/M	A	A	A	O	A	Long-lived tree. Fruit can be too sweet to can.
'Green Gage'	5–9	Avg	M	M	E	S/M	E	E	E	E	E	Mild-flavored old variety, fine for every use.
'Imperial'	5–9	Avg	M/L	M	E	L	E	A	E	E	A	Versatile in the kitchen. Pollenizer: any European variety.
'Italian Prune' ('Fellenburg')	5–9	Avg	M/L	H	E	L	A	A	A	A	A	Hardy, but needs warm spring to bear well. Can overcrop. Self-fertile.
'Late Santa Rosa'	8–9	Avg	L	M	J	M/L	A	A	A	A	A	Firm fruit tends to split. Self-fertile
'Mariposa' ('Improved Satsuma')	8–10	400	M	M	J	L	A	A	A	A	A	One of best for s CA.
'Methley'	6–10	400	E	H	J	S/M	A	A	A	A	A	Best bet for TX. Ripens over long season.
'Ozark Premier'	4–8	Avg	M/L	H	J	VL	A	A	A	A	A	Firm, juicy, tart. Pollenizers: 'Pipestone', 'Satsuma'.
'Pipestone'	4–8	Avg	E	M	J	L	A	A	A	A	A	Among hardiest; needs little heat to ripen. Pollenizer: 'Superior'.
'President'	5–9	Avg	L	M	E	L	A	A	A	P	A	Good in cool-summer N. Pollenizers: 'Imperial', 'Stanley'.
'Queen Ann'	7–9	Avg	M/L	M	J	L	E	E	A	A	A	Weak tree but fine fruit. Pollenizers: 'Laroda,' 'Elephant Heart', 'Redheart', 'Santa Rosa'.
'Reine Claude Conducta'	5–8	Avg	L	M	E	M	E	E	E	E	A	Juicy fruit prized for its flavor. Self-fertile.
'Santa Rosa'	5–10	Avg	E	H	J	M/L	E	A	A	A	A	Widely adapted, ripens over long season. Self-fertile.
'Satsuma'	5–9	Avg	E/M	M	J	S/M	A	A	A	A	A	Widely adapted. Pollenizers: 'Beauty', 'Santa Rosa', 'Wickson'.
'Shiro'	5–9	Avg	E/M	H	J	M/L	A	A	A	A	A	One of best yellow plums in coastal NW. Pollenizer: 'Santa Rosa'.
'Stanley'	5–9	Avg	M/L	H	E	L	A	A	A	A	A	May fruit in Zone 4. Susceptible to brown rot. Self-fertile.
'Superior'	5–8	Avg	L	H	J	L	A	A	A	A	A	Bears young. May bear in Zone 4, overcrop in warmer regions. Pollenizer: 'Pipestone'.
'Wickson'	5–9	Avg	E/M	M	J	L	A	A	A	A	A	Fine flavor. Flesh yellow. Pollenizers: 'Santa Rosa', 'Beauty'.
'Yellow Egg'	5–9	Avg	M	M	E	L	A	A	A	A	A	Another of the fine yellow plums. Self-fertile.

Chart Key:

Ripens:
E/Early, M/Mid, L/Late
Bears:
M/Medium, H/Heavy
Origin:
J/Japan, E/Europe
Size:
S/Small, M/Medium, L/Large, VL/Very large
Fruit quality:
O/Outstanding, E/Excellent, A/Average, P/Poor

*See climate zone maps, pages 84–87.
**Average chilling hours 800–1000. For more information, see pages 84–87.

Japanese varieties are the choice for all parts of the South. They are subject to a few more diseases in humid heat than they are in the dry West, but bear good fruit if given a bit of extra care. Their record is spottier from the Great Lakes east into southern New England. The principle there is that the hardier varieties will bear well and ripen adequately where peaches prosper.

Penn State University extension scientists suggest planting hardy Japanese varieties for general use, and the European varieties 'Damson' and 'Shropshire' only for jams, jellies, or other preserves.

European plums get the experts' nod over the Japanese species in those parts of the northeast quarter of the country where pears do better than peaches. This is so because—compared with Japanese plums—they are hardier, require more chilling hours, bloom later, and ripen their fruit with less summer heat.

European plums are not for the hot Southeast—they ripen there only as prunes, and drying is not an easy art in a humid climate.

The South aside, European plums may do better in the East, as the generality has it, but they are rewarding to grow in much of the West. A large proportion of the country's prunes now come from commercial orchards in California's San Joaquin Valley. Earlier, commercial prunes came mainly from the coastal valleys north and south of San Francisco.

In the cool Pacific Northwest, most garden plums are prune varieties of the European species, and they ripen there just enough to provide excellent eating fresh from the tree.

American hybrid plums dominate in the Dakotas, Minnesota, and the Canadian prairies. They will grow on most of the continent east of the Rockies, but have been replaced by Japanese or European plums wherever these other species will grow, partly because the quality of the fruit from American plums is not quite the equal of the others, and partly because the hybrid trees can be maddeningly resistant to pollenizing. Indeed, the only advice on this latter point is to find a local expert who has succeeded in finding an adequate pollenizer, and imitate success.

No European or Japanese plum is large by the standards of stone fruits. For gardeners pressed for space, European varieties come as semidwarfs, grafted onto 'Nanking' cherry rootstock. Anyone truly pressed for space might investigate the bush-type native plums.

Site & soil

The ideal soil for all plums is a slightly sandy, well-drained loam, pH 6.0 to 6.5; pH 5.5 is good enough. The trees will do nicely in well-drained clay loams, but do not tolerate wet roots so well as pears and some other fruits. Distinctly boggy spots almost surely will lead to root rot.

Further on the point of wet roots, veteran growers recommend against planting plums in lawns. They can thrive at the edge of a sod lawn, though.

Because plums tend to bear heavily, soil fertility is somewhat more important than for other stone fruits.

Plums must have full sun to bear and ripen a crop.

In regions of spring frost, these early-blooming trees should be planted where there is good air drainage.

Propagating & planting

Most nursery plants are cuttings budded or grafted onto disease-resistant or dwarfing rootstock, save for the American hybrids, most of which grow on their own roots.

As with all deciduous fruits, the least expensive way to buy is bare-root for spring planting in most areas, autumn planting in mild-winter zones. Some nurseries stock balled-and-burlapped or container trees for planting the year around.

Oddly—inasmuch as mature plums thrive on fertilizers—some experts advise against putting any fertilizer at all in the planting hole of any Japanese variety. The reasoning is that, even without any boost, they bear too much too soon. Other authorities recommend 1 ounce of dissolved (never dry) ammonium sulfate in the planting holes of all plums, but especially Europeans.

Caring for the trees

Except in humid regions, plums need less care than most other deciduous fruit trees, though they must be pruned vigorously (see caption, page 70).

Watering. Plums are fairly drought-resistant. In most of their range outside of desert areas, the trees are likely to survive on water from rainfall. They grow well on as little as 25 inches of rain per year. However, in any area with dry summers, crops benefit from occasional deep soaking to 4 feet. A useful sign that it is time to water is when the top 3 inches of soil dries. Or plant an indicator such as hydrangea near the plum, and water them together; if the indicator wilts, water both.

Fertilizing. Most expert gardeners recommend some fertilizer annually for all plums, to assure good-size fruit and healthy growth. The trees will thrive on high-nitrogen fertilizers such as ammonium sulfate.

The recommendation for obtaining big crops from mature trees is 1 to 3 pounds of actual nitrogen per year for Japanese varieties, 1 to 2 pounds for European ones. A more cautious recommendation is ½ pound of complete fertilizer (10-10-10 or similar) per tree per year of age, to a maximum of 5 pounds.

Pests and diseases. Plums suffer little from pests or diseases in warm, dry areas, though gardeners must be watchful for aphids, mites, peach tree borers, and scale. The more humid the climate, the more troublesome are the pest curculio, and the diseases bacterial canker, brown rot, and leaf spot.

Aphids, mites, and scale all can be kept in check by a dormant spray. Aphids and borers also can be sprayed with recommended insecticides when buds show white. (See pages 108–111.) In humid areas, brown rot and leaf spot can be controlled with weekly applications of wettable sulfur throughout the growing season (again, see pages 108–111). Bacterial canker has no known cure, but can be inhibited by vigorous pruning and fertilization, and also by a locally designed spray program. Contact a farm advisor for a recommendation.

Pomegranates

Pomegranates grow in many thousands more gardens for their ornamental values than for their fruit, which is flavorful but a considerable nuisance to use.

The fruit, proper, is a thin, gelatinous film around a woody seed, scores of which hide within a leathery ball that is a dusty to bright red. To chew the juicy film is to chew the seeds as well.

As a fruiting plant, pomegranate is narrowly limited to regions with mild winters (USDA Zone 8 or milder) and warm to hot summers. In practice, it ripens best in deserts, but does well enough to be enjoyable in much of the Southwest and Southeast. While trees are hardy to 10°F/ −12°C, fruiting varieties are subject to severe crop loss from spring frosts. Pomegranates, in addition to taking great heat, will survive in soils alkaline enough to kill most other plants.

Nursery plants usually are bought bare-root and planted in January, to allow them to establish root systems before summer heat.

Watering. To establish new plants, water every 2 to 4 weeks during the dry season. Pomegranates need very little water once established, but don't allow the root zone to alternate between wet and dry—this leads to cracked fruit, which spoils quickly. Soils subject to episodic summer rains should be kept moist throughout the growing season; drainage should be good.

Fertilizing. It is seldom required after 2 to 4-ounce applications of

Anatomy of a pomegranate

AT A GLANCE

Climate: Grows best as fruiting plant in deserts; also good in Southeast. Must have summer heat to ripen.

Soil: Widely adaptable; unusually tolerant of alkaline and salty soils.

Trees bear: At 1 to 4 years.

Typical life span: 80 to 90 years.

Typical yield at maturity: 90 to 120 pounds per tree.

Self-pollenizer: Yes.

Semidwarfs and dwarfs available: Yes.

Harvest season: When fully colored.

Principal pests and diseases: Leaf spot.

ammonium sulfate or other nitrogen fertilizer the first two springs in the West. The recommendation for Florida is 1 to 2 pounds of 6-6-6 every 4 months.

Pests and diseases. The plant is subject to few of either. In deserts, the leaf-footed plant bug may drill holes in fruit. Control it with a late spring spray of diazinon or malathion.

Train pomegranate as an open-center tree to about 15 feet, as a fountain-shaped shrub to about 10 feet, or as an informal espalier. Once established, tree need be pruned only to remove crossing and damaged branches, shrub to remove damage, espalier to restrain tip growth of laterals. Fruit seldom requires thinning, except if branches threaten to break from overload toward tips.

Quinces

Typically sparse quince

AT A GLANCE

Climate: Broadly adapted in USDA Zone 5 and warmer.

Soil: Best in heavy soils with good drainage.

Tree bears: At 4 to 6 years.

Typical life span: 35 years.

Typical yield at maturity: 1 bushel per tree.

Self-pollenizer: Yes.

Semidwarfs and dwarfs available: No.

Harvest season: Autumn, after fruit loses green tint.

Principal pests and diseases: Fireblight.

The quince offers to most of the country what the pomegranate offers only to residents of warm places: a tall shrub or squat tree that produces intractable fruit with fascinating flavors.

The tart, fibrous fruit cannot be enjoyed fresh from the tree, but it can be transformed into aromatic jams and jellies, candy, or durably piquant wine.

There is little difference between these varieties in fruit quality or flavor:

'Apple' (also called 'Orange') is an old favorite with good flavor.

'Cooke's Jumbo' produces fruit nearly twice the size of others.

'Pineapple', named for a similarity in flavor with the tropical fruit, has tender flesh.

'Smyrna' has good-size fruit with the strongest quince fragrance.

The tree was a part of almost every pioneer garden in the plains. It grows well everywhere except in the Southwest low desert (where it is prone to fireblight) and in USDA Zones 4 and colder.

Quinces grow best in heavy but well-drained soils, but will tolerate wetter soils than most fruit trees. Once the tree is in place, the ground around it should not be cultivated deeply because of quinces' tendency to shallow rooting.

Quince trees should be planted bare-root in early spring. Plant at the same depth as the tree grew at the nursery.

Watering. Though somewhat drought-resistant, quinces benefit from watering each 4 to 6 weeks if dry spells are common during the growing season.

Fertilizing. It is seldom required. If done, avoid high dosages of nitrogen, because quinces are especially susceptible to fireblight in succulent growth. If needed, use ⅛ pound of 10-10-10 or 5-10-10 per tree per year of age, to a maximum of 5 pounds.

Pests and diseases. Susceptible to almost no insect, and only to fireblight among common diseases.

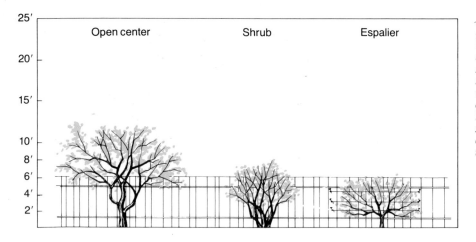

As a tree, quince is best trained to open center, and kept at 10 feet high. It can be grown as a multitrunked shrub or in an informal espalier. Fruit seldom needs thinning, unless a branch bears so heavily it threatens to break. Very little pruning is required of mature trees, except to remove crossing or damaged branches. Heading back and light thinning will keep most trees in prime condition. In heading back, do not remove too many tips; fruit grows there.

Strawberries

Climate: Given correct choice of variety, adapted to every part of U.S., most of populous Canada.

Soil: Tolerant, but most productive in rich, well-drained sandy loam, pH 5.8 to 6.5. Intolerant of saline soils.

Plants bear: In second season.

Typical life span: 2 to 3 productive years.

Typical yield at maturity: 5 to 10 quarts of berries per 10 feet of matted row.

Self-pollenizer: Yes.

Harvest season: Spring for most, spring and fall for everbearing varieties.

Principal pests and diseases: Mites, rose chafer, strawberry root weevil, verticillium wilt, and root rot. Earwigs, slugs, and snails will damage ripening berries.

The cycle—blossom to ripe fruit

Strawberries piled on shortcake. Strawberries mounded over ice cream. Strawberries heaped in a bowl, with or without sour cream and brown sugar for dipping. Strawberry jam lathered on scones. Other berries go into muffins, or make fine accents in salads or desserts, but strawberries come first, and their carriers are merely incidental.

Strawberries are special at the farming end, too. Commercial growers can be as aloof and secretive as mushroom hunters with their breeding programs and tricks of cultivation for bigger, juicier, tastier fruit.

Against these extraordinary images, strawberries are among the easiest fruits to grow in a home garden, and one of the most productive. The plants' lack of longevity and size cause them to respond quickly to attentions bestowed—or forgotten. This and a long fruiting season mean lost ground often can be regained. If all else fails, plants are easily and quickly replaced.

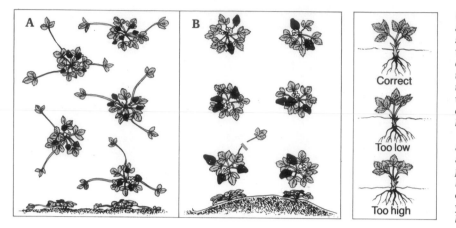

(A) For matted rows, set out plants as shown. Pinch out all blossoms in first season. Allow runners to root anywhere within bed. Weed weekly to minimize competition for water, nutrients. In autumn of second year, grub out about one-third of all plants, focusing on older and weak or diseased ones. Thereafter, grub out oldest, weakest one-third of plants in bed each year.

(B) For hills, set out plants as shown. Pinch off runners as they appear, to force crown growth. (A few plants may be set aside as mothers for bed renewal. Otherwise, a large number of new plants must be bought each year.) If everbearing, blossoms need not be pinched out in first season.

Correct

Too low

Too high

Where they grow

Format calls for an explanation of where strawberries will grow. Fact makes it easier to explain where they will not: in permafrost or on glaciers. The key lies in matching variety and place. Though some varieties are widely adapted, the breeding programs that have spread strawberries all across the continent have made many varieties strict homebodies.

Site & soil

Before planting, soil should be tilled or spaded to a depth of 8 inches or more. Heavy soils should be amended with peat or other organic matter to help drainage; good drainage is imperative. Poor soils benefit from a preplanting application of 1 pound of 10-10-10 fertilizer per 100 square feet of bed.

Subject as they are to verticillium wilt, strawberries should not be planted where eggplants, peppers, potatoes, raspberries, or tomatoes have grown within the preceding 3 years. For the same reason, beds should be moved whenever wilt shows up. Strawberries also should not be planted where lawn has grown recently, leaving grubs and competing weeds.

In hard-winter regions, strawberries are best planted toward the tops of gentle slopes with good air drainage to minimize winter kill and frost damage to blossoms. In USDA Zones 5–7 plants should be protected against freezing in winter by thick mulch, unless the variety has proven hardy where it is growing.

Propagating & planting

Once a bed has been started, propagating new plants from existing ones is almost automatic for most varieties, and is required for all. However, it is best to begin with certified stock from a nursery, and to renew with nursery stock every few years. Plants in gardens tend to weaken steadily from wilts and other diseases. For consistent crops, revitalize the bed each year. Individual plants bear best in their first year, less well in the second, only weakly in the third.

Most strawberry varieties propagate by runners, long stalks that root at the tips, producing new plants. Varieties that produce few or no runners are propagated by dividing the crowns.

Nurseries sell bare-root plants for spring or autumn, flats or containers of them for other seasons. Roots of bare-root plants should be trimmed to 6 inches long and fanned out in the planting holes. However the plants come, they should be set with the base of their crowns at soil level (buried crowns rot), the topmost roots ¼ inch below the soil (exposed roots dry out and die). See illustration, above.

Of the two basic planting methods for strawberry beds, the hill method produces relatively few berries, but those few are large. It is widely used for all varieties west of the Rockies, and for everbearing varieties everywhere. The matted row method yields many more, smaller berries. It is the preferred method east of the Rockies. Spacing and maintenance techniques are noted with the sketches. Strawberries will, of course, grow well in containers for anyone with limited space or meager appetite.

Caring for the plants

Short-lived, soft-tissued strawberries demand constant attention.

Watering. Plants need 1 to 2 inches of water per week from blossom through harvest. Schedule irrigation so the soil stays moist (every 2 or 3 days in sandy soil and dry climates, once a week in heavier soils or rainier regions). June crops may not need irrigation in areas with late spring rains. Everbearers everywhere need summer irrigation. Experts in most regions recommend mulching to help conserve water and to keep the berries clean and dry. Black plastic is the favorite.

Fertilizing. This is where the artist surfaces in a strawberry grower. Recommended basic programs vary by region and berry type; specific programs vary by individual growers.

As starting points: For matted rows of June bearers in most of the country, apply 1 to 2 pounds of ammonium sulfate per 100 square feet just as runners start. (In small patches or for hill plantings, figure 1 teaspoon per plant.) High-nitrogen fertilizers such as ammonium sulfate are particularly recommended in regions of leaching summer rains.

Feed everbearing plants once a year between crops (in August) or twice a year—once when growth begins in spring, again after the first crop. Whether the feeding is split or done all at once, recommendations for fertilizer range from 4 to 5 pounds of a complete fertilizer (usually 10-10-10) to 1 pound of ammonium sulfate per 100 square feet of bed. In cool coastal areas from northern California to British Columbia, growers usually use superphosphate at planting time, high-phosphorus fertilizers in autumn.

Pests and diseases. Spray or dust before fruit has set to control aphids (see page 108) and mites (see page 110). Do not use chemicals after fruit forms. Control slugs and snails by picking them off the plants and stomping them underfoot. Where birds compete for fruit, cover beds with netting.

Strawberries are subject to red stele (root rot), yellows (virus), and verticillium wilt. The most effective control for the latter two is to uproot the bed and plant elsewhere for 2 years. Root rot sometimes can be controlled by improving drainage.

Strawberries

Variety	Plant			Fruit				Chart Key / Comments
	Type	Ripens	Bears	Size	Fresh	Cooked	Frozen	Comments
'Albritton'	J	M	M	M	E	A	A	Well-liked in GA.
'Atlas'	J	M	M	L	E	A	A	Disease-resistant in VA.
'Benton'	J	M	H	L	A	F	E	Major commercial berry for processing in NW.
'Catskill'	J	E	M	L	A	A	E	Widely recommended for VA to MA. Mild to bland.
'Chief Bemidji'	E		H	L	E	A	A	Hardy to −40°F/−40°C; best for cool-summer areas.
'Earlidawn'	J	VE	H	M/L	A	A	A	Blossoms frost-hardy in Va, MO, MA.
'Earliglow'	J	E	H	M/L	E	E	E	Disease-resistant in VA, MO.
'Florida 90'	J	VE	H	L	A	A	A	Favorite in FL, s GA.
'Fort Laramie'	E		H	L	E	A	A	Hardy in mountain states, high plains.
'Guardian'	J	M/L	M	L	E	A	A	Sweet. Resists red stele, verticillium wilt. Liked from MO to MA.
'Lassen'	J	E/L	H	M	A	A	A	For s CA; tolerates warm winters, saline soils.
'Midland'	J	E	M/H	VL	E	A	E	Dark, sweet berries MO to MA.
'Nisqually'	E		M	M	A	A	A	Developed for PNW; mildew-resistant.
'Ogallala'	E		H	M	A	A	A	Top everbearer in lower MW. Blossoms resist frost.
'Ozark Beauty'	E		M	M/L	E	A	E	Adapts to many climates, but quality varies.
'Puget Beauty'	E		M	L	A	A	A	Good in heavy soils in PNW.
'Rainier'	J	M	M	M/L	E	A	E	For w WA, OR, BC.
'Redchief'	J	M	VH	M/L	E	A	E	Resists red stele; recommended in VA, MO, MA.
'Red Rich'	E		M	M/L	E	A	E	Widely adapted; some resistance to salinity.
'Sequoia'	J	E	H	VL	O	A	A	Wins taste tests time and again. Widely adapted.
'Shasta'	J	M	M	L	E	A	A	At best in coastal CA.
'Shuksan'	J	M	M	L	A	A	E	Cold-hardy. Good e of Cascades in WA, OR.
'Sparkle'	J	M/L	H	M/L	E	A	A	Dark; best late berry in MO; fine in MA.
'Surecrop'	J	M	H	L	A	A	A	Mild, reliable. Tolerates drought. Widely recommended in MW, NE.
'Tioga'	J	M	H	L	A	A	A	Outperforms 'Lassen' in CA; good in GA.
'20th Century'	J	M	H	M/L	E	A	A	Good in intermountain, cold-winter areas.

Chart Key:
Type: J/June-bearing, E/Everbearing
Ripens: VE/Very early, E/Early, M/Mid, L/Late,
Bears: L/Light, M/Medium, H/Heavy, VH/Very heavy
Size: M/Medium, L/Large, VL/Very large
Fruit quality: O/Outstanding, E/Excellent, A/Average, P/Poor

Walnuts

English walnut ready for harvest

AT A GLANCE

Climate: USDA Zones 3–9, with careful choice of variety outside of 6–8.

Soil: Deep, well-drained, ideally pH 6 to 6.5, but fairly tolerant.

Trees bear: At 5 to 10 years.

Typical life span: 100 years.

Typical yield at maturity: 1 to 2 bushels; capable of 15. Tend to bear well in alternate years only.

Self-pollenizer: Yes, but much better with second tree.

Semidwarfs and dwarfs available: No.

Harvest season: September–October, as husks split.

Principal pests and diseases: Walnut blight, walnut husk fly, walnut lace bug. Also anthracnose, aphids, codling moth, curculio, mites, scales.

The walnut is a straight, heavy tree, so dark and stolid that it reminds English writer Hugh Johnson of a "puritan waiting to close the theatres." The saving grace is a superb nut, meaty, rich in flavor, easy to eat out of the shell, easy to keep—shelled or unshelled—until the mood strikes to chop them into dressings, drop them into cakes, or sprinkle them through salads.

For people who like to eat walnuts, the trees come in two main groups, one with two subgroups. The main groups are English (or Persian) walnuts, and native black walnuts. The English subdivide into English and Carpathian groups. The questions for eaters are how hardy the tree needs to be, and how hard the proprietor is willing to work at cracking the shells. The question of tree size is not inconsiderable, either. English walnuts grow to about 60 feet. Black walnuts can reach 100 feet west of the Rockies, 150 feet in their native range east of there.

Where they grow

The native range of the black walnut covers most of USDA Zones 6, 7, and

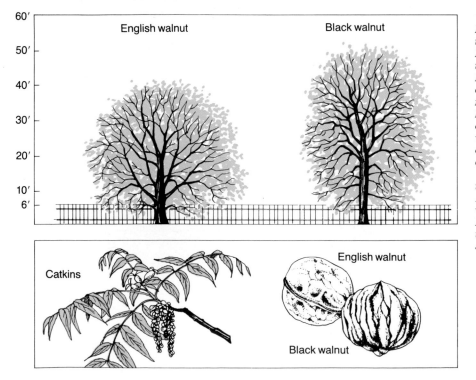

Towering black walnut and smaller English walnut both should be trained to a central leader or modified central leader. The latter establishes two or three tiers of scaffolds from a central leader, then spreads more in the fashion of an open-center tree. First tier of scaffolds should be comfortably above head height, branching between 6 and 8 feet off the ground. Once the basic framework is established, walnuts need little or no pruning except to remove broken or diseased branches.

Catkins of walnuts are less showy than those of chestnuts and pecans. Nuts in their smooth husks are harvested by knocking the branches with long poles, then gathering the crop from the ground. Nuts must be dried on trays after being peeled.

Walnuts

Variety	Tree					Comments
	USDA Climate Zones*	Type	Spring frost risk	Ripens	Bears	Kernel quality	

Chart Key:
Type: E/English, B/Black
Spring frost risk: N/None, L/Low, M/Moderate, VP/Very prone
Ripens: E/Early, M/Mid, L/Late,
Bears: L/Light, M/Medium, H/Heavy, VH/Very heavy
Kernel quality: E/Excellent, A/Average

Variety	USDA Climate Zones*	Type	Spring frost risk	Ripens	Bears	Kernel quality	Comments
'Adams'	4–6	E	L	L	M	A	For E. Hardy Carpathian type. (Second variety of same name for W; much like Franquette.)
'Ambassador'	5–8	E	L	L	H	A	For W. Bears as young as 2 years, usually at 3.
'Broadview'	6–8	E	M	M/L	H	A	For E, but hardy in W. A Carpathian. Only hope in TX. Nut keeps well.
'Burtner'	6–8	E	N	L	M	A	For E. Sheds pollen very late, so readily escapes spring frost damage. Bears annually.
'Carmelo'	9	E	M	M	M	A	For W. Resists sunburn. Bears huge nuts.
'Chandler'	8–9	E	L	M	H	E	For W.
'Chico'	9	E	M	E	H	A	For W. Overbears if not pruned hard. Excellent pollenizer.
'Colby'	7–8	E	L	E	M	A	For E. A Carpathian best adapted n of Ohio River. Thin-shelled nut.
'Concord'	9–10	E	M	M	M	A	For W. Best hope for mild coastal CA.
'Drummond'	9	E	M	E/M	H	A	For W. Big nut with soft shell.
'Elmer Myers'	6–8	B	L	L	M	A	For E. Thin-shelled nut with high proportion of meat.
'Eureka'	8–9	E	M	L	H	E	For W. Slow to begin bearing. Nut cracks easily. Pollenizer: 'Chico'.
'Franquette'	7–9	E	N	L	L	A	For W. At best in NW, regions with late spring.
'Hansen'	6–7	E	M	M	M	A	For E. Widely adapted. Relatively small tree. Nuts are small, thin-shelled, easy to crack. Very high percentage of nuts are filled. Bears annually. Self-pollenating. Resists disease, husk fly.
'Hartley'	8–9	E	L	M	H	A	For W. Slightly susceptible to blight. Pollenizer: 'Franquette' or self.
'Howard'	8–9	E	L	M	VH	A	For W. Small tree. Pollenizers: 'Hartley', 'Franquette'.
'Idaho'	7–9	E	L/N	L	M	A	For W. Disappearing, but useful where frosts come late.
'Lake'	6–8	E	L	M/L	L	A	For E, especially IL, MO. Nut is tasty.
'Mayette'	7–9	E	M	M	M	A	For W. Not winter-hardy in warmest PA.
'McKinster'	6–7	E	L	L	M	A	For E. Favored in OH and MI. Considered self-pollenating. Attractive tree.
'Metcalfe'	6–7	E	L	E	L/M	E	For E. At best in NY.
'Ohio'	6–8	B	L	M	M	A	For E. Resists anthracnose.
'Payne'	9	E	VP	M	H	E	For W. Very susceptible to blight. Pollenizer: 'Chico'.
'Placentia'	9–10	E	M	M	VH	A	For W. Bears young. Needs little chill. Fine in s CA. Pollenizer: self.
'Serr'	9	E	M	M	H	E	For W. Bears young. Highly resistant to sunburn. Pollenizer: 'Chico'.
'Somers'	6–7	E	M	E	M	A	For E. One of earliest-ripening varieties, so a good choice for short-season areas. Apparently resistant to husk fly.
'Sparrow'	5–7	B	L	M/L	H	E	For E. Productive in KA.
'Spurgeon'	5–8	E	N	L	M	E	For W, especially NW. Thin-shelled nut. Pollenizer: self.
'Stabler'	6–7	B	L	M	M	A	For E, especially e PA, MD. Easy nut to crack.
'Ten Eyck'	6–7	B	N	L	H	A	For E. Does well in warmest areas of PA.
'Thomas'	5–7	B	L	L	M/H	A	For E. Among most widely planted varieties of black walnut. Best hope in S.

*See climate zone maps, pages 84–87.

8 east of the Rockies. It can be expected to grow and bear well throughout those areas. Selected varieties also will grow well in Zone 5. The tree itself is hardy to Zone 3, but often fails to fruit because buds are damaged by spring frosts. A near relative, the butternut, is a better choice in Zones 3 and 4, and the colder parts of Zone 5. It is smaller than an English walnut.

The black walnut has adapted very well to most of the West. It can get by with as few as 500 chilling hours, is fairly drought-resistant, and takes summer heat well.

The English or Persian walnut (the trees have grown historically in both places) grow in an even broader range of climates. The subgroup known as Carpathians are extraordinarily hardy, having been bred in the frigid mountains that give them their name, and will fruit in Zone 3. Other varieties will perform tolerably well in the hot, humid South, though walnuts have not become popular there because they crop unreliably and are subject to blights and rots even when they do; theirs is not a record to wean people away from the much better suited pecan.

Most of the commercial orchards are in the West, from California into Oregon.

The thing about English walnuts is that choice of variety is critical. Sturdy as the trees might be, the blossoms are fragile. Each variety must be matched to local climate so that flowering and pollenization take place in the balmiest possible weather.

Site & soil

Big trees, walnuts need deep soil with good drainage. Ideally, the soil should be 4 feet deep, with a soft enough subsoil for the taproot to penetrate easily. An ideal pH is 6 to 6.5; strongly acid soils should be corrected with lime (see page 104). The handy indicator is that walnuts grow well in the kind of soil that grows good corn. They do not grow well in shallow soils on hillsides, or in wet bottom lands.

For all the warnings, walnuts are tolerant.

It does, however, take a dedicated walnut fancier to tolerate the tree in a small garden.

They are better at the edges of lawns than in them because the watering needs of the two are opposed.

Because their shallow feeder roots concentrate at the drip line, there should be no competing plants there. This is a problem they tend to take care of themselves, for the roots of all commonly planted walnuts, especially black walnuts, keep competition out from underfoot by poisoning other plants—including their own seedlings. They are most poisonous to tomatoes, rhododendrons, and azaleas, but are hard on all flowers and vegetables.

Walnuts certainly will have aphids in such numbers that the exuded honeydew makes them unwelcome hanging over patios or automobile parking places.

Finally, to round out the negatives, many people are allergic to wind-borne walnut pollen.

Propagating & planting

Like all large nut trees, walnuts are not for the instant gardener. Seedlings need as many as 20 years to bear. Grafted plants from nurseries need 5 to 10 years to begin yielding useful crops.

A majority of nursery plants are English walnuts grafted onto black walnut rootstock (for disease resistance) because the softer-shelled nuts of the English varieties are widely preferred, and because the tree is far smaller. However, black walnut varieties can be found without much trouble. Most are improved varieties grafted onto seedling rootstock.

The least expensive tree is, as always, a bare-root one. In all cold-winter climates, bare-root walnuts must be planted in spring. They can be planted in autumn where the ground does not freeze.

The planting hole should be surrounded immediately with a watering basin.

Caring for the trees

Steady, deep watering and steady attention to pests and diseases are the keys to large crops of walnuts.

Watering. The trees are drought-resistant but need water for full crops. Deep, slow, infrequent irrigation in basins is the ideal. (The basin should have an inner ring to keep the base of the trunk dry, avoiding fungus and rot attacks. Walnuts in lawns should have a foot-wide collar of coarse gravel or rock extending down to the first roots.)

To help bring nuts to full ripeness in the Southwest, experienced growers run a sprinkler for 4 to 6 hours just 2 weeks before harvest, soaking the ground evenly to the drip line.

Fertilizing. Young trees in good soil do not need fertilizers so long as the leaves stay a healthy green. Older trees may benefit from annual applications of 1 to 4 pounds of actual nitrogen each spring just as buds swell. The trees also may need fair amounts of potassium, so complete fertilizers are the general recommendation.

Pests and diseases. Black walnuts are susceptible to walnut anthracnose, or leaf blotch, a fungus that destroys the leaves. The symptoms are many dark-brown spots (which sometimes merge to form yellow-edged dead spots) and early defoliation. The crop is poor and the weakened tree subject to winter freeze injury. Bordeaux mixture as a dormant spray is a preventive; locally recommended fungicides will control the disease.

Walnut husk fly is the principal pest. The symptom is a blackened husk that clings to a disfigured nut. The numbers can be minimized if fallen nuts are kept cleaned up at all times. Serious infestations can be controlled by spraying malathion or sevin on a locally advised schedule.

Walnut husk fly traps can be bought readily in regions with walnut orchards, or from mail-order garden supply houses.

The walnut lace bug is a problem east of the Rockies. It sucks the juices from leaves, leaving them gray or yellow; they drop early, and the tree fails to ripen its crop. It, too, yields to malathion. The walnut caterpillar can be controlled mechanically by pruning infected shoots. Aphids, codling moth, curculio, mites, and scales all may be found in walnuts; see pages 108–111 for controls.

Subtropicals

GUAVA

Climate: Guava in USDA Zone 10 only; much easier to grow in Hawaii and Florida than California; needs ample summer heat. Lemon guava and strawberry guava (separate species from guava) in Zones 8–10; need less heat than guava; grow well in California and Arizona (except hottest regions), and in Florida.

Soil: Best in rich soils. Can take some drought after well established.

Standard tree size: Guava to 25 feet trained to open center. Lemon and strawberry guava 10 to 15 feet as shrubs; smaller in containers.

Favored varieties: As under "Climate."

Self-pollenizer: Yes.

Typical life span: At least 30 years.

Trees bear: At 1 to 2 years.

Typical yield at maturity: To 100 pounds per tree.

Harvest season: Autumn in California; June into October in Florida.

Fertilizer needs: Much the same as citrus, see pages 39–40.

Principal pests and diseases: Caribbean fruit fly, nematodes, red alga, scale, whitefly.

JAPANESE LOQUAT

Climate: USDA Zones 7–10; needs some summer humidity. Hardy to 20°F/–7°C; has survived to 12°F/ –11°C, but with considerable damage.

Soil: Tolerant of soil type, but needs good drainage.

Standard tree size: 15 to 30 feet; train to central leader.

Favored varieties: 'Advance', 'Champagne' (needs highest heat), 'Gold Nugget' (sweet, does well in moderately cool coastal climates), 'MacBeth' (largest fruit), 'Oliver', 'Thales' (ripens late), 'Wolfe'.

Self-pollenizer: Yes.

Typical life span: At least 40 years.

Trees bear: At 3 or 4 years.

Typical yield at maturity: 100 to 150 pounds per tree.

Harvest season: February into May in Florida; March into June in California.

Fertilizer needs: Takes complete fertilizer (8-4-8 or similar) three times a year in Florida, twice in California.

Principal pests and diseases: Anthracnose, Caribbean fruit fly, fireblight. Will sunburn in desert.

KIWI

Climate: USDA Zones 7–9. Well proven in most areas of California, Willamette Valley of Oregon, Puget Sound basin of Washington. Little tried elsewhere.

Soil: Needs good drainage. Best in loam. Does not tolerate salt. Must be kept well watered; benefits from mulching.

Standard vine size: Train as cordon on head-high trellis.

Favored varieties: 'Chico', 'Hayward'. Also 'Abbott', 'Bruno', 'Monty'.

Self-pollenizer: No; must have male and female plants.

Typical life span: Uncertain; at least 20 years.

Vines bear: At 2 years.

Typical yield at maturity: To 200 pounds per vine.

Harvest season: October and November.

Fertilizer needs: Minimal; easily burned by over-fertilizing.

Principal pests and diseases: Few, save for gophers.

MACADAMIA

Climate: USDA Zones 8–10. Best adapted in Hawaii, but does very well in California (especially along the southern coast) and Florida. Not much tested elsewhere, but not for desert.

Soil: Best in deep, rich loam. Resists drought, but grows slowly and bears lightly if dry.

Standard tree size: To 60 feet in Hawaii; trained to open center in California, 25 to 30 feet (and almost as wide); to 40 feet in Florida.

Favored varieties: Two species. Smooth-shelled (the Hawaiian nut)—'Beaumont', 'Keauhou', 'Ikaika'. Rough-shelled—'Cata', 'Stephenson'.

Self-pollenizer: Yes.

Typical life span: 75 to 100 years.

Trees bear: At 4 to 6 years.

Typical yield at maturity: 150 pounds per tree.

Harvest season: When nuts drop; smooth-shelled late autumn into May; rough-shelled autumn through February.

Fertilizer needs: Benefit from light feedings of nitrogen in California; in Florida, needs phosphorus, zinc, and iron.

Principal pests and diseases: Rodents, root rot, stinkbugs, thrips.

MANGO

Climate: Zone 10. Survives in southern California, but much better adapted in Florida.

Soil: Tolerates poor, shallow soils, but bears best in deeper ones. Needs steady moisture.

Standard tree size: To 50 feet in Florida. To 25 feet as open-center tree, but usually shrubby in southern California.

Favored varieties: 'Villasenor', 'Aloha' in the West; 'Carrie', 'Kent' in Florida.

Self-pollenizer: Yes.

Typical life span: At least 50 years.

Trees bear: At 2 years.

Typical yield at maturity: 3 to 5 bushels per tree.

(Continued on next page)

Harvest season: Autumn to winter in California; May into September in Florida.

Fertilizer needs: Fed much like citrus, see pages 39–40.

Principal pests and diseases: Anthracnose, mites, powdery mildew, scab, scale, thrips.

PAPAYA

Climate: USDA Zone 10, especially Florida, Hawaii, southern California coast. Must have warm soil in winter; cold, wet soil is as lethal as frost. Good bet for greenhouses outside of ideal climate range.

Soil: Rich, well drained. Trees need frequent watering.

Standard tree size: To 20 feet as straight-trunked tree.

Favored varieties: None named, but avoid ornamental species.

Self-pollenizer: Some bisexual plants available; otherwise, must have 3 to 5 male and female plants.

Typical life span: 3 to 6 years of good production; for steady supply of fruit, develop new plant(s) and destroy oldest one(s) each year.

Trees bear: At 1 to 2 years.

Typical yield at maturity: To 200 pounds per tree.

Harvest season: About 8 months after flowering in California, 3 to 4 months in Florida.

Fertilizer needs: Feed frequently (every other month) with nitrogen; dosages uncertain—establish by trial and error.

Principal pests and diseases: Root rots (keep quick-draining soil warm in winter), crown rot (keep mulch away from trunk), papaya fly. Also nematodes.

PASSION FRUIT

Climate: USDA Zone 10 regions having only infrequent frosts—essentially southern Florida.

Soil: Tolerant. Bears best with steady watering, but is drought-resistant.

Standard vine size: Semievergreen or evergreen vine 30 to 80 feet long. Will overgrow unless given stern annual pruning to keep it open.

Favored varieties: Several varieties of passion vine bear fruit, including some hardy to 0°F/ −18°C, but only passion fruit is notable for fruit.

Self-pollenizer: Yes.

Typical life span: 5 to 10 years.

Vines bear: In 1 or 2 years.

Typical yield at maturity: 15 pounds per plant.

Harvest season: Summer to late autumn.

Fertilizer needs: Complete fertilizer (6-6-6 or similar) each quarter.

Principal pests and diseases: Crown rot, caterpillar of the gulf fritillary butterfly, nematodes.

PISTACHIO

Climate: USDA Zones 7–10 where summers are hot and dry, especially California's central valley and southern California's inland areas.

Soil: Must drain well. Tree resists drought; irrigate deeply but infrequently.

Standard tree size: To 30 feet, trained to open center.

Favored varieties: 'Kerman' as female fruiting variety; 'Peters' as pollenizing male variety.

Self-pollenizer: No; see "Favored varieties."

Typical life span: At least 30 years.

Trees bear: At 5 to 8 years.

Typical yield at maturity: 1 to 2 bushels.

Harvest season: August and September.

Fertilizer needs: Spring feeding of complete fertilizer (10-10-10 or similar) is useful.

Principal pests and diseases: Oak root fungus, verticilium wilt.

Mail order sources for unusual varieties

For gardeners seeking unusual varieties of any fruit, the following mail-order sources may be of help. Some catalogs are free; for others there is a fee.

Bountiful Ridge Nurseries
Princess Anne, MD 21853
Free. Broad range of fruit.

Cumberland Valley Nurseries
P.O. Box 430
McMinnville, TN 37110
Free. Specialists in peaches, plums, nectarines.

Greenmantle Nursery
3010 Ettersburg Rd.
Garberville, CA 95440
Fee. Many fruits, but specialist in old-time apples.

New York State Fruit Testing Cooperative Association
Box 462
Geneva, NY 14456
Fee. Broad range of new and old-time varieties.

Owen's Vineyard and Nursery
Georgia Highway 85
Gay, GA 30218
Fee. Specialist in muscadine grapes, rabbiteye blueberries.

Pacific Tree Farms
4301 Lynwood Dr.
Chula Vista, CA 92010
Fee. Avocados and other subtropicals. Also low-chill temperate-zone fruits.

Southmeadow Fruit Gardens
Lakeside, MI 49116
Fee. Broad, deep range of old-time varieties.

Stark Brothers
Louisiana, MO 63353
Free. Wide range of dwarf varieties.

Dave Wilson Nursery
Box 90 A
Hughson, CA 95326
Fee. Broad range of fruits, berries, European grapes.

GARDENERS' PRIMER

United States & Canada

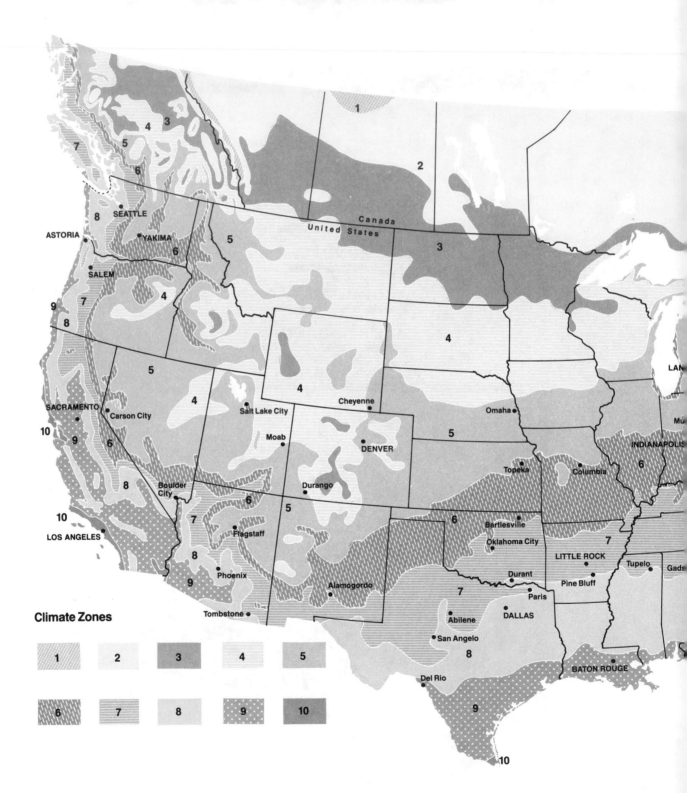

Climate Zones

1   2   3   4   5

6   7   8   9   10

The zones on this map show minimum expected winter temperatures. Selection of this measure over others as a guide to planting has a simple basis: minimum temperatures can be shown easily, and they are the prime factor in plant survival.

Other plant-growth factors of importance include first and last frost dates, seasonal precipitation, humidity, soil characteristics, and duration and intensity of sunlight during the growing season. These cannot be mapped readily, but statistics for 17 key cities show typical climate patterns within each hardiness zone to help define profitable growing regions for the major fruits and nuts, and thus the prospects for individual gardeners. Also, in the charts in each of the major fruits, the climate range of each variety is keyed to this map as a more detailed help.

Temperatures listed in weather summaries are in Fahrenheit. To convert a Fahrenheit temperature to Celsius, use this formula: $(F° - 32) \times 5/9 = C°$.

In the notes following each weather summary, the "Best bets," "Good," and "Difficult" entries are not descriptions of the quality of the fruit—only of the ease or difficulty of keeping the plant healthy and bearing in that region.

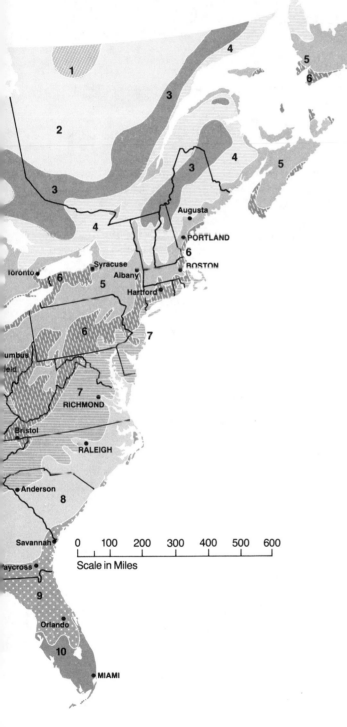

Zone 10

Physically the smallest of the USDA zones, this one is defined by predictable winter lows ranging no lower than 30°F/−1°C. At its northern boundaries in Texas and Florida, Zone 10 experiences about 400 winter chill hours, ranging to 200 or fewer farther south. In drier California the range is wider, from 600 to 200. Summer temperatures rise quickly inland from such shoreside stations as Los Angeles. In addition to the areas shown on the map, much of Hawaii qualifies.

MIAMI, FL

Temp.	Jan	Feb	Mar	Apr	May	Jun	Jul	Aug	Sep	Oct	Nov	Dec
Max.	76.6	76.6	79.5	82.7	85.0	88.0	89.1	89.9	88.3	84.8	79.9	76.6
Min.	58.7	59.0	63.0	67.3	70.7	73.9	75.5	75.8	75.0	71.0	64.5	60.0
Precip.	2.15	1.95	2.07	3.60	6.12	9.00	6.91	6.72	8.74	8.18	2.72	1.64

Best bets: citrus, mango, pecans. Good: avocados, (rabbiteye) blueberries, (Muscadine) grapes, strawberries. Difficult: apples, pears.

LOS ANGELES, CA

Temp.	Jan	Feb	Mar	Apr	May	Jun	Jul	Aug	Sep	Oct	Nov	Dec
Max.	63.5	64.1	64.3	65.9	68.4	70.3	74.8	75.8	75.7	72.9	69.6	66.5
Min.	45.4	47.0	48.6	51.7	55.3	58.6	62.1	63.2	61.6	57.5	51.3	47.3
Precip.	2.52	2.32	1.71	1.10	0.08	0.03	0.01	0.02	0.07	0.22	1.76	1.75

Best bets: avocados, citrus, pistachios. Good: almonds, (European) grapes, peaches, walnuts. Difficult: apples, cherries, pears.

Zone 9

Zone 9 is defined by lowest predictable winter temperatures ranging between 30 and 20°F (−1 and −7°C). East of the Rocky Mountains it has winter chill hours ranging between 400 on the boundary with Zone 10 and 800 on the boundary with Zone 8 (the 600 hour mark stays almost exactly halfway between the boundaries). Because Zone 9 extends all the way up the Pacific coast from the southern California desert into shoreside British Columbia, the winter chill hours in the West range far more widely. So does summer heat, from searing desert to the cool, humid coast of the Northwest.

BATON ROUGE, LA

Temp.	Jan	Feb	Mar	Apr	May	Jun	Jul	Aug	Sep	Oct	Nov	Dec
Max.	61.5	64.5	70.6	79.0	85.2	90.3	91.2	91.1	87.2	80.4	70.3	63.7
Min.	40.5	43.2	48.7	57.7	64.3	70.3	72.7	72.1	67.7	56.6	46.9	42.0
Precip.	4.40	4.76	5.14	5.10	4.39	3.77	6.51	4.67	3.79	2.65	3.84	5.03

Best bets: berries, pecans. Good: persimmons. Difficult: apples, cherries, pears.

SACRAMENTO, CA

Temp.	Jan	Feb	Mar	Apr	May	Jun	Jul	Aug	Sep	Oct	Nov	Dec
Max.	53.0	59.1	64.1	71.3	78.8	86.4	92.9	91.3	87.7	77.1	63.6	53.3
Min.	37.1	40.4	41.9	45.3	49.8	54.6	57.5	56.9	55.3	49.5	42.4	38.3
Precip.	3.73	2.68	2.17	1.54	0.51	0.10	1.01	0.05	0.19	0.99	2.13	3.12

Best bets: almonds, apricots, avocados, nectarines, persimmons, pomegranates. Good: apples, cherries, peaches, pears. Difficult: berries, citrus.

(Continued on next page)

ASTORIA, OR

Temp.	Jan	Feb	Mar	Apr	May	Jun	Jul	Aug	Sep	Oct	Nov	Dec
Max.	46.5	50.6	52.1	55.6	60.3	63.8	67.7	68.3	67.6	61.0	53.4	48.6
Min.	34.6	36.6	36.7	40.0	44.3	49.1	52.2	52.2	49.1	44.5	39.6	36.9
Precip.	9.73	7.82	6.62	4.61	2.72	2.45	0.96	1.46	2.83	6.80	9.78	10.57

Best bets: blackberries, (highbush) blueberries. Good: apples. Difficult: apricots, cherries, pears.

Zone 8

Zone 8 is defined by minimum predictable winter temperatures of 10 to 20°F (− 12 to − 7°C). East of the Rockies, nearly all of the zone is marked by moderately to distinctly humid summers ranging from very warm to hot. In the West, the summer patterns range from very hot and dry in the high deserts and California's great Central Valley (see Sacramento in Zone 9) to cool and rather humid in the coastal Pacific Northwest and British Columbia.

RALEIGH, NC

Temp.	Jan	Feb	Mar	Apr	May	Jun	Jul	Aug	Sep	Oct	Nov	Dec
Max.	51.0	53.2	61.0	72.2	79.4	85.6	87.7	86.8	81.5	72.4	62.1	51.9
Min.	30.0	31.1	37.4	46.7	55.4	63.1	67.2	66.2	59.7	48.0	37.8	30.5
Precip.	3.22	3.32	3.44	3.07	3.32	3.67	5.08	4.93	3.78	2.81	2.82	3.08

Best bets: apples, berries, peaches, pecans, plums. Good: cherries, pears, persimmons. Difficult: apricots.

DALLAS-FORT WORTH, TX

Temp.	Jan	Feb	Mar	Apr	May	Jun	Jul	Aug	Sep	Oct	Nov	Dec
Max.	55.7	59.8	66.6	76.3	82.8	90.8	95.5	96.1	88.5	79.2	67.5	58.7
Min.	33.9	37.6	43.3	54.1	62.1	70.3	74.0	73.7	66.8	56.0	44.1	37.0
Precip.	1.80	2.36	2.54	4.30	4.47	3.05	1.84	2.26	3.15	2.68	2.03	1.82

Best bets: berries, figs, peaches, pears, pecans. Good: (American) grapes, persimmons, plums. Difficult: apples, cherries, walnuts.

SEATTLE-TACOMA, WA

Temp.	Jan	Feb	Mar	Apr	May	Jun	Jul	Aug	Sep	Oct	Nov	Dec
Max.	43.4	48.5	51.5	57.0	64.1	69.0	75.1	73.8	68.7	59.4	50.4	45.4
Min.	33.0	36.0	36.6	40.3	45.6	50.6	53.8	53.7	50.4	44.9	38.8	35.5
Precip.	5.79	4.19	3.61	2.46	1.70	1.53	0.71	1.08	1.99	3.91	5.88	5.94

Best bets: apples, berries. Good: peaches, pears, plums. Difficult: apricots, nectarines, figs.

Zone 7

The defining predictable winter minimums are 0 to 10°F (− 18 to − 12°C). Summers east and west of the Rockies are much the same as those of Zone 8, with the same dividing line.

RICHMOND, VA

Temp.	Jan	Feb	Mar	Apr	May	Jun	Jul	Aug	Sep	Oct	Nov	Dec
Max.	47.4	49.9	58.2	70.3	78.4	85.4	88.2	86.6	80.9	71.2	60.6	49.1
Min.	27.6	28.8	35.5	45.2	54.5	62.9	67.5	65.9	59.0	47.4	37.3	28.8
Precip.	2.86	3.01	3.38	2.77	3.42	3.52	5.63	5.06	3.58	2.94	3.20	3.22

Best bets: apples, berries, peaches, pecans, walnuts. Good: cherries, nectarines, pears. Difficult: almonds, apricots.

LITTLE ROCK, AR

Temp.	Jan	Feb	Mar	Apr	May	Jun	Jul	Aug	Sep	Oct	Nov	Dec
Max.	50.1	53.8	61.8	73.5	81.4	89.3	92.6	92.6	85.8	76.0	62.4	52.1
Min.	28.9	31.9	38.7	49.9	58.1	66.8	70.1	68.6	60.8	48.7	38.1	31.1
Precip.	4.24	4.42	4.93	5.25	5.30	3.50	3.38	3.01	3.55	2.99	3.86	4.09

Best bets: apples, berries, peaches, walnuts. Good: cherries, pears, pecans, plums. Difficult: almonds, figs.

SALEM, OR

Temp.	Jan	Feb	Mar	Apr	May	Jun	Jul	Aug	Sep	Oct	Nov	Dec
Max.	45.3	51.4	54.9	61.0	68.1	74.0	82.4	81.3	76.5	64.0	53.0	47.1
Min.	32.2	34.4	35.4	38.5	43.3	48.4	50.7	50.9	47.3	42.3	37.4	34.7
Precip.	6.90	4.79	4.33	2.29	2.09	1.39	0.35	0.57	1.46	3.98	6.08	6.85

Best bets: apples, berries, cherries, filberts, pears, walnuts. Good: figs, grapes, peaches, plums. Difficult: almonds, apricots, persimmons.

Zone 6

Zone 6 is defined by predictable winter minimum temperatures of 0 to − 10°F (− 18 to − 23°C). Other aspects of the climate run from near-desert conditions in eastern Washington and Oregon and the Southwest to distinctly humid ones along the New England coast. The Great Lakes moderate the weather along their southern shores enough to produce Zone 6 conditions well to the north of much of Zone 5. The Atlantic Ocean provides even more dramatic examples of the same effect; parts of Newfoundland fall within the zone.

BOSTON, MA

Temp.	Jan	Feb	Mar	Apr	May	Jun	Jul	Aug	Sep	Oct	Nov	Dec
Max.	35.9	37.5	44.6	56.3	67.1	76.6	81.4	79.3	72.2	63.2	51.7	39.3
Min.	22.5	23.3	31.5	40.8	50.1	59.3	65.1	63.3	56.7	47.5	38.7	26.6
Precip.	3.69	3.54	4.01	3.49	3.47	3.19	2.74	3.46	3.16	3.02	4.51	4.24

Best bets: apples, berries, chestnuts, walnuts. Good: cherries, (American) grapes, peaches, pears, plums. Difficult: apricots, figs, hazelnuts.

INDIANAPOLIS, IN

Temp.	Jan	Feb	Mar	Apr	May	Jun	Jul	Aug	Sep	Oct	Nov	Dec
Max.	36.0	39.3	49.0	62.8	72.9	82.3	85.4	84.0	77.7	67.0	50.5	38.7
Min.	19.7	22.1	30.3	41.8	51.5	61.1	64.6	62.4	54.9	44.3	32.8	23.1
Precip.	2.86	2.36	3.75	3.87	4.08	4.16	3.67	2.80	2.87	2.51	3.10	2.71

Best bets: apples, berries, chestnuts, walnuts. Good: cherries, (American) grapes, peaches, pears, plums. Difficult: apricots, figs, hazelnuts.

YAKIMA, WA

Temp.	Jan	Feb	Mar	Apr	May	Jun	Jul	Aug	Sep	Oct	Nov	Dec
Max.	36.4	46.1	54.8	64.1	73.1	79.7	88.1	85.9	78.3	64.7	48.5	39.1
Min.	18.6	25.2	28.8	34.8	42.6	49.3	53.3	51.2	44.3	35.4	28.3	23.5
Precip.	1.33	0.78	0.58	0.51	0.55	0.73	0.16	0.25	0.31	0.58	1.07	1.15

Best bets: apples, cherries, (American) grapes. Good: apricots, hazelnuts, peaches, pears, plums, walnuts. Difficult: almonds, figs.

Zone 5

The definition is predictable winter minimum temperatures of − 10 to − 20°F (− 23 to − 29°C). Somewhere in Zone 5 is the boundary line for many deciduous fruit trees, either because they are not hardy at the temperature extreme, or because spring frosts kill fruit blossoms most years. In the West, Zone 5 is mostly mountainous or high desert. East of the Rockies it covers a substantial amount of lowlands from the Plains east into New England, including regions of notably heavy winter snows.

PORTLAND, ME

Temp.	Jan	Feb	Mar	Apr	May	Jun	Jul	Aug	Sep	Oct	Nov	Dec
Max.	31.2	33.3	40.8	52.8	63.6	73.2	79.1	77.6	69.9	60.2	47.5	34.9
Min.	11.7	12.5	22.8	32.5	41.7	51.1	56.9	55.2	47.4	38.0	29.7	16.4
Precip.	3.38	3.52	3.60	3.34	3.33	3.10	2.61	2.60	3.09	3.31	4.86	4.06

Best bets: apples, berries, cherries, plums. Good: pears. Difficult: figs, persimmons.

LANSING, MI

Temp.	Jan	Feb	Mar	Apr	May	Jun	Jul	Aug	Sep	Oct	Nov	Dec
Max.	29.9	32.0	41.7	57.0	68.1	78.4	82.6	81.1	73.0	62.1	46.0	33.9
Min.	15.3	16.0	24.1	35.9	45.5	55.8	59.2	57.8	50.4	41.0	30.8	20.2
Precip.	1.91	1.62	2.36	2.90	3.32	3.47	2.82	2.79	2.63	2.31	2.26	2.00

Best bets: apples, berries, cherries, plums. Good: pears, persimmons, walnuts. Difficult: figs.

DENVER, CO

Temp.	Jan	Feb	Mar	Apr	May	Jun	Jul	Aug	Sep	Oct	Nov	Dec
Max.	43.5	46.2	50.1	61.0	70.3	80.1	87.4	85.8	77.7	66.8	53.3	46.2
Min.	16.2	19.4	23.8	33.9	43.6	51.9	58.6	57.4	47.8	37.2	25.4	18.9
Precip.	0.61	0.67	1.21	1.93	2.64	1.93	1.78	1.29	1.13	1.13	0.76	0.43

Best bets: apples, berries, walnuts. Good: cherries, peaches, pears. Difficult: apricots, figs.

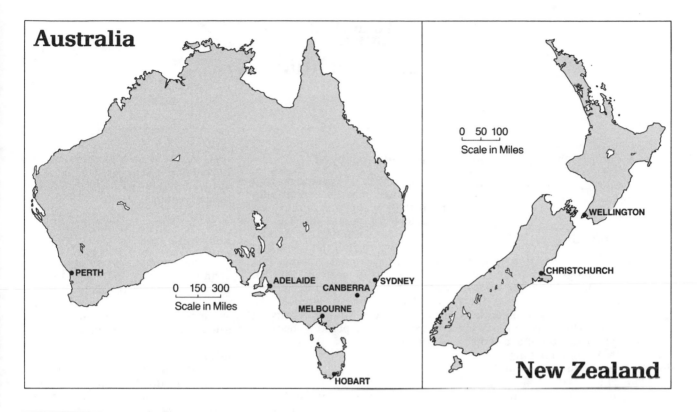

The climate of Australia

While there has been no official classification of climate zones in Australia equivalent to the USDA Zones of the United States, virtually all of Australia's great population centers fall neatly into the equivalents of Zones 9 and 10. The notable exceptions are Tasmania, where Hobart's climate is most nearly like warm USDA Zone 8, and Canberra, which approaches USDA Zone 7.

Summer climates in the Australian North are fairly similar to those in the American Gulf States. Suggestions for this region (from east Texas across Louisiana and Georgia to Florida) should be generally helpful, though some summer climate patterns are closer to North Carolina and Virginia. Summer climates of southern Australia come closer to the American Southwest. Southern Australia is not quite so dry, but enough so that any advice for the central or southern California coast is reasonably applicable. Tasmania most nearly resembles western Washington and Oregon.

Fahrenheit to Celsius aside, the only translation that needs to be made is in months. Where this book suggests March and April for spring fertilizing and planting, September and October are the counterparts. Where it suggests June through August as harvest months, the Australian equivalents are December through February.

ADELAIDE, South Australia

Temp.	Jan	Feb	Mar	Apr	May	Jun	Jul	Aug	Sep	Oct	Nov	Dec
Max.	85	85	80	73	66	60	59	61	66	72	77	82
Min.	61	62	59	55	51	47	45	46	48	52	55	59
Precip.	.8	.8	.9	1.7	2.7	2.8	2.6	2.4	2.0	1.7	1.2	1.0

CANBERRA, Federal District

Temp.	Jan	Feb	Mar	Apr	May	Jun	Jul	Aug	Sep	Oct	Nov	Dec
Max.	82	80	76	67	59	54	52	55	60	66	72	79
Min.	56	55	51	44	37	34	33	33	37	42	47	52
Precip.	2.4	2.4	2.1	1.9	1.9	1.5	1.5	1.8	2.0	2.9	2.5	2.2

HOBART, Tasmania

Temp.	Jan	Feb	Mar	Apr	May	Jun	Jul	Aug	Sep	Oct	Nov	Dec
Max.	71	71	68	63	58	53	53	55	59	62	65	68
Min.	53	53	51	48	44	41	40	41	43	45	48	51
Precip.	1.9	1.7	1.8	2.2	1.9	2.3	2.1	1.9	2.0	2.5	2.2	2.2

MELBOURNE, Victoria

Temp.	Jan	Feb	Mar	Apr	May	Jun	Jul	Aug	Sep	Oct	Nov	Dec
Max.	78	78	75	68	62	57	56	59	63	67	71	75
Min.	57	58	55	51	47	44	42	44	46	49	51	55
Precip.	1.9	2.0	2.1	2.8	2.2	2.0	1.9	2.0	2.7	2.7	2.3	2.3

PERTH, Western Australia

Temp.	Jan	Feb	Mar	Apr	May	Jun	Jul	Aug	Sep	Oct	Nov	Dec
Max.	85	86	82	76	69	65	63	64	67	70	76	81
Min.	64	64	62	57	53	50	48	48	50	53	57	61
Precip.	.31	.43	.8	1.8	4.9	7.3	6.9	5.4	3.2	2.2	.8	.5

SYDNEY, New South Wales

Temp.	Jan	Feb	Mar	Apr	May	Jun	Jul	Aug	Sep	Oct	Nov	Dec
Max.	78	78	76	72	67	62	60	63	67	71	74	77
Min.	65	65	63	58	52	48	46	48	51	56	50	63
Precip.	3.9	4.5	5.2	5.0	4.8	5.2	4.1	3.2	2.7	3.0	3.1	3.1

The climate of New Zealand

Except in its uplands, New Zealand's climates echo those of eastern Australia at the same latitudes. If anything, they are more tempered by the sea. Though not quite like any station in the United States, they equate to USDA Zones 9 and 10, being cooler than the Southeast but rainier and more humid than the Southwest. The summer weather patterns are not unlike those of Virginia.

CHRISTCHURCH

Temp.	Jan	Feb	Mar	Apr	May	Jun	Jul	Aug	Sep	Oct	Nov	Dec
Mean	62	61	58	53	48	43	42	44	49	53	56	60
Precip.	2.1	1.8	2.1	2.0	2.7	2.6	2.6	2.1	1.8	1.8	1.9	2.1

WELLINGTON

Temp.	Jan	Feb	Mar	Apr	May	Jun	Jul	Aug	Sep	Oct	Nov	Dec
Mean	62	62	60	57	52	49	47	48	51	54	56	60
Precip.	3.2	3.2	3.3	3.9	4.8	4.9	5.5	4.8	3.9	4.2	3.5	3.6

The basic techniques

There are at least three cultural options in buying a new tree at a nursery. Each has advantages and disadvantages.

Bare-root planting

Nearly all deciduous fruit trees may be bought as bare-root plants from late autumn (in mild-winter areas) through early spring. Price is the primary advantage; easy transportation is another. The drawbacks are a relatively short season of availability, and the risk of damaging or losing the tree during transplanting.

The key to successful transplanting lies in keeping the roots moist from purchase until permanent planting. The nursery will wrap the roots in some sort of protection for the trip home. Thereafter, the tree should be heeled in— placed with its roots in loose peat, planting mix, or soil—until its permanent site is ready.

Balled-and-burlapped

Both deciduous and evergreen fruit and nut trees may be bought with the rootball wrapped in burlap. One advantage is minimal shock to the roots at transplanting, and thus faster growth during the tree's first season in the ground. Another is a longer planting season. Finally, maturer trees may be bought this way. The two possible drawbacks are initial cost, and difficulty in transporting and planting because of weight.

Container trees

If destined to be planted in the ground, container trees can be viewed as a variation on balled-and-burlapped planting, and handled in much the same way. Often they are younger and smaller than balled trees. One possible drawback is that container trees can be slightly to severely rootbound. In the case of trees meant to be kept permanently in containers, this may be a modest virtue in that the root system will be properly shaped.

Planting a tree

Thinking on how to plant a tree has changed sharply in recent years. The old notion was to plant the tree with its crown at grade level, in a symmetrical, smooth-sided hole filled with a carefully mixed, ideal soil. But close study suggests two fallacies. First, the grade-level planting can lead to crown rot when the tree is flood-irrigated, so new thinking is to plant the tree with its crown above grade level. Second, in all but light soils a smooth-sided hole full of ideal soil becomes for all practical purposes an underground container for the roots. The new approach is to plant a tree in an irregularly cut hole filled with the same soil as that surrounding.

Bare root

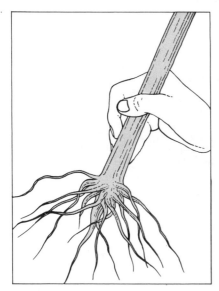

Container

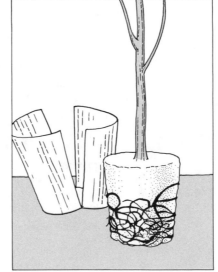

Balled-and-burlapped

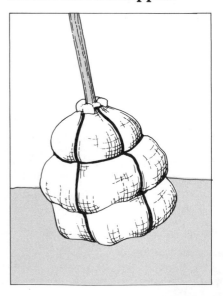

1. *Dig hole so that loosened soil forms a convex bottom that will support plant with crown 3 to 4 inches above grade level. Cut irregular walls to help steer roots into surrounding earth.*

2. *If tree is in a container, remove it. Wash away earth from outer inch or so of roots. Straighten kinked ones; trim off any that will not straighten. Balled-and-burlapped trees can be left wrapped if burlap is natural, not synthetic.*

3. *If tree is bare-root, spread roots evenly over mound of soft soil in bottom of planting hole. Press roots firmly into place before beginning to add soil on top of them. Dampened soil will hold roots best.*

4. *With tree in position, fill hole with earth dug from it. To eliminate air pockets around roots, tamp earth lightly and also water as you go. If stakes are needed, set them at this time.*

5. *To form a watering basin, build berms nearly but not quite as high as crown; do this within 6 inches of trunk and just outside drip line. (Break berm in spots each winter to avoid drowning roots.)*

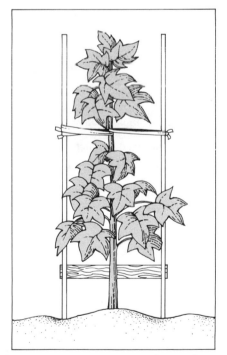

6. *In high traffic areas, use short stakes to protect trunk against injury from mowers or tricycles. In windy areas or with fast-growing or willowy trees, use long stakes for support.*

Terms & techniques

Effective training establishes a sturdy, healthy tree. Consistent pruning keeps it that way, and delivers optimum-size crops yearly . . . well, almost.

There are two principal styles for training trees are open-center and central-leader. Each is preferable for some trees, optional for others, and ill-advised for the rest. Programs for training trees to these shapes are on pages 92–95.

A few other terms and techniques are worth knowing. Paired with the drawing on this page, the terms are self-evident. The techniques run, with illustrations, at the bottom of the facing page.

Pinching out. *Removes tender tip buds to slow or stop outward growth and/or force branching.*

Leaf bud. *Small and triangular bud that lies flat against a branch.*

Heading back. *Lops off ends of upper or outer branches at a chosen point to keep a tree within a selected size. That is, it does belatedly what pinching out can do.*

Shoots. *Twigs or branches of current year's growth.*

Fruit bud. *Thick bud, swells first in spring; it can lie against a branch or be on a twiglet called a fruiting spur.*

Lateral. *Branch growing outward from trunk or scaffold; carries fruit, foliage, or both.*

Watersprout. *Tall shoot growing vertically from a scaffold or other branch. Will sap energy, is unproductive, so should be removed by pinching when it appears. If left, prune out in proper season.*

Fruiting spur. *Several deciduous fruits bear on stubby twigs; some spurs are long-lived, others last only 2 to 4 years. Trees must be pruned to maintain large numbers of them (or other fruit buds).*

Stub. *Length of branch beyond the last bud on it. Stubs die back to bud and can be an entry point for disease if left on a tree.*

Scaffold. *Main branch off trunk; function is to carry weight of fruiting and foliage branches.*

Hanger. *Downward-growing branch; undesirable. Should be pruned back to lateral or scaffold from which it grows.*

Sucker. *Branch growing from a root or from below bud union. Never desirable; may be rootstock rather than fruiting variety. Remove at earliest moment.*

Crotch. *Joint between a lateral and a scaffold, or a scaffold and trunk. Must be wide to be strong.*

Tools of the trade

Clipper. *For branches to ½-inch diameter. Two types, anvil (cutting blade meets flat surface) and scissor (overlapping blades). Choice between them is personal.*

Lopping shears. *For branches to 1¼-inch diameter.*

Curved narrow pruning saw. *For branches to 2-inch diameter, especially in tight spots.*

Pruning hook. *For high branches, alternative to lopping shears.*

Extension saw. *For high branches, alternative to curved narrow pruning saw.*

Pruning knife. *To smooth edges of pruning cuts, promoting quick healing.*

Pruning compound. *To seal cuts more than ½ inch in diameter. Some experts advise against its use; others recommend it.*

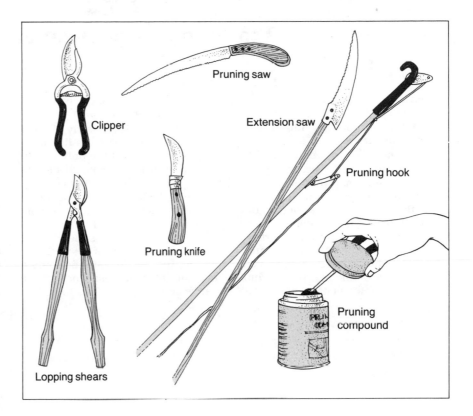

Tricks of the trade

Directing growth. *Prune to an outward-facing bud to help an upright branch spread; prune to an inward or upward-facing bud to help a spreading branch turn up.*

Removing heavy limb. *To avoid tearing bark and splitting wood, 1) undercut limb a short distance from trunk, 2) cut through limb from above just outside undercut, and 3) trim off stub flush with bark collar on trunk.*

Correct cut above bud. *As shown, cut should angle at about 45°; lowest point (on opposite side of branch from bud) should be even with top of bud. All other cuts shown are incorrect.*

Correct cut of an entire shoot. *Hold shears so cutting edge of blade is flush against trunk or scaffold at top of branch to be cut. Lower edge of cut should not be flush. Saw cuts should follow same pattern.*

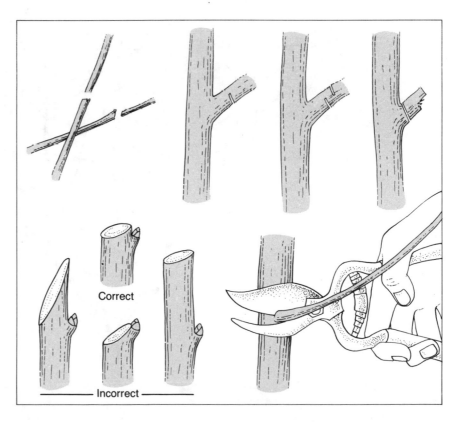

Training an open-center tree

Open-center training has several advantages.

- It helps get light into the center of dense trees.
- It helps control height.
- It divides the risk of disease among several main limbs.

The primary disadvantage is that the tree is not as strong as one trained to a central leader.

Open-center training is particularly recommended for apples, apricots, peaches, pears, and plums. (Specific recommendations accompany the sketches that show tree sizes and shapes in each section on an individual fruit or nut.)

Step 1, cutting a newly planted sapling back to a stub, is the hardest one to take, but the only way to end up with a well-shaped mature tree able to bear consistent crops.

In addition to aiming for such a tree, it is not a bad idea to work toward a tree that will not need severe pruning later in its life. The old goal of making dozens of small cuts and no big ones means not only a healthier tree, but less work for the gardener.

Because the trees that are best served by open-center training tend to be the ones that grow most upright, it is particularly important to ensure that the scaffold branches spread widely. Otherwise the tree will have weak crotches, and the center may be too crowded to ripen fruit on interior branches.

Using a wooden clothespin to direct soft new shoots is easy, and a proven success. Stiffer, longer spreaders cut from wood will help later, but cannot do a good job if the crotch is already narrow.

1. At planting, cut whip back to a healthy bud no higher than 24 inches off the ground for a dwarf, 36 inches for a standard tree. Be sure there are three to six healthy buds distributed around trunk, for scaffolds.

2. During first growing season, use clothespins or other spreaders to make sure that selected scaffold branches spread widely. Pinch any competitor buds from trunk to direct maximum energy to scaffolds.

3. During first dormant season, prune scaffolds back to strong, outward-facing lateral buds. Prune best laterals back to strong buds. Thin out hangers, crossing branches, weak or damaged branches.

4. During second growing season, pinch tip growth to force branching where desired.

5. During second dormant season, prune scaffolds back again, but not as far as in previous dormant season.

6. In subsequent seasons, continue pruning so no scaffold or lateral exceeds 30 inches without branching.

Training a central-leader tree

Central-leader training also offers advantages.

• It promotes the strongest possible framework.

• It lets a tree attain maximum height.

The primary disadvantages are the possibility of excessive height, and the risk of losing the heart of the tree to disease—risks greater than with open-center training.

Central-leader training is universally recommended for chestnuts, pecans, persimmons and wal-nuts. In cold regions where trees grow slowly, it is sometimes recommended for apples, cherries, and pears. This training also is advised for many dwarf apples regardless of climate. (Specific recommendations accompany the sketches that show tree sizes and shapes in each section on an individual fruit or nut.)

One aspect of central-leader training is the same as for open-center: step 1, cutting a newly planted sapling back to a stub, is still the hardest one to take, and still the only way to end up with a well-shaped, steady bearer that is relatively easy to prune.

Another factor is also the same, but for a different reason: scaffold branches must be spread, but it is mainly the lowest tier. Without this, they become shaded and unproductive. More important, they interfere with higher tiers, as the sketches show. Using a clothespin to direct soft new shoots is the first step. Later use of longer spreaders is more important than with open-center trees, because the limbs must be forced outward farther.

1. At planting, cut whip back to a healthy bud no higher than 24 inches off the ground for a dwarf, 36 inches for a standard fruit tree, head height for one of the taller nut trees. Be sure three healthy buds are distributed around trunk, for scaffolds.

2. During first growing season, use clothespins or other spreaders to ensure that selected scaffold branches spread widely. Allow other branches to grow through season without training.

3. During first dormant season, leave scaffolds intact. Prune out all competitors. Head central leader back to a promising set of buds about 3 feet above first tier of scaffold.

4. During second growing season, use longer spreaders set farther out along scaffolds.

5. During second dormant season, establish second set of scaffolds, pruning out competition to both sets.

6. Subsequent seasons, continue pruning so no scaffold or lateral exceeds 30 inches without branching.

Reclaiming an untended tree

A tree that has not been pruned for some years, or has been pruned badly, can be reclaimed. A much overgrown tree is best restored to good shape over a span of 2 or 3 years to minimize shock, but you should have a complete plan before beginning to cut. The worst-case situation:

1. *Select and remove two or three weak or crowding competitors to most fruitful scaffolds. Trim them first, then take them out in sections to minimize damage to rest of tree.*

2. *Thin the tree, beginning with broken and crossing smaller branches, continuing with poorly placed ones. Work from top down to see how well center is opening. This should conclude first season's work.*

3. *In second season, if tree has grown too large, head it back to strong laterals. Include branches due to come out and those meant to stay. Again, thin the shoots, saving newest ones where possible.*

4. *In third season, continue or complete removal of unproductive scaffolds, still trimming them, then cutting them into lengths. Prune rest of tree normally, as described on preceding pages.*

Replacing a leader or scaffold branch

As trees mature, the original major branches may bend down from carrying the weight of the fruit each year, and eventually become weak and unproductive. Such branches can be replaced in stages. This is the one occasion when encouraging a watersprout serves a useful purpose.

1. *Select an upright shoot (**D**) near trunk as eventual new leader. Encourage growth of two laterals (**C**, **B**) beyond selected shoot.*

2. *Cut off original leader (**A**) as (**C**) and (**B**) gain strength.*

3. *Cut off (**B**).*

4. *Cut off (**C**) as selected new leader matures.*

Training trees on wires

Espaliers in all their variety are the most fruitful means of saving space in a garden. Apples, pears, apricots, cherries, and plums, in about that order, are the favorite fruit trees for espaliering. Grapes and other vines, as well as citrus, take to the same training.

Apples, cherries, citrus, and grapes take readily to the formal espalier, or cordon. Their limbs conform readily to horizontal wires.

Pears and plums lend themselves more readily to the informal espalier, because of their strong

Formal espalier (cordon)

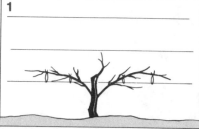

(1) *At planting, select two branches for lowest wire; trim all others off, and head leader back to near height of wire. Begin to bring selected branches down to wire.* (2) *During first growing season, con-*

Informal espalier

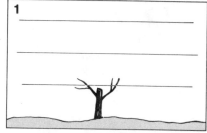

(1) *Cut vertical branch back to a point just below first wire. Choose two lateral branches, trimming off the rest.* (2) *During first growing season, avoid a vertical*

Hedgerow

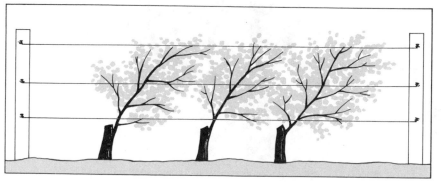

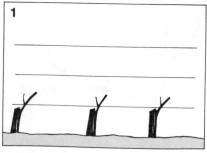

(1) *Bend whip in direction of greatest space. Head it back to help force laterals*

tendency to grow upright. Apricots are marginally better as informal espaliers.

The hedgerow is of use when a number of trees are to be planted tightly in a row. All of these fruits accept the shape readily.

In cool climates, plants can be set against a south wall for reflected heat. In hot climates, an east wall spares them excessive heat. In any case, the wires should be at least 4—better 12—inches from the wall for air circulation and ease of maintenance.

Use galvanized pipe or 4 by 4 wood posts, or anchor the wires to a wall, if one is available. Set supports no more than 15 to 20 feet apart. Generally, it is easier to keep wires at that length, too. Trying to obtain good tension over longer distances is difficult without special tools.

Use 14-gauge wire stretched tightly by means of turnbuckles.

Set the first wire about 14 inches off the ground; space higher wires 12 inches apart.

Most espaliers designed as hedges run 6 to 8 feet tall; so do those set against side walls. However, where landscaping dictates a taller espalier, there is nothing to stand in the way, save the natural limits of the trees being used. Using semidwarf varieties, our editors found excellent examples that reach up 15 feet and more.

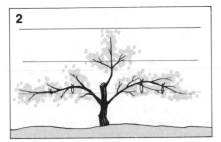

tinue slowly bending branches to wire; keep newly sprouted leader erect. (3) During first dormant season, head vertical branch back near second wire; select two branches for second wire and

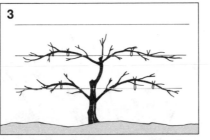

trim off all competitors; prune laterals on first-wire branches to two buds. Do not cut off any fruiting spurs. During second growing season, keep vertical

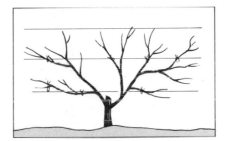

branch upright; bend second tier of branches slowly onto second wire. In succeeding seasons, repeat until tree is at top wire.

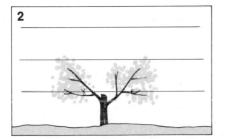

branch; encourage frequent forks in laterals. (3) During first dormant season, select two branches for second tier

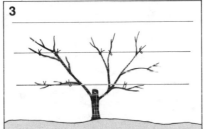

of laterals, trimming off all competitors. If first tier branches are 12 to 14 inches away from second tier, encourage them

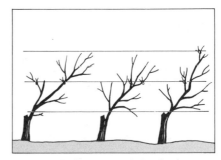

to fork. Retain any spurs; trim laterals to two buds. Repeat in succeeding seasons.

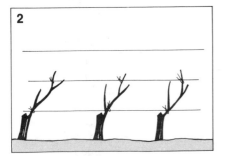

to develop. As laterals, save branches 12 to 14 inches apart on upper side of whip.

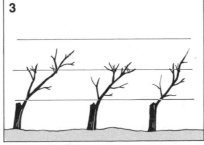

(2) Tie developing laterals to wires so they are roughly parallel to each other. Trim off any competitors to selected

laterals. (3) Head laterals back when they reach within 6 inches of adjoining main trunk.

Propagating techniques

Nurseries use several techniques regularly to establish fruiting varieties on rootstocks. Home gardeners may find budding, grafting, or layer-ing a practical way to add a pollen-izing branch to a single tree, or to change an old tree over to a new fruiting variety. Because both bud-ding and grafting take some skill, first efforts may go unrewarded, but most trees will forgive a few mis-takes if the scale is modest.

Grafting

Grafting joins stock and scion of sub-stantially differing girth, so is commonly used with stock older than 3 years. Most often the purpose is to change the fruit-ing variety of a tree from one to another (called "topworking"). Sometimes grafts are used to add a second fruiting variety to the first for the reasons noted under "Budding."

Budding

Budding joins stock and scion of ap-proximately equal girth, so this method is used with stock 1 to 3 years old. It can take either of two roles: to add a fruiting variety to a rootstock; or to add a second fruiting variety to the first—as a space saver or a pollenizer, or to prolong the fruiting season.

Buds can be taken directly, or they can come from cuttings that have been taken in autumn, wrapped in wet paper, sealed in plastic film, and stored until spring in a refrigerator.

The tools of the trade are simple: a sharp knife, and ½-inch-wide rubber or plastic strips that are 4 to 6 inches long.

Scion

Grafting

Stock

Bud

Budding

Scions ideally are hardened first-year or second-year wood ⅜ to ¾ inch in diameter with three or four mature buds (no fruiting buds, no terminal bud). They are stripped of leaves before use. They can be taken directly from a tree for use, or can be taken in autumn, wrapped in wet paper, sealed in plastic film, and stored in a refrigerator until spring.

Depending on method, tools may in-clude pruning saw, pruning shears, sharp knife, grafting tool (or hatchet and small wedge) or fine-toothed saw, as well as tape and wound dressing.

Tip layering

Simple layering

Layering

Layering will produce a new plant of the same variety as layered. In an era when most trees are on rootstocks different from the fruiting variety, layering is un-likely to produce a tree identical to the existing one. Useful exceptions are figs, hazelnuts, and olives, produced by sim-ple layering. Tip layering is used most to propagate trailing blackberries and black raspberries.

T-budding

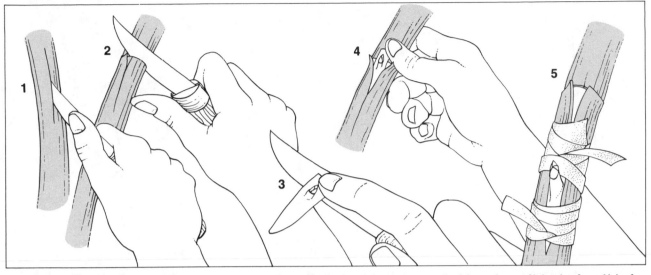

The commonest budding technique for both deciduous and evergreen species is one of the simplest ones. Buds can be cut fresh from a selected tree, summer through autumn. In spring, they can be taken from cuttings refrigerated since the previous autumn. Select a location on the stock free of any growth for a space of 2 to 3 inches; bark in the area should be as smooth as possible.

(1) Make vertical cut 1 inch long through bark to wood. (2) With knife blade tipped slightly downward, make horizontal cut one-third the diameter of stock at top of vertical cut. If both cuts are to a proper depth, top flaps will open slightly from pressure of knife.

Select a healthy bud. Cut through leaf stalk (petiole) about ¼ inch from shoot to provide a handle for bud. Cut bud from shoot, slicing in about ½ inch below bud and extending a curving cut to ½ inch above it. As cut is finished, bud should be pressed lightly against knife by a thumb. (3) Carry bud on knife blade to stock. (4) Insert bud, bottom edge first, into T-cut. Push it down until it is firmly seated inside flaps of T (this matches cambium layers). (5) Wrap bud and T-cut with rubber or plastic strips.

Patch budding

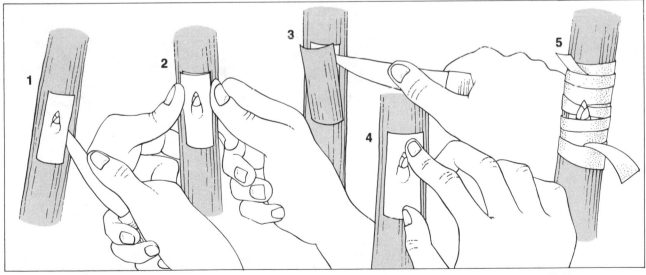

For thick-barked trees (especially walnut and pecan), the patch bud often outperforms either a T or chip bud. Budwood for these species usually is ½ to 1 inch in diameter, about twice as thick as typical budwood for T-budding.

(1) Cut a square or rectangular patch (including a bud) of material to be propagated. (2) Force it free by squeezing from opposite sides with thumbs; this brings with bud the wood necessary for its future growth. (3) From tree onto which bud will be placed, cut a patch of bark precisely the same size as bud patch. (4) Push bud tight against wood. (5) Secure bud with rubber strips.

Chip budding

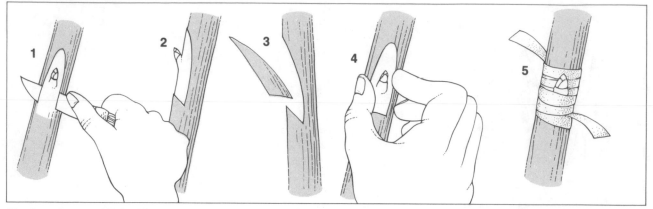

Used mostly to establish a Vitis vinifera fruiting variety on native American grape rootstock, chip budding can be used on all thin-barked deciduous fruit. It is difficult but crucial to get perfect match of cambium layers.

(1) Cut bud from scion with 45° cut starting ½ inch above bud and extending ½ inch below it. **(2)** Make second cut straight down to meet first cut. **(3)** In case of a vine where bud is to become the sole fruiting variety: On strongest shoot of rootstock, try to make cut identical to that used to remove bud from cane, except slightly deeper, so bud can rest firmly in it. This cut should be as near ground as possible to minimize future suckers.

(4) Seat bud and **(5)** wrap tightly with strip of rubber. Trim all rootstock shoots back to two or three buds each (these will be insurance if first bud fails to take). Bury bud at least 4 inches deep in loosely mounded dirt. In following spring, brush mounded earth away. If new bud has taken, cut away all other shoots and train desired shoot on a stake. If garden is subject to invasion by rabbits, place an open-ended milk carton over new shoot, and stake to protect it.

In the case of a tree where the bud is to add the fruiting variety to a rootstock: Locate an advantageous spot for the new bud, as in "T-budding." Make both cuts as for vines, and secure the bud in place with rubber strips. Do not cut away material above the bud until it has taken and is growing well.

Cleft grafting

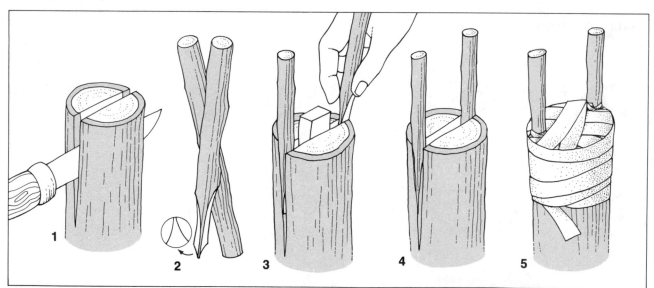

Simplest of the grafting techniques, this is used especially for apples, pears, and persimmons older than 3 years. It must be done in spring, before growth begins. (After growth begins, bark grafting is more reliable.) Cut off limb at desired point (minimum diameter 1 inch, better 2 to 3).

(1) Split stock as shown, or with grafting tool; do not split knots. Spread split with grafting tool, screwdriver, or similar. **(2)** Cut ⅜ to ¾-inch-diameter scion to wedge shape, one side more abruptly than other. **(3)** Seat scions in split, narrow edge in; cambium layers must match. **(4)** Remove wedge, **(5)** wrap stock with tape, and paint with wound dressing. Eight weeks later, cut tape; leave it to fall away by itself.

Bark grafting

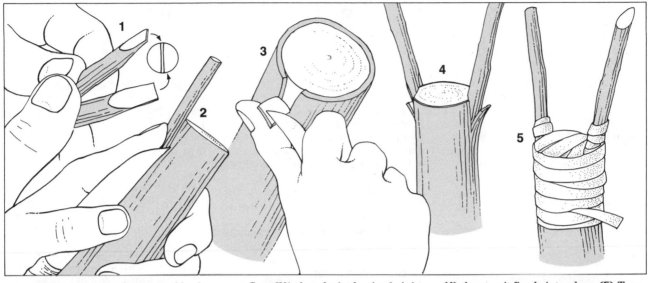

After spring growth has begun, and bark will peel freely from wood beneath, this technique works well with the same roster of trees (apples, persimmons, pears). It is only slightly more difficult than cleft grafting. Initially weak unions (the drawback) may need special attention.

Cut off limb at desired point (minimum diameter 1 inch). (1) Make unequal slanting cuts on scions gathered just as they are to be used. (2) Holding scion in position against stock, make parallel cuts in bark. (3) Peel bark back just enough for scion to be seated,

(4) then tap it firmly into place. (5) Tape stock and paint with wound dressing. Eight weeks later cut tape; leave it to fall away on its own. If scion grows rapidly, tack a splint on stock and tie scion to it.

Saw-kerf grafting

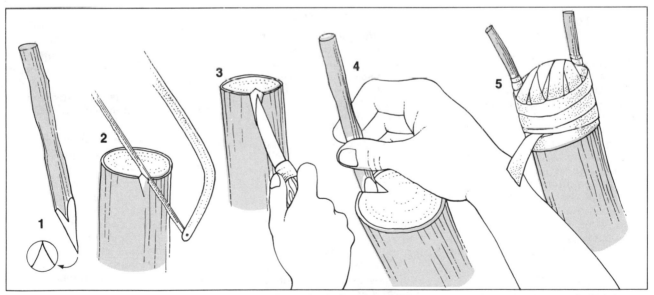

Like cleft grafting, this must be done before spring growth begins. It requires the greatest skill of any grafting technique to get a cambium match, but is preferable for knotty woods that do not split well (plums, peaches, nectarines).

Cut limb of stock at desired point (minimum diameter 1 inch). (1) Cut end of scion to wedge shape, with lowest bud on outside. (2) Make angled cut with fine-toothed saw, matching cut to size of scion. With scion in position, mark stock; (3) with saw or knife, cut notch to

fit. (4) Seat scion, leaning it slightly outward to ensure cambium match. When cambium match is certain, drive scion firmly into place. (5) Cover all cuts, including top of scion, with wound dressing.

Soils

To care for a tree, a gardener needs to unlock the mysteries of fertilizing and watering. The key to that is knowing three related sets of facts about the soil a plant is to grow in:

- Its type, which governs its capacity to retain water and fertilizers.
- Its pH—that is, its acidity or alkalinity.
- Its fertility.

Soil types

Science has devised seemingly endless classifications for soil types. Fortunately, it takes just three general descriptive terms—clay, sand, and loam—to cover the multitude of soils. Particle size and the way particles fit together are the determining factors.

Clay particles are tiny and flattened; they pack together tightly, in the manner of a pile of playing cards. In contrast, sand particles are large and roughly rounded; they gather rather loosely, in the fashion of a boxful of tennis balls. Both clay and sand are essentially mineral. Loam has a distinct content of organic matter mixed with varying proportions of clay and sand.

Because a clay soil has so many particles per volume, there is scant space for air and water between particles. However, once water penetrates, its moisture-holding capacity is far greater than sand's. Clay remains wet longer, and holds nutrients in solution longer for use by plants. The drawback of clay lies in this slowness to accept and to release water. During wet periods it can remain saturated too long for root health, while a dry clay may take considerable time in accepting water throughout the root zone of a wilted plant.

In sand, water penetrates easily and quickly, guaranteeing adequate supplies of air. The drawbacks are the reverse of clay's. Both water and nutrients can pass through the root zone too swiftly for the plant's maximum benefit.

Loam, the gardener's "ideal soil," contains clay, sand, and in-between-size particles, *plus* organic matter. It accepts water more quickly than clay, dries more slowly than sand, and contains enough air for good root growth. It also may have nutrient value.

It is impossible to overstress the potential value of organic matter to a productive, healthy soil. Simply stated, organic matter is formerly living material (usually plant remains or animal manures) in a state of continuing decay. Its coarser texture loosens clay soils, allowing easier penetration of water and air. In sand, it helps clog drain channels and also acts as a sponge.

Texture alone tells all a gardener needs to know to plan a successful watering program. Chemical analysis may be needed to work out the other qualities of a particular patch of ground, and thus a program of fertilizing.

pH (potential hydrogen)

One of the most important properties soil analysis will reveal is acidity or alkalinity, measured as pH. The scale ranges from 0 (acid) to 14 (alkaline), with pH 7 being neutral. Commonly, the soils of rainy regions are acid, and those of dry areas are alkaline. Most widely grown fruits do best in slightly acid soils, from pH 4 to 6 or 6.5. Some desert plants thrive in somewhat alkaline soils, but will tolerate slight acidity.

A secondary function of pH is its effect on mineral nutrients. Alkaline soils, for example, bind iron, leading to chlorosis in some plants.

As often as not, a short talk with a county farm advisor or a local nursery staffer will provide enough information about pH. Simple soil-test kits for measuring pH are available at nurseries and garden centers, and by mail order. For true problem sites, more elaborate—and expensive—tests to determine mineral or other deficiencies are performed by professionals. Check with the county extension office, or look in the Yellow Pages under "Soil Laboratories."

Adjusting pH

The actual correction of an unbalanced soil is only a matter of digging an active agent into the planting plot. A number of limestones are available to raise pH (or to reduce acidity). Sulfur also may be used for this purpose. Several commonly available fertilizers lower pH (or increase acidity).

To lower pH/raise acidity in alkaline soils (excess of calcium, sodium):

- Add ordinary powdered sulfur in amounts recommended by a county farm advisor; he or she will need to know the soil type and its pH reading to make the recommendation. This means test results must be in hand before the advisor is consulted.
- Use an acidifying fertilizer, preferably ammonium sulfate, but any one containing ammonium.
- Mulch with acidic material, especially pine needles, leaf mold, or acidic peat moss.

Some plants may also require periodic addition of chelates.

To raise pH/lower acidity in acid soils (deficiency of calcium, magnesium, sodium, potassium):

- Add finely ground dolomitic limestone in amounts recommended by a county farm advisor; he or she will need to know the soil type and its pH. Dolomitic limestone contains magnesium; common limestone does not. The process may have to be repeated every third or fourth year.
- Use fertilizers other than those containing ammonium.
- Mulch with nonacidic material such as poultry litter or firbark.

Up or down, the first suggestion can produce a large change; the last only a small shift.

Fertilizing

The 16 nutrients essential for plant growth come from three sources: air, water, and soil. Plants obtain oxygen and carbon from the air, hydrogen and oxygen from water. Soil functions as the reservoir for the other 13 nutrients, which may be divided into three groups—major, secondary, and trace—based on the amounts required.

Major nutrients

The big three are nitrogen, phosphorus, and potassium. These are the elements common to all complete fertilizers carrying such number identities as 10-10-10, 23-15-18, and a host of others.

Nitrogen is the growth nutrient, and supplying it is the primary reason for fertilizing. With too little, a plant makes scant new growth, and may be paler green than normal. Too much produces exuberant, succulent growth at the expense of flowering and fruiting; much too much may burn the roots. Though nitrogen is available naturally from rainfall, decaying organic matter, and nitrogen nodules on the roots of certain plants, it almost surely will be in short supply.

Nitrogen comes in several chemical states of differing utility. *Nitrate nitrogen* is immediately usable by plants. Both potassium nitrate and calcium nitrate are nitrate nitrogens. *Ammonium nitrogen* is changed in the soil into nitrate nitrogen over a period of 2 weeks to 3 months, sometimes longer. Ammonium phosphate and ammonium sulfate are ammonium nitrogens. *Organic nitrogen* must be changed into ammonium nitrogen on the way to becoming nitrate nitrogen. The first step in that process takes several days to several years. Urea is one organic nitrogen ("organic" in this definition refers to chemical primitiveness, not to an "organic" source).

Phosphorus is used by plants to form nucleic acids to assist in producing early growth, roots, and seeds. Starved of phosphorus, a plant will be stunted, leaf tips will brown, some leaves will turn purplish, and seeds won't develop properly.

Potassium helps move sugars and starches throughout the plant and is essential to the plant's ability to grow roots, resist diseases, and produce fruit. Without potassium, leaf edges will brown, plants will grow slowly, and fruit will stay small.

In manufactured fertilizers, phosphorus will appear on the label as "phosphoric acid," and potassium as "potash." Even if water soluble, these nutrients bond chemically with soil particles in the top 2 inches of soil. To reach the root zone of a plant, the fertilizer must be dug into trenches, or poured into holes bored down into the root zone, or introduced in the form of fertilizer spikes.

Secondary nutrients

Calcium, magnesium, and *sulfur* are the secondary nutrients, usually present in adequate supply in most soils but potentially lacking, and trouble when they are.

Trace nutrients

The remaining seven—*iron, zinc, manganese, boron, molybdenum, copper,* and *chlorine*—are trace elements, usually present in minute but adequate amounts, yet able to cause real damage when soil contains too little—or too much—of one or another of them.

Lack of available iron leads to chlorosis, symptomized by yellowed leaves with dark green veins. The problem occurs most often in alkaline soils. Too little zinc is betrayed by clusters of under-size leaves at the tips of branches that otherwise lack foliage along their lengths. Too much boron results in burned or dried-looking leaves; plants in boron-rich soil often die.

When and how much?

The theory and practice of fertilizing is as splendidly complicated as the rules of golf, but less certain.

The minimalist school says, in effect, if it ain't broke, don't fix it, and does not fertilize until symptoms of deficiency appear.

Commercial growers stand at the other pole, fertilizing yearly to keep plants healthy, growing, and bearing maximum crops.

Picking a ground—even a middle ground—and holding to it is not easy. Regional climates make a great difference. Soils add complications. So do the tree in question and plants near it. Two general points make a beginning point for designing a program:

• Nitrogen will be needed in greater volume and more often than other nutrients. Under the circumstances, it may be economical to use all-nitrogen fertilizers two or three years out of four, a complete fertilizer only at longer intervals. (There may be some regional exceptions. In the Pacific Northwest, nitrogen appears to be in greater supply than in other regions, while phosphorus lacks to an unusual degree.)

• In cold-winter climates, fertilizer containing nitrogen should be applied only in spring, at the end of frost season, because soft new tissue resulting from a later feeding is likely to be damaged by autumn frosts. The same fertilizer may be applied in spring and again in summer in milder-winter regions. In frost-free Florida, where rains leach soils quickly, it makes sense to fertilize lightly every second or third month, the year around.

In the sections on individual fruits, we give other programs devised for other parts of the country. They differ from these programs and each other, sometimes wildly.

There is nothing for it but to pick a path that makes local sense, and to adjust if need be.

Overall, it is better to underdo fertilizing than overdo.

Fertilizers & what's in them

Fertilizers have a language all their own.

"Organic fertilizer" qualifies for its name by being the remains or by-product of a once-living organism (for example, bone or blood meal, animal manure, fish emulsion) or by being a naturally occurring material (such as ground phosphate rock).

"Inorganic" or "chemical" fertilizers are manmade products that combine raw materials through chemical reactions. Virtually all complete fertilizers fall in this category.

Complete fertilizers

"Complete" or "balanced" fertilizers contain all three major nutrients—nitrogen (N), phosphorus (P), and potassium (K). The proportions vary dramatically from one fertilizer to another. Some examples: 23-15-18, 7-40-6, 3-8-7, 10-10-10. There are scores more. By law, the analysis must be accurate, and the numbers must appear on the fertilizer package, indicating the nutrients in an established order: nitrogen, phosphorus, potassium. If nitrogen is present in more than one form (usually a fast-release and a slow-release), the required *guaranteed analysis* listing on the package will show the percentage of each kind.

Complete fertilizers come as granules, pellets, pegs or stakes, and liquids (or as granules or powders that must be dissolved in water before application). When only nitrogen is needed, complete fertilizers can be expensive, compared to nitrogen-only fertilizers.

"Specialty fertilizers" are nothing more nor less than complete fertilizers balanced to a presumed optimum for a particular plant or group of plants. "Citrus food" is an example. Others are "rose food" and "azalea food." You needn't restrict the fertilizers to the plants on the label; it is the nutrient proportions that are important.

Simple fertilizers

"Simple" fertilizers are those that contain just one of the three major nutrients. Most important of these are the nitrogen-only fertilizers.

Among the simple nitrogen fertilizers, you can find fast, medium, and slow-acting kinds, depending on whether the nitrogen is nitrate, ammonium, or organic. Here are some examples.

Ammonium nitrate (33-0-0) is half nitrate nitrogen and half ammonium nitrogen, so it is immediately available but also releases nitrogen over time. It is granular: measure very accurately to avoid burning roots; then spread it and water it in. Because it is highly flammable under certain conditions, it is less commonly available for home gardens than for commercial farming. More often it is a component in complete fertilizers. Calcium nitrate (15-0-0) and sodium nitrate (16-0-0) are totally nitrate (fast-acting) nitrogen. Potassium nitrate (13-0-44) brings a rich potassium source in addition to nitrogen (taking it beyond the realm of a simple fertilizer).

Ammonium sulfate (21-0-0) is the most widely available source of ammonium nitrogen, a quick but not instant source. This, too, is granular: to avoid burning roots, measure carefully and spread evenly, and water it in. This is among the most cost-effective fertilizers.

Organic and synthetic organic nitrogen are the slowest to act.

Of the strictly organic nitrogen sources, blood meal is virtually nitrogen-only at around 10 percent. It is granular and must be scattered and scratched into the soil, and watered in.

Fish emulsion (5-1-1) is used mainly for its nitrogen, though it qualifies (barely) as "complete." It is a liquid concentrate; you dilute it in water, then apply the solution to the soil.

Animal manures vary in their amounts of nitrogen, but even the strongest (poultry) is too low to be counted on to supply significant nitrogen amounts.

Urea (45-0-0) is synthetic organic nitrogen, packaged as granules or pellets. Other formulations are ureaform (38-0-0), sulfur-coated urea (which also increases soil acidity), and IBDU (isobutylidene diurea); these release urea slowly over several months.

FERTILIZER/NITROGEN CONVERSION TABLE																	
Actual nitrogen (in lbs.)	Percentages of nitrogen in common fertilizers																
	4%	5%	6%	7%	8%	9%	10%	11%	13%	15%	17%	19%	21%	23%	25%	29%	33%
¼	6¼	5	4	3¼	3	2¾	2½	2¼	2	1½	1½	1¼	1¼	1	1	¾	¾
½	12½	10	8¼	7	6¼	5½	5	4½	3¾	3¼	3	2½	2¼	2¼	2	1¾	1½
¾	18¾	15	12½	10¾	9¼	8¼	7½	6¾	5¾	5	4½	4	3½	3¼	3	2½	2¼
1	25	20	16¾	14¼	12½	11	10	9	7¾	6¾	5¾	5¼	4¾	4¼	4	3½	3

This table will help you figure out how many pounds of fertilizer you need to buy to attain a given amount of nitrogen. For example, to get ¼ pound actual nitrogen from any 10% nitrogen fertilizer, look under 10% and you'll see that you need 2½ pounds of fertilizer.

Watering

The watering requirements of plants make their fertilizer needs seem like kindergarten stuff. Still, there are sensible rules to follow.

Soil soaked to the maximum has as thick a film of water as each particle can retain against the pull of gravity—it has reached its *field capacity*. When the film of water surrounding each soil particle becomes so thin that its molecular attraction to the soil particle is stronger than the ability of the root tips to absorb it, a plant will wilt.

The simple basic is this: water should be applied before a plant reaches the wilting point, but is a waste applied to soil already damp. The trick lies in finding a conservative balance point.

Clay soils hold more water and hold it longer than loamy soils, and loamy soils hold more water longer than sandy soils. Compared to loams, clays need more water per soaking but need it less often. Sands need less water per soaking than loam, but need more water overall because they must be soaked oftener.

Hot, dry air dries out any soil (and plant) faster than cool, humid air. Desert gardens need water oftener than coastal gardens of a similar soil type, even if the coastal rainfall is hardly more than the desert's in summer.

On any dry day, wind causes more rapid evaporation (from plants and soil alike) than does still air.

These factors (plus water tables and a few more variables) make a mockery of almost any generalization about how much water to give any sort of fruit.

In western Washington and Oregon, for example, trees almost never need irrigation, even in drought years, while other regions with as much or more rainfall need regular summer irrigation. However, the accompanying table of water volumes and depths of penetration offers a starting point. Other notes with each fruit add a few more reference points.

The table is not absolute, either—only a close approximation. The gallons-per-minute from a hose turned on full force are dramatic, but all by themselves they are misleading. They cannot include runoff, which may range from nil to considerable. (Note that water moves *down* through soil; there is slight lateral movement in clay, virtually none in sand.) Also, the figures do not take into account how the water is delivered. Overhead spray irrigation does not get as much water to the roots as flood irrigation, which in turn may not deliver as much usable water as drip irrigation.

Ways to water

No method of irrigation is the perfect substitute for rainfall; each has advantages and disadvantages.

Sprinkling—overhead irrigation—attempts to imitate rainfall. Sprinklers can cover a large area from one location. One catch is that no sprinkler delivers an even amount of water to the entire area it moistens, no matter which of several patterns it follows. The other disadvantage is the relatively high proportion of evaporation loss. And uneven watering patterns and evaporation loss are worsened by windy weather.

To be effective, sprinklers need to be set to compensate for variations in their patterns, and must be left running long enough to soak to the desired depth.

Flood irrigation is likely to cut down on evaporation loss and to work more quickly than overhead sprinkling, but is limited to relatively flat sites. To avoid runoff from an open area, the flow rate must be adjusted so it does not exceed the absorption rate, and the hose end must be moved several times to ensure even soaking of a root zone.

A quicker alternative is a system of miniature levees erected to contain the water until it can soak in. Such a levee system must form a watering basin that encompasses the entire root zone of the tree. For rows of berries, a trench along each side of each row has the same effect that a watering basin has for a single tree.

Drip irrigation can replace flood irrigation if water conservation is paramount. In essence, such a system waters plants a drop at a time through emitters strategically placed along low-pressure plastic tubing. Nurseries and garden supply centers sell components and kits. Another advantage is that drip systems require less attention than flood irrigation or sprinkling while they work.

Sloping sites pose special problems for which there are practical solutions. Drip systems are one. For trenches and/or watering basins, substitute soaker hoses—in effect temporary drip systems—that keep all of the water from running to the low end of a depression. Another answer is a deep root irrigator, in effect a giant hypodermic needle that guarantees getting water deep into the root zone of a plant fast. The irrigators are so swiftly effective that some flat site gardeners use them in preference to drip irrigation, though they are more laborious. These tools, too, are available at nurseries and garden supply centers.

Gallons of water per 10 sq. ft. needed to penetrate to various depths in different soils.

Soil	Desired depth (in inches)							
	4	8	12	16	20	24	28	32
Clay	6	12	18	24	30	36	42	48
Loam	3	6	12	18	24	30	36	42
Sand	2	4	6	12	18	24	30	36

The figures indicating depth of penetration are general, for three pure soil types. Most soils will fall between some two of the soil types for composition, and thus for volumes of water needed to soak to a selected depth.

Symptoms & controls

Aphids

Attack: Most trees.

Symptoms: Curled and disfigured leaves, especially tender ones on new shoots; sticky, sooty-black mold on leaves; white, cottony tufts in case of wooly apple aphid. Unlike other aphids, wooly apple aphids will attack the trunk of a tree at or just below the ground line. Once on roots, they can be hard to eradicate.

Controls: *Live*—Lacewings or lacewing larvae. *Physical*—Sprayed-on soapy water. *Packaged*—Malathion or diazinon; if aphid colony tended by ants, ants must be controlled. Use diazinon or dursban granules; they will not harm birds or other natural predators of aphids.

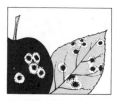

Apple Scab

Attacks: Apples, crab apples.

Symptoms: Brownish spots on young fruits; leaves that enlarge and become corky. Fruit can become disfigured, drop before ripening; affected leaves also may drop.

Controls: *Live*—None. *Physical*—In dormant season, thorough cleanup of fallen leaves and fruits of previous season. If tree is small and infestation light, pick and destroy infected fruits, leaves. *Packaged*—Dormant lime-sulfur spray just before flower buds show color; at colored bud stage, again when most petals have fallen, spray with benomyl, captan, or ferbam.

Birds

Attack: Many ripe and near-ripe fruits.

Symptoms: Holes in fruit where birds have pecked; rot may set in after bird damage.

Controls: *Live*—None. *Physical*—Reflectors, scarecrows, pinwheels, and the like may temporarily keep birds away, but none is reliable enough to protect a crop. Only sure protection is caging or netting over the bearing plant. Nylon broad-mesh netting (¾ inch) is most popular for protecting fruit trees. Two to three weeks before fruit is due to ripen, enclose tree with netting; tie off nets where lowest branches leave the trunk. Remove nets at harvest time. *Packaged*—None.

Brown Rot

Attacks: Stone fruits, almonds.

Symptoms: Early in flowering period, some flowers and new leaves wilt, then brown; many remain on tree. Some twigs die back; brown, sunken cankers form. Infected tissues produce spores that spread by wind and rain to developing fruits, where they produce small brown spots. As fruits mature, spots enlarge and rot fruits; infected fruits often show patches of fuzzy gray spores. Disease lives from year to year on infected twigs, fruits (both those fallen to ground and shriveled and hanging on tree).

Controls: *Live*—None. *Physical*—Cut out all infected twigs; remove shriveled fruits from tree; thoroughly clean up all fallen debris from beneath tree. *Packaged*—Spray with benomyl or captan. Check with farm advisor for recommended spray schedule in your area.

Cedar-apple rust

Attacks: Apples, crab apples (primarily east of Rocky Mountains).

Symptoms: Small, light yellow spots on leaves, fruits, in mid to late spring. Spots grow larger, turn orange with tiny black dots; leaf undersides beneath spots show small cup-shaped structures. Fruits may be stunted; fruits and leaves may fall prematurely. Disease requires junipers (especially Eastern red cedar) as alternate host for part of its life cycle.

Controls: *Live*—None. *Physical*—Eliminate all junipers from vicinity of apple, crab apple planting (this control potentially ineffective if junipers remain within several miles of planting); remove corky, round galls from junipers. *Packaged*—Spray with ferbam or zineb at colored bud stage, again when most petals have fallen, again 10 days later.

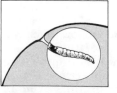

Cherry fruit fly, Apple maggot

Attacks: Apple, cherry.

Symptoms: Apples—Brown streaks on skins, early fruit drop. Cherries—Premature fruit drop.

Controls: *Live*—None. *Physical*—Remove all fallen fruits: maggots enter soil from fruits, pupate, emerge as flies next spring to lay eggs in new crop of fruits. *Packaged*—Spray with diazinon, malathion when you see small black flies in late spring; spray twice again at 2-week intervals.

Cherry slug, Pear slug

Attacks: Cherry, pear, plum.

Symptoms: In early summer, leaves show irregular patches that look like tissue paper and turn brown; these appear where leaf surface has been eaten away between veins.

Controls: *Live*—None. *Physical*—None. *Packaged*—Spray with malathion or methoxyclor to control small, sluglike fly larvae when you first see their damage.

Codling moth

Attacks: Apple, pear.

Symptoms: The superficial one is a blackened, crusted hole somewhere on the skin of each affected fruit. The hole betrays the presence inside the ripening fruit of a small, white worm, the larval form of the codling moth.

Controls: *Live*—None. *Physical*—None. *Packaged*—Spray with diazinon or methoxychlor, but only if infestation is severe. (These controls also kill bees and some predators, harming pollenation and leaving tree subject to attack by other pests.) Spraying must be timed to catch hatch of eggs laid on leaves and shoots. Soon after leafout, begin using pheromone trap to obtain count; spraying is needed only when trapped moths number more than 20 per week between early March and late May. If done then, repeat in mid-June, early August.

Crown gall

Attacks: Most fruit and nut trees.

Symptoms: Tumorlike, rough-textured growths up to several inches in diameter at or close to the soil line; galls also may grow on roots. Plant growth may be slower than normal, weakened, stunted; occasionally plant will die.

Controls: *Live*—None. *Physical*—Remove galls with sharp knife (this is no guarantee against regrowth); dig out and destroy badly infected plant; don't do further planting in same location. *Packaged*—None.

Crown rot

Attacks: Many fruit, nut trees.

Symptoms: Variable, depending on organism. Often first sign is wilting of leaves on one or more limbs; leaves then turn brown and die. Bark at ground level may show sign of decay or rot.

Controls: *Live*—None. *Physical*—Most crown rot organisms proliferate in poorly drained, overly moist soil. To control, remove all diseased wood and keep area exposed to air. Check with local farm advisors for specific diagnosis and any possible remedial measures. *Packaged*—None.

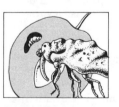

Curculio

Attacks: Apple, apricot, cherry, peach, nectarine, pear, plum, quince—east of Rocky Mountains.

Symptoms: Developing fruits marked by deep scars with crescent-shaped margins; fruits may be misshapen, decaying inside where pale, brown-headed larvae are feeding. Adult brown beetle has characteristic long, curved snout.

Controls: *Live*—None. *Physical*—Collect and destroy all damaged fallen fruits; remove and destroy all damaged fruits from tree. *Packaged*—Spray with malathion or methoxyclor immediately after tree blossoms; spray later in season according to schedule recommended by farm advisor.

Fireblight

Attacks: Apple, crab apple, pear, quince.

Symptoms: Flowering shoots, leafy young stems wilt and turn brownish to black with fire-scorched appearance. Infection spreads down stems to form dark, sunken cankers on larger branches.

Controls: *Live*—None. *Physical*—Cut out and destroy all affected shoots; make each cut at least 12 inches below infected tissue, and disinfect shears with rubbing alcohol or 5 percent solution of household bleach after each cut. Avoid high-nitrogen fertilizers and heavy pruning, both of which stimulate particularly susceptible rank, succulent growth. *Packaged*—Spray with streptomycin or fixed copper at intervals of 5 to 7 days, from time flower buds swell until bloom is finished.

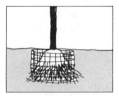

Gophers

Attack: Many plants by eating or girdling roots.

Symptoms: Sudden wilt of part or all of plant, or plant toppled over or pulled into the earth. Telltale volcano-shaped mound of pulverized earth (residue of gopher tunneling activity) may appear nearby.

Controls: *Live*—Some cats are adept gopher catchers, but not to be counted on. *Physical*—Trapping is most successful control. Clear away mound of soil to expose gopher hole, then dig down to main horizontal runway. Set *two* traps in runway, one in either direction; attach each trap with wire or chain to a stake driven into soil about 2 feet from hole. Plug hole with folded carrot tops, fresh green grass, or other fresh, tender greens—their scent attracts gophers. Then place a board or soil over greens and top of hole to exclude all light. Check traps daily. If gopher pushes soil into traps, clear tunnel and reset traps. *Packaged*—None.

Gummosis

Attacks: Many fruit and nut trees.

Symptoms: Drops or globules of brownish, sticky sap appear on limbs or trunk. (Note, though, that this does not always indicate disease. Stone fruits tend to secrete sap even though healthy. Sap production can be triggered by injury: pruning, breakage, any bark wound, including drilling by woodpeckers, sapsuckers, flickers. Trees growing under stress of too much or too little water or experiencing sudden fluctuations in weather may excrete sap.) Borers—the larvae of various moths and beetles—may cause sap to ooze from tunnels they make in branches; sometimes you will note sawdust in sap or nearby on bark or ground. Also, disease infection can produce bark cankers that bleed sap.

Controls: *Live*—None. *Physical*—Both borers and canker-forming fungi or bacteria are difficult to control. If small branches are involved, cut them out (when dealing with cankers, disinfect shears with rubbing alcohol after each cut). *Packaged*—Best advice will come from

local farm advisor, who can make diagnosis, recommend possible control measures and best timing for your area.

Leaf roller

Attacks: Apple (especially) and pear; in California, citrus, walnut, and many deciduous fruits.

Symptoms: Individual leaves rolled up and held together by webbing inside, or two or more leaves bound to one another by webbing; inside webbing is dark-headed green worm about ¾ inch long that chews irregular holes and notches in leaves and fruits.

Controls: *Live*—Bacillus thuringiensis during spring after leaf-out. *Physical*—Squash worms within rolled leaves, or pick and destroy such leaves. *Packaged*—Spray deciduous trees with dormant-strength oil just before growth begins; spray with carbaryl, diazinon, or malathion during spring at intervals recommended by county farm advisor.

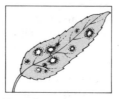

Leaf spot

Attacks: Many fruit and nut trees.

Symptoms: Red, brown to black, or yellow spots on leaves and stems; sometimes spots drop out, leaving "shot hole" condition. Several bacteria and fungi can cause a variety of leaf spotting.

Controls: *Live*—none. *Physical*—Thoroughly clean up all fallen leaves and fruits of previous growing season during autumn and winter; disease may live over winter in this refuse. *Packaged*—Check with nearest farm advisor for diagnosis of exact causal organism, suggested treatment and timing. Wet weather and warm tempera-

tures favor development of leaf-spot organisms. Benomyl, captan, folpet, thiram are common growing-season controls; lime-sulfur may be recommended for dormant-season use.

Mites

Attack: Many fruit and nut trees during hot weather.

Symptoms: Leaves have yellow to silvery stippling; in severe infestation, leaf undersides show white webbing, then turn brown and drop prematurely. Use magnifying glass to verify presence of tiny insects at first sign of stippling, before web appears.

Controls: *Live*—Lacewing larvae, mite-eating mites (*Phytoseiulus persimilis*). *Physical*—Frequent washing of leaves (especially undersides) with jet of water from hose. *Packaged*—Spray with kelthane or diazinon at sign of infestation, then at least twice again at intervals of 7 to 10 days to eradicate newly hatching mites.

Oriental fruit moth,
Peach twig borer

Attacks: Apricot, cherry, peach, nectarine, plum, quince.

Symptoms: New tip growth suddenly wilts, dies; cut-open stem reveals small worm—pinkish white (oriental fruit moth) or red brown (peach twig borer). Later in season, new generations infest fruits, leave holes filled with sticky gum.

Controls: *Live*—None. *Physical*—Dispatch worm when found in wilted stem. *Packaged*—Spray with diazinon, malathion, or methoxyclor during growing season to kill adult moths.

Peach leaf curl

Attacks: Peaches and nectarines; also may affect almond, cherry, plum.

Symptoms: New leaves thicken and pucker along midribs, causing leaves to curl or twist; distorted leaves may be pink to red or orange, turning yellowish to light green and then falling. New growth that follows can be infected if weather continues cool and wet.

Controls: *Live*—None. *Physical*—None effective. *Packaged*—Spray entire tree with lime-sulfur or Bordeaux mixture after autumn leaf drop, again in spring just as buds begin to swell, no later than when flower buds begin to open. Peach leaf curl appears to be borne by winter or spring rains; timing the spray can be difficult in a wet spring. As a rule of thumb, early during bud swell is better than later, but not if continuing rains wash off the spray.

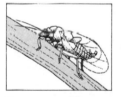

Pear psylla

Attacks: Pear, quince.

Symptoms: Sticky honeydew on leaves and developing fruits, usually with sooty black fungus that lives on honeydew. Fungus is unsightly but basically harmless (can be washed off). However, psyllids—sucking insects related to aphids—can cause leaf yellowing and some leaf drop if unchecked.

Controls: *Live*—None. *Physical*—None. *Packaged*—In early spring just before budbreak, spray trunk and limbs with dormant oil spray to kill recently laid eggs. If infestation persists during growing season, spray with carbaryl or malathion in summer oil. Check with local farm advisor for timing.

Powdery mildew

Attacks: Apple, especially; may infest various other fruit and nut trees.

Symptoms: Irregular, mealy or powdery-appearing gray to white patches on leaves. Severe infestations cover new growth, causing stunting, distortion; may also affect developing fruits. Disease is encouraged by humidity, cool temperature, shade, poor air circulation.

Controls: *Live*—None. *Physical*—None. *Packaged*—Sprays of dinocap or cyclohexamide will kill actively growing powdery mildew; must be repeated as new outbreaks occur. Benomyl will prevent development of the disease—follow product directions. For previously infected deciduous fruit trees, spray with benomyl as new leaves unfold.

Rabbits, Mice

Attacks: Many fruit and nut trees.

Symptoms: Chewed bark at or near ground level (rabbits and mice); nipped-off stems (rabbits). In snow country where snow builds up around trees, bark damage can occur higher on tree, at snow line.

Controls: *Live*—For mice: cats. Otherwise, none practical. *Physical*—Encircle tree trunk with cylinder of wire mesh. To be effective, cylinder should be 2 feet high (higher where snows are expected), embedded 2–3 inches beneath soil surface, and be securely staked. To discourage mice, keep ground clear around bases of trees; this eliminates protective cover mice need. *Packaged*—For rabbit control, especially where snow buildup is expected, paint trunk and lowest limbs for about their first foot of length with the following mixture: 1 pound thiram mixed into 1 quart ex-

terior-grade, water-soluble latex paint to which you have added 1 pint of water for easy application.

Scales

Attacks: Many fruit, nut trees.

Symptoms: Clusters or patches of small, bumpy growths—rounded and flattened, or irregularly shaped—on branches or leaf undersides; each bump is protective covering for sucking insect beneath.

Controls: *Live*—Aphytis wasps. *Physical*—Where infestation is slight, scrape off scales, pick and destroy infested leaves. *Packaged*—Spray in spring (timing as advised by local farm advisor) with diazinon or malathion to kill crawlers. During dormancy, spray deciduous trees with oil, or oil plus diazinon or malathion to kill adult scales.

Tent caterpillar

Attacks: Most fruit and nut trees.

Symptoms: Gauzelike webbing forms "tents" surrounding forks of tree branches in early spring; inside the tents live immature caterpillars that venture out to chew foliage. There is one generation each year; in summer, moths lay eggs on tree branches, surround them with varnishlike substance. (Tents that appear in late spring through late summer are of the fall webworm; several generations per year are possible—moths lay eggs on leaf undersides.)

Controls: *Live*—Bacillus thuringiensis while caterpillars are small. *Physical*—Remove and destroy tents while caterpillars are in residence; in winter, prune out egg masses found on twigs. *Packaged*—Spray caterpillars with carbaryl, diazinon, malathion, or methoxyclor.

Index